Practicing Truth

Practicing Truth

Confident Witness
in Our
Pluralistic World

Edited by David W. Shenk
and Linford Stutzman

Foreword by Paul G. Hiebert

2674
Herald
Press

Scottdale, Pennsylvania
Waterloo, Ontario

Cataloguing in Publication Data
Practicing truth: confident witness in our pluralistic world / edited by David
W. Shenk and Linford Stutzman ; foreword by Paul Hiebert
     p. cm.
  Includes bibliographical references.
  ISBN 0-8361-9107-2 (alk. paper)
    1. Religious pluralism—Christianity. 2. Christianity and other religions.
3. Religious pluralism—Anabaptists. 4. Anabaptists—relations. I. Shenk,
David W., 1937– II. Stutzman, Linford, 1950–

BR 127 .C59 1999
261.2—dc21   99-046099

The paper used in this publication is recycled and meets the minimum requirements of American National Standard for Information Sciences—
Permanence of Paper for Printed Library Materials, ANSI Z39.48-1984.

PRACTICING TRUTH
Copyright © 1999 by Herald Press, Scottdale, Pa. 15683
        Published simultaneously in Canada by Herald Press,
        Waterloo, Ont. N2L 6H7. All rights reserved
Library of Congress Catalog Number: 99-046099
International Standard Book Number: 0-8361-9107-2
Printed in the United States of America
Book design by Michael A. King, Pandora Press U.S., in consultation with Jim
Butti, Herald Press
Cover design by Jim Butti, Herald Press

10 09 08 07 06 05 04 03 02 01 00 99 10 9 8 7 6 5 4 3 2 1

To order or request information, please call
1-800-759-4447 (individuals); 1-800-245-7894 (trade)
Website: www.mph.org

To
Lesslie Newbigin,
who as a twentieth-century global Christian
was a confident witness for Jesus Christ
in our pluralist world

Contents

Witness
Cultural Transformation
Conclusion

Foreword

The world is undergoing a sea change, and the church in the West is caught in the transformation. Underlying the change is the West's encounter with Others and Otherness. During the Age of Exploration, the West found people who had no place in its medieval worldview. The Western response was to label them barbarians and savages—half humans. With the coming of modernism and the theory of evolution, these others became primitives—fully human but backward and aboriginals—like ancestors of the West.

Postmodernism challenges the arrogance of this view and affirms the equality and dignity of all human communities but sees Others as natives—inscrutably and wholly other. It argues that true intercultural communication is impossible and that there is no basis for seeking universals and truth. It offers no way to break down walls of ethnicity, class, culture, and religion that divide us and generate injustice and violence.

How should the church in the West respond to the cultural and religious pluralism engulfing it? Many Christians in the West are trying to restore Christendom by establishing Christian states. Others argue that postmodernity is a good corrective and that we should recognize that the gospel of Jesus Christ is one gospel among many. All human knowledge, they argue, is located in particular cultural and historical contexts; none can be shown to be truer than another.

Does Anabaptist theology offer a distinct and valid response to the challenges of modernism with its Western arrogance and denial of spiritual realities, and of postmodernism with its self-centered narcissism, cognitive and moral relativism, and inability to address global human crises? Can it point us beyond these to what Houston Smith calls a post-postmodern world—a world in which diversity is recognized and affirmed but in which Truth is sought and proclaimed? Can Christians truly witness with boldness in the turmoil of our age?

This book's writers wrestle with such questions and point a way beyond the current impasse. Their responses are rooted in Scripture and

11

Anabaptist theological perspectives. Rather than a definitive Anabaptist view of proclaiming truth in a pluralistic world, this volume highlights key themes that must be part of such a theology.

First, the writers examine different ways in which unity and diversity relate to each other. Some point out that pluralism is not a modern/postmodern discovery. Africans, Muslims, Hindus, and others have developed their own responses to pluralism. Some examine how the Old and New Testaments deals with others and otherness. Some trace the logic of Christendom that dominated the West in the Middle Ages and justified the conquest of the world by the church and state working in partnership. Some examine the emergence of pluralism as a "problem" in the West as postmodernism has challenged the arrogance and intellectual hegemony of modernism. They show the inconsistencies of postmodernism and its inability to address the world's growing problems of violence, starvation, injustice, alienation, and sin.

Against this backdrop, the writers examine the early Anabaptist rejection of Christendom and call for all cultures to be judged not by earthly criteria but by the standards of the kingdom of God. This call has included asking Christians truly to love their Others—enemies, pagans, sinners, heretics, savages—not as Others but as Neighbors, as truly Us. They also show how the Anabaptist understanding of unity and diversity provides a way to proclaim truth that goes beyond the triumphalism of modernism and communitarian response of postmodernism.

A second theme has to do with the nature of truth and its relationship to revelation. The writers point out that Anabaptists make a distinction between the gospel as divine revelation and human understandings of that revelation. Early Anabaptists boldly affirmed the truthfulness of Scripture for all, not because it is the highest and best of human search for truth, but because God reveals his truth to humans through the Bible and definitively through the person of Jesus Christ.

The Anabaptists recognized that their understanding of that revelation was always partial and perspectival, so they refused to absolutize any theological system. They did not seek to prove the truth of the gospel on the basis of reason, nor did they claim ownership of the gospel or their own spiritual superiority because they were recipients of God's revelation. Rather, they sought to hear and obey the gospel as it was revealed to them in the particularities of their lives, and they proclaimed the Gospel for all to hear and believe.

Anabaptists have held that revelation is always given in the particularity of human cultural and historical contexts. The God of the Bible did not speak to humankind in general. He spoke to Abraham, David, and Mary in the contexts of their daily living. Above all, he revealed himself definitively in the person of Jesus.

Anabaptists do not seek to construct universal systems of truth. Rather, they ask what is God saying in this particular situation. They believed that authentic Christianity is not a set of disembodied doctrines, but a faith woven into and expressed in real-life contexts. At the heart of the gospel for them is not a body of knowledge—but a relationship with God incarnate in Jesus Christ. The greatest threat to Christianity in the West today does not come from without, but from within—in the loss of the universal claim of the gospel to offer definitive divine revelation through God incarnate in Jesus.

A third theme has to do with Christ's return and the establishment of his kingdom on earth. Anabaptists see the reign of God as having already begun in the person of Jesus Christ. That reign is embodied visibly in the life of the church and invisibly through the work of God in human hearts and the affairs of nations. This rule is not exercised to dominate, but to manifest love, mercy, peace, and purity.

A fourth theme is Anabaptist stress on personal witness rather than argument about abstract truths. Early Anabaptist lives were transformed by an existential encounter with the living Christ. They gave public testimony of what they had seen and experienced. They did not seek like lawyers to convince people of the truth of their positions. They empowered spiritually hungry people by inviting them to join a living community of forgiveness, belonging, and service—a community that is but a foretaste of the reign of God that some day will be rooted in personal experience. For them the gospel was not simply information to be believed. Rather, it was a divine call not to be debated but obeyed.

These writers challenge us to bear confident witness in our modernist/postmodernist world. They chart a course beyond Christian triumphalism and religious relativism. They point out that the Anabaptist witness is rooted in conviction that God has indeed spoken through Christ, Scripture, and our life-transforming experience with that revelation. They remind us that to witness with confidence we must not only know the gospel and how it views Others and Otherness. A living experience of that gospel must also constantly transform our lives.

—*Paul G. Hiebert*
  Associate Dean of Academic Doctorates and
  Professor of Mission, Anthropology, and South Asia Studies,
  Trinity Evangelical Divinity School
  Deerfield, Illinois

Editor's Preface

Linford Stutzman

Jesus was confident. He knew who he was, what his mission was, and what truth the world needed. Jesus practiced truth in the context of religious debate, unsuccessful attempts at recovering the kingdom, and competing claims to be the Messiah. While Jesus' context was not one of Western pluralism as we know it today, it was a context of moral ambiguity, of disagreeing religious groups all claiming to speak the truth, all seeking adherents.

Genuine Christian witness is inseparable from Jesus' confidence. "All authority in heaven and on earth has been given to me," Jesus told the eleven. "Go therefore and make disciples of all nations" (Matt. 28:18-19a). At that point, when eleven persons heard Jesus' mandate and promise, there existed no church, no plans of world evangelism, and little evidence that the kingdom of God would ever have a chance of succeeding to take root and grow in the empire of Rome.

But like mustard seed and leaven, the mandate of Jesus has been carried forward with confidence and hope by Jesus' followers for two millennia. The Christian movement has spread into every nation, entering virtually every tribe, people, and language on earth, to the point that a third of the world's population now claims Christian identity. The predictions are that this percentage will continue to increase, especially in regions outside of the West.

Confidence once characterized Western Christianity. Believers had confidence in the truth of Jesus' claims, the finality and effectiveness of his life, death, and resurrection, the reliability of Scripture, and the universality of the gospel. Missionaries, students from Harvard and Yale, lay workers, men and women once volunteered by the thousands for distant shores, ready and willing to die for the chance to let others know of the gospel. They were heroes and martyrs. They were confident witnesses.

15

However, in the history of Christian missions, genuine Christian confidence seems only a small step away from witness characterized by arrogant presuppositions of cultural superiority. What had begun as confidence based in Christ was gradually replaced after the Enlightenment by self-confidence—confidence in human reason, in science, and in human ability to overcome the contingencies of nature and the dark side of human hearts and societies. Confidence was not the casualty; *Christian* confidence was. As Lesslie Newbigin has written,

> We no longer use the kind of language that was natural for Christians in 1910. We feel a proper sense of guilt about the wrongs done in the name of our "Christian" civilization, and we are impressed by what other cultures have to teach us. Yet we continue without embarrassment to export our science and technology, and the rest of the world not only receives it eagerly but surpasses us in its development (*Toward the 21st Century in Christian Mission*, ed. James M. Phillips and Robert T. Coote, Grand Rapids: Eerdmans, 1993).

To practice confidence without Jesus is potentially and demonstrably destructive, as David Shenk describes in the Introduction. For if ultimate authority does not belong to Jesus, to whom does it belong? The destructive nature of human confidence has haunted people who possess a sense of justice and compassion. If human self-confidence is so easily channeled into arrogance and self-aggrandizement at the expense of others, perhaps tentativeness and conditional conclusions about everything that matters are more healthy for the global community.

So confidence itself has become an endangered social feature of a postmodern, pluralistic world of doubt, agnosticism, and contingency science. As the universal "truth" of Marxism has been rejected by many nations, as Darwinian social theories have deteriorated in the evil of ethnic cleansing, human self-confidence on a grand scale is in trouble.

The autonomous individual, although small and insignificant among the six billion other individuals, remains the irreducible center of reference. Technology available to the individual, from handguns to personal home pages on the Internet, increases the sense of self-reliance as well as the potential threat to others.

Jesus was a witness of the kingdom of God and shaped the witnessing character of Christianity. Christian witness included the confession of the truth of Jesus to all—to the lost, to those of other religions and cultures. This witness was personal, convincing, and self-understood.

Missions were organized witness. Though in too many times and places mission activity reflected domination and arrogance, in other times and places it embodied the presence of the kingdom of God.

Jesus practiced truth in a world of argument over the truth. The righteousness of the kingdom of God was made real, present, powerful, and believable through Jesus' actions of love, healing, and exorcism and his words of explanation, rebuke, affirmation, and hope. Christians, in the context of pluralism, must be and do the same as Jesus, the confident witness who practiced the truth of the kingdom of God.

The voices in this volume are many. They present a variety of perspectives. Though they speak in different voices, they address a common area of both concern and conviction—that truth is not only something we say but something we do.

Christian witness in pluralism can no longer rest on any real or apparent vestiges of Christendom consensus. The case for Christ must be made through lives that show Jesus' presence and make the kingdom of God real and relevant. Our pluralistic world forces us to practice truth, and as such is an ideal context for faithfulness.

This volume is a resource for recovery of confidence, witness, and the practice of truth in our world. At the turn of the twenty-first century, with millennial anxieties demonstrating once again that we are afraid of ourselves, and with good reason, I am grateful for Jesus' words of confidence, direction, and promise: "And remember, I am with you always, to the end of the age" (Matt. 28:20b).

As I close this preface, let me stress my gratitude to Eastern Mennonite Missions for helping to initiate and support the conference from which this volume has emerged; to Eastern Mennonite Seminary's John Coffman Center for allocating resources that made both the conference and this volume possible; and to Pandora Press U.S. (which helped prepare this book for Herald Press) for helping to shape all this wisdom into book form.

—Linford Stutzman
Harrisonburg, Virginia

Introduction

David W. Shenk

This book is not for armchair theologians. It is about life and death issues. It is about the destiny of human history and the destiny of each of us.

I am writing this introduction in the safety of Klaipeda, Lithuania, on Easter weekend, 1999. Yet I am troubled and angry. In another part of Europe, Yugoslavia is in flames; hundreds of thousands of refugees are fleeing from Kosovo.

The Balkan conflict, like this book, is about pluralism and truth, and about lies masqueraded as truth. I have friends caught in the violence. They are doing their theology in the trenches where young men and boys are killed, young women raped, factories bombed, and homes burned—and where some people reach out to one another in compassion and loving concern.

As this book heads toward publication, the violence amid which I first wrote has given way to a militarily imposed peace. It is an uneasy peace indeed. Kosovo is astride Europe's ethnic and religious fault line, where Islam and the Orthodox Church meet. Ideally, both religious systems provide space for alternative communities, but the instinct of each is to circumscribe and control any alternative groups. Historically, both Islam and Orthodoxy have a profound compulsion to insist that religion, nation, culture, government, and territory are indivisible.

Communist ideology presented a similar example. For half a century, eastern Europe was ruled by Marxist belief systems that tried to control and even eradicate other systems. It is, therefore, not surprising that after the collapse of the communist empire, issues of tolerance and pluralism have haunted most of the nations of the former Soviet bloc.

Like Yugoslavia, Lithuania was ruled by communists. Moreover, the religious history of Lithuania, like that of Yugoslavia, has been one of conflict and violence.

Our history books describe the eleventh- to thirteenth-century Crusades into the Middle East. However, in the thirteenth and fourteenth centuries, Crusaders also invaded the northern lands of Europe. For nearly a century and a half, knights of the Teutonic Order made war against the "pagan" Lithuanians until they were successful in establishing a Christian kingdom. These Christian warriors from the West also confronted the Orthodox Church reaching into Lithuania from the East. In time the hegemony of the Western church prevailed.[1]

Despite such historical parallels to Yugoslavia, Lithuania has taken a fundamentally different approach to the challenge posed by diversity. Lithuania's way of dealing with ethnic and religious affinities is exceedingly pertinent to the issues of truth and pluralism addressed in this book.

A Quest for Pluralist Society in Lithuania

Lithuania Christian College, where my wife Grace and I now serve, was founded in 1991. It began because Lithuanian education officials forthrightly sought to establish a Christian institution that would equip leaders to strengthen the moral and spiritual foundations necessary to develop a pluralist culture, civil society, and democracy.

The story of the college really begins during the late 1970s and early 1980s. Soviet Christians of German ethnicity discovered that exit permits to emigrate to Germany were more easily acquired in Lithuania than in most other Soviet republics. Nevertheless, the wait for permits could take several years. While in Lithuania, some of these Christians in transit learned the Lithuanian language, shared the gospel, and formed unobtrusive churches.

Consequently, a young Lithuanian couple, Otonas and Raimonda Balciunas, became believers. Otonas was trained to be a high school teacher. However, his career evaporated because no Christian could be a school teacher. Raimonda was apprehended by the security police, who told her that her life goals were finished. She could not continue her university education. The couple feared Otonas would be deported to Siberia.

Courageously, however, the couple persisted in their faith. Over time, they negotiated the registration of what is believed to be the first Christian charity in the Soviet Union, the Lithuania Christian Fund. The couple also planted congregations that became known as the Christian Free Church. These churches were the first to break from the homogeneity of the traditional Catholic or Protestant systems. They were pushing the boundaries, dangerously so, in a nonpluralist Soviet Union antagonistic toward challenge.

As the Soviet system came under strain at the beginning of the 1990s, Lithuania was the first Soviet republic to declare its independence. President Gorbachev insisted that this was an impossibility. Soviet tanks surrounded the Lithuanian Parliament.

In the midst of that confrontation, Lithuanian educational and political authorities began a remarkable conversation with Otonas and several of his colleagues. The officials asked if the Lithuania Christian Fund would consider expanding its mission and establishing a nonsectarian Christian liberal arts college.

Lithuania is traditionally Catholic. In the early 1990s, there were probably no more than 10,000 practicing Protestants in the whole country (Protestant affiliation was about 40,000). Yet Lithuanian political and educational leaders were deliberately reaching for the formation of an educational institution that would sow seeds of healthy diversity in Lithuanian society. It would be ecumenical, with a good dose of Protestant ethos, as exemplified in the nontraditionalist Christian Free Church.

The birth of the college in 1991 (first as an English language institute with thirty students) was a tremendous jolt to the monocultural hegemony that the atheistic guardians of "truth" had acquired under the communist regime. The college's founding also challenged the traditionalist, pre-Vatican II ethos of the Catholic Church. Thus the college began amid intense public debate concerning whether Lithuania should indeed become a pluralist society.

That the school would be religious in nature was never in question. The Lithuanian authorities who spoke with Otonas had a profound suspicion of scientific ideologies. These concerns were expressed by Professor Leonidas Donskis, chair of the Klaipeda University Department of Philosophy, when he spoke at the third LCC graduation in 1998.

One of the most dangerous ideas ever produced throughout history, Professor Donskis said, is the notion that true science has to put aside such things as human values and free choices. The professor described Nazism and Marxism as examples of this dangerous and antipluralist idea. In the enlightened twentieth century, he noted, these supposedly objective systems brought immense destruction and suffering on the Lithuanian nation.[2]

Professor Donskis observed that the Christian faith has nurtured humane qualities, respect for the person, and freedom in Western civilization. Christian faith, he said, has sustained pluralist society and made possible the respectful dialogue that is essential for democracy.

The Defense of Truth

The conversation about truth and pluralism faces two fundamental questions: First, what is truth? Second, how should the truth be established? These questions have been answered one way in the Balkans and in a very different way by the founders of the college in which I now serve. In various ways the essays in this volume seek to wrestle with these two fundamental issues.

George M. Marsden's 1994 book, *The Soul of the American University, From Protestant Establishment to Established Nonbelief,* demonstrates how intractable truth questions have been in the American university experience. Harvard is an archetype of the issues.

Harvard was the first American university, established in 1636. It was established by the Puritans, only 16 years after the Pilgrims landed in Plymouth.

Harvard served both church and state. The first college laws stated, "Every one shall consider the main End of his life and studies, to know God and Jesus Christ which is Eternal life."[3]

Each student was required to engage in daily private prayer and twice-a-day reading of Scripture. There was considerable debate as to whether pagan philosophers such as Plato or Aristotle should be admitted into the curriculum. As the Massachusetts Puritans began to experience pluralist societies, serious stresses soon projected into this tight system of truth preservation and communication. Especially problematic was the assumption that a church-dominated college could fully serve the interests of the state. The conflict between the church, as the steward of the truth, and the pluralistic commitments of the state became increasingly intractable.

During the mid- and later-nineteenth century, science began to usurp revelation as the basis for objective truth. In the twentieth century that assumption deepened. The anticipation was that objective science could cut through the issues that pluralist culture presented. Not all might agree that the Bible is God's Word, but all would agree that the virus sighted in the microscope was pernicious.

The church as a whole was astonished at this turn of events. The founders of Harvard and many other universities had assumed that science is the vocation of exploring God's creation, and that science and biblical faith would always walk hand in hand. That science would usurp revelation as the source of truth was an astonishing development. Yet to many educators this seemed necessary if the university was to faithfully reflect the philosophies of pluralism that America's increasingly diverse society demanded.

So it is not surprising that some three centuries after the founding of Harvard, the professors of that university concluded that notions of biblical authority were contrary to the pluralism the university had to nurture. In the influential Harvard Report of 1945, entitled "General Education in a Free Society," the professors advised against offering religious studies in the undergraduate school. Science, not the revelation of Scripture, had become the source for truth.

In the sixteenth century, Protestantism had rejected papal authority. Likewise, Harvard now found it helpful to "reject the unique authority of the Scriptures. . . . "[4] Great literature would replace religious studies in the core curriculum. The reason for this necessary transformation was the reality of American pluralistic culture with "its varieties of faith and even of unfaith."[5]

Certainly an impositional approach to Christian faith has contributed to the revulsion against revealed authority that characterizes Harvard and many other universities today. There is a widespread assumption among academics that those who embrace biblical authority are a danger to democratic, pluralist society. A decade ago an editorial in *Christianity Today* observed, "A recent poll reveals that one in three academics now view evangelicals as a 'serious threat to democracy.'"[6]

It is ironic, however, that universities have sidelined the study of Scripture in their alleged defense of democratic pluralism. At Harvard and throughout most of public American academia today, the truth claims of the gospel are not admissible for serious study.

Even a century ago, Protestantism was the establishment truth center in American public academia; today nonbelief reigns as the establishment creed in America's public universities.[7] It appears that neither "Protestant establishment nor established non-belief"[8] has been conducive to nurturing a healthy pluralistic ethos. Nevertheless, in my judgment, "established non-belief" is far more pernicious in its affront to pluralist society than was the "Protestant establishment."

The university experience in the United States is in continuity with the mainstream of Western culture. In the liberal pluralistic democracies of Europe and North America, there is profound aversion to universal truth claims.

It is far easier for me to converse about truth claims with Muslim friends than with friends who embrace an ideology of pluralism or science-centrism. Muslims believe truth is revealed. So do I. We debate and dialogue about that truth.

But not so with my friends who are secularists. For them science, not revelation, is the source of truth data; agnosticism must reign in any region of human existence that science cannot probe. And in any event all religions are fundamentally the same, and all values are relative to one's culture. That relativistic commitment is the truth. Any other stance would undermine the ideology of pluralism that is fundamental to democratic institutions.

Lesslie Newbigin's Contribution

Lesslie Newbigin spent many decades in church leadership in India. Following his return to England, he discovered that the ideology of pluralism, and the paradoxical confidence in science as the source of all truth, were tenaciously central to the worldview of the people of his Birmingham parish. In India he had encountered relativism but not the deep-seated scientism of England. He responded by writing prolifically about the gospel and pluralism.[9]

We had hoped that Newbigin would participate in the March 1998 conference that provided the impetus for this book and that he would contribute an essay in this volume. However, his wife took ill, and then the Lord called him home shortly before the conference.

Newbigin sometimes quoted an excerpt from the Westminster Confession: "We are created to glorify God and enjoy him forever." We rejoice that Lesslie Newbigin is now celebrating that truth, enjoying God forever.

This volume is dedicated to Newbigin. Our hope is that this compendium of essays will encourage many to continue Newbigin's commitment to faithfully represent the gospel with neighbors, among those who have not yet heard the gospel, and in the public squares of our pluralistic villages everywhere.

Pluralist Society and Ideologies of Pluralism

As we begin to explore the essays that follow, it is helpful to keep in mind the difference between *pluralistic* and *pluralism*. We live in a world that is indeed pluralistic—with many religions and cultures. Pluralism, however, is an ideology or philosophy. This philosophy holds that the only authentic way to live harmoniously in diversity is to become relativists: to insist that there is no such thing as universal truth. Values that are relative to a culture are acceptable, but not universal truth.

A commitment to pluralist societies, however, does not necessarily mean that one embraces pluralism as a philosophy. The writers of the essays that follow believe that a commitment to Christ requires genuine respect for the dignity, freedom, and eternal significance of the person.

We believe that a confession of faith in Christ, when given in the servant spirit of Jesus the Christ, does nurture the respect for the person that is essential to pluralist, democratic, civil society.

The authors of these essays seek to encourage the kind of pluralist culture that provides an arena for open debate about truth. We believe the church should nurture that kind of culture. It is for this reason that this compendium will address ideologies of pluralism that reject any ultimate truth claims except the "truth" of relativism or the data of scientism.

The Essays in this Book

As noted earlier, this book grows out of presentations originally given at a consultation.

The first essay is by Gerald H. Anderson. "Christian Mission in Our Pluralistic World" surveys the challenge and critique to mission that ideologies of pluralism present. The concluding essay by Chris Wright, "What Difference Does Jesus Make?" summarizes and pulls together the soul of this volume in the spirit of a confessional commitment to faithfulness to the gospel.

In the current debate concerning Christian faith in a pluralistic world, participants often assume that the church is today facing the challenge of diversity for the first time. However, the chapters by biblical scholars (Elmer Martens, J. Nelson Kraybill, and Wright) demonstrate that the issues of covenant commitment to God in a world of multiple faith loyalties are as old as Scripture.

John D. Roth's essay on the Anabaptist movement of the sixteenth century focuses on the commitment of that community to recapture the New Testament commitment to discipleship. The Anabaptists believed that a New Testament church is always a discipling community among alternative communities and commitments.

Of course, it is not just the Christian movement that is engaged with pluralism. Three essays look at very different ways other systems—Islam, Hinduism, and postmodernism—address pluralism. There is also an essay from a Christian perspective beyond Europe and North America; Tite Tienou comments on the pluralistic African experience.

Five essays interact with the biblical and Anabaptist experience as they address modern realities. The North American setting is the explicit theme of the essay by Wilbert Shenk, "The Church in Pluralistic North America." Calvin Shenk reflects on the relationship of the gospel to other religions. Linford Stutzman gives particular attention to the challenge of confessing the gospel as public truth in the public square and the cultural transformation that this kind of confession anticipates.

Two essays address global village concerns. Tom Finger reflects on our pluralistic world and Sara Wenger Shenk on the challenges and privileges of living as global Christians in a global community. The truth is nonsense, she says, unless it can be seen and experienced; the faithful church is the in-history hermeneutic of the gospel. The book ends with a testimonial of personal commitment to Jesus by a global church person, Donald R. Jacobs.

The Intention

Finally, I reproduce the statement of intention for the consultation and the essays:

> [This book] is built on the central confession of the Anabaptist movement that Jesus Christ of the Scriptures is both Lord and Savior. We affirm this confessional tradition and are committed to following Christ in faithful discipleship and inviting others to join us in this way of life. This confession and invitation has always been challenged by the dominant culture. As the twentieth century comes to a close, this confession is undergoing intense critique. The root of the critique is multi-faceted.
>
> Several themes which especially challenge the confession "Jesus is Lord" are these:
> * Modern mobility and communication have introduced Christians everywhere to the reality that we do, indeed, live in a pluralistic world.
> * Pervading assumption, especially in Euro-American culture, that truth claims are always relative to one's particular culture.
> * Embarrassment about the expressions of cultural arrogance that sometimes accompanied the nineteenth- and twentieth-century missionary movement.
> * Disconcerting awareness that Western "Christianized" societies are becoming increasingly decadent, and that these same societies have nurtured colossal global conflagrations in this so-called Christian century.
> * A widespread assumption in Euro-American culture that the foundations of Christian faith are mythical.
>
> We believe that we must reaffirm the confession "Jesus is Lord" in light of these issues and reshape our commitments to address the present situation. In doing so, we hope to offer insights of

the Anabaptist heritage to the larger Christian family which is struggling with the same issues. We believe this perspective offers an alternative to both a mainline Protestantism troubled by the demise of establishment Christianity and a type of Evangelicalism that dreams of restoring the church's social dominance.[10]

This book aims to equip disciples of Jesus who desire to commend the way, the truth, and the life of Jesus in our pluralistic world.

Notes

1. Saulius Suziedelis, *The Sword and the Cross, A History of the Church in Lithuania* (Huntington, Ind.: Our Sunday Visitor Publishing Division, 1988), 19-26.

2. Dr. Leondias Donskis, Chair, Department of Philosophy; Director, Center for the Study of Comparative Civilizations, Klaipeda University, Commencement Address, Lithuania Christian College, May 9, 1999.

3. George M. Marsden, *The Soul of the American University: From Protestant Establishment to Established Nonbelief* (New York: Oxford University Press, 1994), 43.

4. Ibid., 389.

5. Ibid., 389.

6. John N. Akers, editorial, "Evangelism's Search for Tomorrow," *Christianity Today*, September 2, 1988, 11.

7. Marsden.

8. Marsden, title page.

9. See, for example, Lesslie Newbigin, *The Gospel in a Pluralist Society* (Grand Rapids, Mich.: Eerdmans, 1989); *Truth to Tell: The Gospel as Public Truth* (Grand Rapids: Eerdmans, 1991); *A Word in Season* (Grand Rapids: Eerdmans, 1994).

10. "Introduction," *Practicing Truth, Confident Witness in our Pluralistic World* (consultation at Eastern Mennonite Seminary, sponsored by Eastern Mennonite Missions and John Coffman Center for Evangelism and Church Planting of Eastern Mennonite Seminary, March 26-28, 1998).

Practicing Truth

CHAPTER ONE

Christian Mission in Our Pluralistic World[1]

Gerald H. Anderson

We cannot begin this volume without thinking about Lesslie Newbigin, who died January 30, 1998. In my view, no one in the last half of the twentieth century did more than Bishop Newbigin to help us think about the issues of "Christian Mission in Our Pluralistic World." It is our great loss that he is no longer with us.

Bishop Newbigin will be widely remembered as a missionary statesman, but above all he was a global evangelist. At eighty-seven he was still traveling around the world, preaching and persuading people to believe the gospel of Jesus Christ—that it is historical, factual, and true. In his last contribution to the *International Bulletin of Missionary Research* he said, "There cannot be any greater task, or any deeper joy, than to tell the world what God has done for us in Jesus Christ and to enable others to know, love, and serve him as Lord and Savior."[2]

We praise God for the life and legacy of Lesslie Newbigin on behalf of Christ's mission to the world. I will include his views at several points.

A Personal Beginning

My own reflection on mission and religious pluralism began in my senior year at Boston University School of Theology. In those days we had a one-semester required course in Christian world mission. The course was taught by visiting professor Fred Field Goodsell, who had recently retired as general secretary of what was then known as the American Board of Commissioners for Foreign Missions.

One morning Goodsell said to us, "I want you to imagine that you are riding in a compartment on a train in India. Sitting across from you is an Indian gentleman who is a Hindu. During the course of your conversation, he learns that you are a Christian, and he asks you, 'What does Christ mean to you, and why should I become a Christian?'

"You have three minutes to give your answer," Goodsell said, "and we will go in alphabetical order. Anderson, you go first. Come up here in front of the class and tell us—or rather, tell the Hindu man on the train—what Christ means to you, and why he should become a Christian."

I do not remember anything I said. I only remember how nervous I was, and wishing that my name was Zabrisky! But I never forgot the question, and it started me thinking about the challenge of communicating the gospel in a context of religious pluralism.

Little did I realize then that in my lifetime this would become the most critical, controversial, and divisive issue in mission. It involves a theology of religions in which Christians articulate their understanding of the relationship between God's redemptive activity in Jesus Christ and people of other faiths. Since World War II there has been a resurgence and expansion among some of the other world religions, along with the emergence of a number of aggressive new religious movements. Christians in the West, like those in the non-Western world, now find themselves increasingly living in community with people of other faiths. The problem is that we are not theologically equipped to deal with this. In the ecumenical movement, the concern for Christian mission has not kept up with the concern for Christian unity.

This is apparent in the increasing marginalization of mission and evangelism in the World Council of Churches, where there is a loss of memory about the roots of the ecumenical movement in the missionary movement of the nineteenth century. The result, as I have been saying for years, is that while there may be more consciousness of religious pluralism today, the churches in the West are not prepared to deal with it missiologically. The fruits of long missionary experience in the encounter with people of other faiths in other parts of the world have not been appropriated in the West.

Krister Stendahl reminds us that "the birth of the true understanding of other religions actually came through missionaries who were courageous enough to think about what they experienced. The real theological depth of the comparative study of religions would not have existed in the West had we not had the missionary movement of the eighteenth and nineteenth centuries."[3]

It is ironic that anthropologists today tend toward general suspicion of and cynicism about missionaries. John Peel of London University's School of Oriental and African Studies points out that, in the end, village people in many parts of the world do not remember the anthropologists who studied them. They don't name their children or schools for them as they do missionaries who came and lived and died among them.[4]

The Gospel and People of Other Faiths

The relation of the gospel to people of other faiths has always been an issue in Christian mission. Yet never before has it been so urgent and critical for study and discussion.

In recent decades an extremely wide divergence of views on this has developed in the church. We recall, for instance, the message of the Jerusalem meeting of the International Missionary Council in 1928. This classic Christocentric statement was drafted and read by William Temple, who later became archbishop of Canterbury. It echoed the message from the 1927 World Conference on Faith and Order.

"The message of the church to the world is and must always remain the Gospel of Jesus Christ," the Jerusalem statement declared. Indeed, the very nature of the gospel "forbids us to say that it may be the right belief for some but not for others. Either it is true for all, or it is not true at all. . . . We cannot live without Christ and we cannot bear to think of [others] living without Him." Addressing non-Christians, the message said:

> We rejoice to think that just because in Jesus Christ the light that lighteth every man shone forth in its full splendor, we find rays of that same light where He is unknown or even is rejected. We welcome every noble quality in non-Christian persons or systems as further proof that the Father, who sent His Son into the world, has nowhere left Himself without witness. . . . [We invite everyone] to share with us the pardon and the life that we have found in Christ.[5]

This contrasts sharply with the message from the Conference on World Mission, sponsored by the World Council of Churches at Salvador, Brazil, in 1996. The Salvador statement has no explicit mention of the uniqueness, the universality, or the adequacy of the gospel of Jesus Christ for the salvation of humanity. There is no suggestion that everyone (or anyone!) needs the gospel, no urgency or passion for evangelism. In fact, it is difficult to determine from the message of the conference just what the gospel is.

The theme of the conference was "Called to One Hope: The Gospel in Diverse Cultures." After one session, Bishop Newbiggin said to me that the participants were obviously more interested in culture than in the gospel. In the conference message, the only mention of the gospel's relation to people of other faiths said:

> Christians in many places around the globe are engaging in serious dialogue with people of other faiths, telling the Christian story, listening attentively to the stories of others, and thus gaining a clearer and richer understanding of their own faith and helping to build a "community of communities" to the benefit of all.[6]

In his reflections after the conference, Bishop Newbigin wrote, "I must say that I missed very much the sense that we do have a Gospel—that we have good news, and that it has been entrusted to us as a precious treasure on behalf of the world. . . . In the plenary discussions and in the findings [of the Salvador Conference] there were few references to evangelism." The World Council of Churches, he said, needs to give "much more evidence of being filled with a longing to bring the Gospel to all peoples. . . . It does seem to have lost the missionary passion that was the vital force that created the ecumenical movement."[7]

This critical assessment from Bishop Newbigin is significant because it exposes the theological malaise and disarray in the WCC regarding Christian mission and religious pluralism. Indeed, the greatest threat to the Christian mission today comes not from outside—from Islam, communism, or authoritarian governments. The church can deal with those. The greatest threat to mission today comes from inside the church itself, from a rampant, radical, theological relativism that denies the unique, ultimate, and universal claims of the gospel.

This relativism is eating away at the spiritual fabric of the church like a cancer, yet unlike cancer it is unfortunately contagious. Most of our churches are infected with it. The results are apparent in terms of decline in membership, decline in support for world mission, and decline in passion for evangelistic outreach.

I recently heard a group of seminary students argue that, while the gospel is valid and important for those who are in the church, to say that everyone needs the gospel or to try to evangelize people of other faiths would be arrogant and imperialistic. Jesus, they said, may be our savior, but he is not the only savior; we have our covenant with God through Jesus Christ, but other people have other covenants that serve them. For these seminary students the gospel was not a matter of life and death; it was relative, depending on culture, custom, or perhaps convenience.

It is not hard to find examples of where this has come from. Some years ago in *Christian Century*, Deane William Ferm, then of Mount Holyoke College, wrote:

Except for a phalanx of conservative rearguard figures, I know of no mainstream theologians today, Catholic or Protestant, who are brazen advocates of the uniqueness and once-for-allness of the Christian revelation. . . . Both Catholics and mainstream Protestants are renouncing the efforts to evangelize Jews. We are increasing contact with other religions of the world, and an insistence on the uniqueness of the historical Jesus can only be a hindrance. . . . It is just too preposterous to believe that God gave her/his world-embracing love uniquely through Jesus.[8]

While Ferm is not a theological heavyweight, it is hard to respond to him without engaging in metaphysical speculation quite apart from the biblical testimony. Rarely, I have noticed, does any argument for radical relativism in theology and mission refer to the Bible.

Let me give some additional illustrations. Shubert Ogden, longtime professor of theology at Southern Methodist University, says in his book *Is There Only One True Religion or Are There Many?* that there can be many true religions. "Religions other than Christianity can as validly claim to be formally true as it can," he says. Therefore, he sees no need for an evangelistic mission to people of other faiths.[9]

John B. Cobb Jr. for many years was professor of theology at the School of Theology in Claremont, California. He says he "locates salvation in the future as that toward which history moves . . . anticipated in Jesus Christ . . . but in its fullness it is not yet here." This salvific future, he says, "will contain the contributions of other religious traditions as well as Christianity" because each religion has "its own irreplaceable role to play in the economy of God's salvation of the world." Cobb holds "the view that we move toward the fullness of God's purpose for humankind as we learn from others and are thus transformed. . . . This means that Jesus Christ and our witness to him play a unique role in the salvation of the world. But it does not mean that other religious communities have nothing to contribute to that salvation."[10] Therefore, he proposes no mission of evangelization to people of other faiths.

Two other U.S. theologians who have contributed to the problem are Gordon Kaufman, professor of divinity at Harvard Divinity School, and Langdon Gilkey, professor of theology at the University of Chicago. Both have essays in *The Myth of Christian Uniqueness*, edited by John Hick and Paul Knitter.[11]

The authors in this volume propose that Christians should abandon claims about the uniqueness of Christ and Christianity, or about having any definitive revelation. Instead, Christians should accept instead that there is a plurality of revelations and a parity of religions, with

Christianity simply one among many religions through which people may be saved.

For Kaufman, Christian theology is not based on divine revelation, but on "human imaginative response," informed by "modern historical consciousness." This modern historical consciousness, he claims, liberates us from belief in divine inspiration and revelation, enabling us to see that our religious traditions are the product of human imaginative creativity[12] and that our theological statements and claims are simply "the product of our own human study and reflection."[13]

The problem with this—as Lesslie Newbigin pointed out—is that Kaufman takes it for granted that the Christian gospel is not true. Newbigin reminds us that "'modern historical consciousness' is also a culturally conditioned phenomenon and does not provide us with a standpoint from which we can dispose of truth-claims of the Bible. . . . [It] provides no grounds on which it is possible to deny that God might have acted decisively to reveal and effect the divine purpose for human history."[14]

Langdon Gilkey, in his essay, admits that what the authors in this volume are doing represents what he calls "a monstrous shift" from a belief that Christianity contains "the definitive revelation among other religions to some sort of plurality of revelations" and a "rough parity" of religions, with "recognition of the co-validity and the co-efficacy of other religions." This position, he says, involves *all* theological doctrines, not just some of them,"[15] and it "has devastating theological effects," which he believes are desirable.[16] The problem, he admits, is that soon "we have no grounds for speaking of salvation at all, a situation of relativity far beyond asking about the salvation of all."[17] However, he finds that a position of absolute relativity "seems to defy intellectual resolution," so he opts instead for "relative absoluteness"—with "one part absoluteness and two parts relativity."[18]

What does Gilkey propose then as the center for theological understanding? He proposes "the absolute as *relatively* present in the relative—as the clue to the center of theological understanding."[19] That is as relative as you can get—relatively speaking, of course. Or as Lesslie Newbigin said, "I remain totally unconvinced by the idea of an absolute that is available on call when it is relatively necessary."[20] It is hard to imagine that anyone would ever be converted or want to join the church on the basis of this "clue to the center of theological understanding." Can you imagine that anyone would ever be willing to die for this? Or that John Wesley would have had his heart strangely warmed by "the absolute as relatively present in the relative"?

As I mentioned earlier, it is characteristic that those who are proposing a radical theological relativism rarely refer to the Bible. And that is the case with Shubert Ogden, John Cobb, Gordon Kaufman, and Langdon Gilkey. In the writings I have cited, they do not mention the Bible.[21] They take for granted, without discussion, that the Bible has little or nothing to offer.

In fact, the Bible has much to contribute to the discussion. Sadly, however, we face the problem of biblical illiteracy, even in our churches. *The New York Times* reported a survey recently in which 33 percent of U.S. adults say they read the Bible at least once a week. Of those who claim to read the Bible weekly, however, 54 percent cannot name the four Gospels. Sixty-three percent don't know what a Gospel is. Fifty-eight percent can't name five of the Ten Commandments, and 10 percent think Joan of Arc was Noah's wife.[22]

The Bible is a missionary book, about a missionary God, who sends Jesus as a missionary, and the church that continues his mission. This is summarized most clearly in the so-called Great Commission of the risen Christ, which is generally considered the premier text for the world mission of the church: "Go therefore and make disciples of all nations, baptizing them in the name of the Father and of the Son and of the Holy Spirit, and teaching them to obey everything that I have commanded you" (Matt. 28:19-20). Parallels of it appear in all four Gospels and in Acts 1.

According to Karl Barth, "The great commission is truly the most genuine utterance of the risen Jesus." It is the great turning point in history, Barth said. The temporary restriction of going only to the house of Israel (Matt. 10:5) is lifted after the resurrection, and the apostles are sent to make disciples of all nations.[23] Moreover, according to David J. Bosch, "There can be little doubt that Matthew himself understood the last verses of chapter 28 to be the key to his entire Gospel."[24]

These texts for the great commission illustrate and highlight what is pervasive throughout the New Testament and, indeed, the whole Bible: that God is a revealing and redeeming God, a sending and seeking God, a missionary God. A few years ago the Catholic bishops in the United States issued a Pastoral Statement on world mission that began with the affirmation, "Jesus was a missionary."[25] The great commission is a passionate and urgent directive. The risen Christ tells his followers to continue his mission by discipling, baptizing, and teaching all nations—all people, without exception, to the ends of the earth.

Continuity and Discontinuity

Even for those who recognize the inspiration and authority of Scripture, and who take seriously the lordship of Christ, there are difficulties in describing and defining the relationship between the gospel and people of other faiths.

In Scripture and in the history of Christian doctrine, there are two major streams or traditions regarding the relationship of God's redemptive activity in Jesus Christ and God's activity among people of other faiths.[26] One tradition, while recognizing the uniqueness and universality of Jesus Christ, emphasizes the *continuity* of God's revealing and redeeming activity in Christ with God's activity among all people everywhere. It views Christian faith as the climax of a divine revelation that began long before human history and has been available to everyone.

Jesus Christ in this view is crucial, normative, and definitive, but not exclusive. What is true of Jesus Christ in a focal way is pervasively true of the whole cosmos. He is the key or clue to the rest of God's working. But the Word of God is not limited to and did not end with the revelation in the historic person of Jesus. There is much biblical and patristic testimony in support of this tradition, which is summed up in the statement that God "has not left himself without a witness" among all nations, even those who had no knowledge of the biblical revelation (Acts 14:16-17).

The other tradition emphasizes a radical *discontinuity* between the realm of Christian revelation, which is unique, and the whole range of non-Christian religious experience. In this view, the non-Christian religions are the various efforts of human beings to apprehend their existence, whereas Christianity is the result of the self-disclosure of God in Jesus Christ. God has spoken to humanity only in the person of Jesus Christ, and "there is salvation in no one else" (Acts 4:12). This tradition—which is the narrow, exclusivist tradition—is equally, if not more strongly, represented in Scripture and the history of Christian doctrine.

These two streams of teaching and tradition are hard to reconcile; they seem almost contradictory. Yet they are often found almost side-by-side in the New Testament. For instance, in John's Gospel, we are told that Jesus was "the true light, which enlightens everyone" (1:9). Yet in the same passage we are told that "The light shines in the darkness" (1:5; not everything was light!), and it was only to those "who believed in his name, [that] he gave power to become children of God" (1:12).

John 3 tells us that God sent his only son into the world that the world might be saved through him. Those who believe in him are not condemned; those who do not believe are condemned. In John 10, Jesus says, "I am the gate. Whoever enters by me will be saved," but there are "other sheep that do not belong to this fold. I must bring them also.... So there shall be one flock, one shepherd."

In John 14:2, Jesus says, "In my Father's house, there are many dwelling places," which some pluralists quote to suggest that there are many religions in the kingdom of God, of equal value. But in that same chapter Jesus also said, "I am the way, and the truth, and the life. No one comes to the Father except through me" (14:6).

Similarly, in Acts we find Peter telling some Gentiles, "I truly understand that God shows no partiality, but in every nation anyone who fears him and does what is right is acceptable to him" (10:34b-35). Then Peter tells them that all who believe in Jesus receive forgiveness of sins, whereupon "the Holy Spirit fell on all who heard the word" and Peter "ordered them to be baptized in the name of Jesus Christ." (10:44, 48)

My point is that both these streams are part of the Christian tradition. Both have support in Scripture and patristic teaching. Both have been well represented in the history of Christian missions. The problem is that the church tends to swing its emphasis in different periods from one extreme to the other and thereby distorts its message and mission, presenting only a partial gospel.

Unfortunately, it is easier to present a partial, simplistic gospel than the full gospel, which is seldom simple. Both of these traditions in Christian thought must be maintained in balanced tension. This is hard to do when those from one tradition offer continuity with doubtful uniqueness, and those from the other side urge uniqueness without continuity. Needed in our theological understanding about Christian mission and religious pluralism is uniqueness *with* continuity.[27]

It is generally recognized that Christ is present and active among non-Christians. The more difficult question is whether Christ is present in non-Christian religions as such, and whether they may thereby be considered ways of salvation.

I recall many years ago asking D. T. Niles whether non-Christians could be saved in and through their own religions, without explicit faith in Christ. "If they are saved," he replied, "they are saved because of what Christ has done for them."

Niles elaborated on this in his book *The Preacher's Task and the Stone of Stumbling*. In it he said, "It is outside the preacher's competence or commission to pass judgment on what others claim to be their experience of salvation; his business is only to invite them to acknowledge Jesus Christ as their Saviour."[28]

Pope John Paul II expressed his views on this issue in his general audience on February 4, 1998, when he said:

> Apart from Christ there are no other autonomous sources or ways of salvation. . . . Therefore, in the great religions, which the church views with respect and esteem, . . . Christians recognize the presence of salvific elements that operate dependent on the influence of Christ's grace. . . . These religions can thus contribute, by virtue of the Holy Spirit who 'blows where he wills,' to help men along the path to eternal happiness.

But such activity, the pontiff said, is always "the result of Christ's redeeming action."[29]

"To the Jew First"

The foundation for a Christian theology of religions begins with the relationship of the gospel to the Jewish people. That is where the Christian mission began. If we cannot get that right in our missiology, then it is likely that nothing else will be right in our theology and our efforts to deal with religious pluralism.

While the relationship of the gospel to the Jewish people is distinctive, it is not totally different or separate from the relationship of the gospel to people of other faiths. There is no exemption of the Jewish people from the Christian mission.

Initially Jesus saw himself as "sent only to . . . the house of Israel" (Matt. 15:24; cf. 10:5-6), and for Paul the pattern of mission was "to the Jew first" (Rom. 1:16). It was only after the resurrection that the mission expanded beyond Israel to include the Gentiles and "all nations." This caused the first major controversy in the primitive church, over whether anyone *other than* Jews should be discipled.

It is ironic that today the controversy is just the opposite—whether Jews themselves should be discipled. It is also ironic that the reticence of early Jewish Christians to share the gospel with Gentiles is matched today by the reticence of Gentile Christians to share the gospel with Jews. Another irony is that whereas in the primitive church there was a controversy over whether Gentiles had to become Jews to be Christians, today there is a controversy over whether Jews have to become Gentiles and give up their Jewish heritage to be Christians.

It would never have occurred to Peter and Paul to think that they were no longer Jews after they came to faith in Jesus as the Messiah. Paul commonly spoke in synagogues wherever he went and proclaimed that Jesus was the Messiah. There are not two covenants with God, one for Jews and one for Christians. Rather God's covenant with Israel was fulfilled by Jesus, who proclaimed, "I have come not to abolish but to fulfill" the law (Matt. 5:17).

Today, however, it is considered theologically correct among many Protestant and Catholic theologians to say that Jews do not need the gospel of Jesus Christ because—it is said—Jews have their own covenant with God through Abraham, which renders faith in Jesus as the Messiah unnecessary. This concept is foreign to the New Testament and creates a flawed foundation for a Christian theology of religions. If a theologian says that Jews do not need the gospel, that same theologian will likely also deny that people of other faiths need the gospel. Thus, we end up with a theological relativism that rejects the Christian mission to *all* people of other faiths.

As F. Dale Bruner states in his commentary on Matthew, "The litmus test today on whether one really believes that Jesus is the Savior of the world is the position one takes on the evangelism of the Jewish people."[30] A theology of religions for Christian mission in our pluralistic world needs to begin with the affirmation that everyone—Jews and Gentiles alike—needs faith in Jesus Christ. There are no exemptions or exceptions to the universal mission of Christ. Remember the message of the Conference on World Mission at Jerusalem: "Either [the gospel] is true for all, or it is not true at all." A theology for Christian mission and religious pluralism must begin with the Jews and build on it for our understanding of mission to people of other faiths.

Interfaith Dialogue

In my work of editing the *Biographical Dictionary of Christian Missions*, I became increasingly aware of the important place that interfaith dialogue has had in Christian witness down through the centuries. One only has to mention the names of Mateo Ricci, Robert de Nobili, Robert Allen Hume, J. N. Farquhar, A. G. Hogg, Karl Ludwig Reichelt, Lewis Bevan Jones, and E. Stanley Jones to bring to mind just a few of the great missionary figures who have pioneered in interfaith dialogue.

Today the place of dialogue has grown in prominence and also in controversy over the proper role and relationship of dialogue to mission. There are three basic issues here. First, there is the fear and suspicion on the part of non-Christians that Christians are simply using dialogue as a device for evangelism—that dialogue is the new name for evangelism. Therefore, they question the motives of Christians who want to engage them in dialogue. Second, there is a suspicion in some Christian quarters that dialogue may lead to theological compromise and religious syncretism. Third, some Christians deny the validity of mission and claim that dialogue is the only viable form of Christian witness in the midst of religious pluralism. There is a great deal that could be said about these three issues, but I will comment very briefly on each.

First, *dialogue has its own integrity* as a mode of Christian witness to establish understanding, personal relationships, and cooperation with persons of other faiths. Dialogue, however, should not be used as a device with the intention of evangelism. As the World Conference on Mission and Evangelism at San Antonio, Texas, said in 1989, "We affirm that witness does not preclude dialogue but invites it, and that dialogue does not preclude witness but extends and deepens it. Dialogue has its own place and integrity and is neither opposed to nor incompatible with witness or proclamation."[31]

Second, there is always the possibility that *dialogue could lead to compromise and syncretism.* Some reckless statements by advocates of dialogue heighten that concern. Yet we really cannot avoid dialogue with people of other faiths today, so the responsible thing is to engage in dialogue, without compromise of our convictions. We should do so with full expectation that God is there in the midst of our effort, that we may be used by God, and that we may learn something in the process.

Third, *the claim that dialogue is the only valid mode of mission today leads to an unfortunate polarization* that must be avoided. Dialogue and mission are complementary modes of witness, each with its own integrity and validity. Dialogue is not to be used for evangelization, and mission is more than dialogue. Yet dialogue can provide opportunities for mutuality of witness.

I recall an incident at an interfaith consultation in which I participated a few years ago. A Christian theologian, Donald G. Dawe, proposed that

> the pattern of new being encoded in "the name of Jesus" is one that is encountered in many religious traditions. Christians identify it and celebrate it because of what they know through Jesus Christ. Other traditions live out of this power of new being in accordance with the names by which they encounter and participate in ultimate reality.

Dawe concluded that

> The finality of Jesus Christ is in the unconditioned way in which he points beyond himself, even to the point of surrendering his personal

selfhood, so that humankind may find healing in the Unconditioned. . . . The Christian religion will receive new life when it is willing to die to the demonic forms its claim to finality has taken. It will then enter fully into the power of the "name of Jesus." Christians must be willing to accept death of their ideologies to enter into the resurrection of new being.[32]

I am sure I was not the only Christian there who felt uncomfortable with this reduction of "the name of Jesus" to a code that is found in many religious traditions. But it was interesting that the most critical response to Dawe came not from a Christian but from a Jewish theologian, Eugene B. Borowitz. He said that in Dawe's concern to be inclusive, "he brings universalism to the brink of relativism. He gives us criteria for judging other faiths that are so broad . . . that it is not clear what, if any, religious way of life might give him Christian pause."

Borowitz was especially critical of Dawe's attempt to "departicularize Christianity." He cautioned the Christian theologian not to deny his roots, because in his desire "to humanize Christianity he has made it dispensable." Finally, the Jew asked the Christian whether he thought there would be "any *theological* loss if Christianity should disappear as an identifiable religion? Or would it mean the loss of merely another socio-cultural humanizing faith? We Jews," said Borowitz, "are much more particularistic than that."[33]

Here we have an example of interfaith dialogue at its best, of faith meeting faith and "speaking the truth in love" (Eph. 4:15), in an exchange of witness. We see the Christian admonished by the Jew to adhere more closely to historic Christian faith. The Jew knows the danger to identity and belief that comes from "the cumulative effect of . . . denial of our roots," and he laments "the potential death of a covenant partner." There is "no inherent need," Borowitz said, "to departicularize one's faith because one is drawn to its universal vision of humanity." Rather, he said, we should "acknowledge our simultaneous assertion of particular and universal truths and see how we can envision our particularity so as not to violate our universality."[34]

Christians need to learn this lesson about interfaith dialogue, and our partners from other faith communities need to remind us when we forget: namely, that minimal formulations of faith are neither accurate nor adequate expressions of the Christian tradition. As such, they do not serve in the long run to advance the cause of interfaith understanding and relations. Rather, they build on sand and betray our partners in the dialogue, who expect and deserve to hear the full gospel.

Conclusion

So if anyone asks, "What does Christ mean to you, and why should I become a Christian?" remember the words of 1 Peter 3:15, that you should "always be prepared to make a defense to anyone who calls you to account for the hope that is in you, yet do it with gentleness and reverence."

Notes

1. I have written on this subject many times, most recently in "Theology of Religions and Missiology: A Time of Testing," *The Good News of the Kingdom: Mission Theology for the Third Millennium*, ed. Charles Van Engen et al. (Maryknoll, N.Y.: Orbis Books, 1993), and "Theology of Religions: The Epitome of Mission Theology," *Mission in Bold Humility: David Bosch's Work Considered*, ed. Willem Saayman and Klippies Kritzinger (Maryknoll, N.Y.: Orbis Books, 1996). Some of what I have said elsewhere is included here.

2. Lesslie Newbigin, "The Dialogue of Gospel and Culture," *International Bulletin of Missionary Research* 21 (April 1997): 50.

3. Krister Stendahl, "Toward a New Generation: A Report to the CCJP from Its Moderator," London-Colney, June 22, 1981. Mimeographed, World Council of Churches, 1981, 1.

4. John Peel in discussions at a consultation of the Research Enablement Program in Nashville, Tennessee, May 1997.

5. *The Christian Life and Message in Relation to Non-Christian Systems: Report of the Jerusalem Meeting of the International Missionary Council, March 24-April 8, 1928* (London: Oxford University Press, 1928), 481ff.

6. "Conference Message from Salvador: Conference on World Mission and Evangelism, Salvador, Bahia, Brazil, November 24-December 3, 1996," *International Bulletin of Missionary Research* 21 (April 1997): 54.

7. Newbigin, "Dialogue of Gospel and Culture," 50, 52.

8. Deane William Ferm, "'The Road Ahead in Theology' Revisited," *Christian Century* (May 9, 1979): 525, 527.

9. Shubert M. Ogden, *Is There Only One True Religion or Are There Many?* (Dallas: Southern Methodist University Press, 1992), 83-84.

10. John B. Cobb Jr., "Salvation: Beyond Pluralism and Exclusivism," *Circuit Rider* 17, no. 1 (1993): 7-8.

11. John Hick and Paul Knitter, eds., *The Myth of Christian Uniqueness* (Maryknoll, N.Y.: Orbis Books, 1987).

12. Ibid., 8.

13. Ibid., 12.

14. Lesslie Newbigin, "Religious Pluralism and the Uniqueness of Jesus Christ," *International Bulletin of Missionary Research* 13 (April 1989): 50.

15. In Hick and Knitter, 41.

16. Ibid., 40.

17. Ibid., 44.

18. Ibid., 47.

19. Ibid.

20. Newbigin, "Religious Pluralism and the Uniqueness of Jesus Christ," 52.

21. Actually, Kaufman does allude to the Bible once when he says, "In the biblical documents God is portrayed as a quasi-personal or agential reality—that is, the model in terms of which the notion of God is constructed is the human self or agent" (p. 10).

22. Russell Shorto, "Belief by the Numbers," *New York Times Magazine*, December 7, 1997, 61.

23. Karl Barth, "An Exegetical Study of Matthew 28:16-20," *The Theology of the Christian Mission*, ed. Gerald H. Anderson (New York: McGraw-Hill, 1960), 67.

24. David J. Bosch, "The Structure of Mission: An Exposition of Matthew 28:16-20," *Exploring Church Growth*, ed. Wilbert R. Shenk (Grand Rapids, Mich.: Eerdmans Publishing Co., 1983), 223.

25. National Conference of Catholic Bishops in the U.S.A., "To the Ends of the Earth: A Pastoral Statement on World Mission," *International Bulletin of Missionary Research* 11 (April 1987): 50.

26. See my article on "Continuity and Discontinuity," *Concise Dictionary of the Christian World Mission*, ed. Stephen Neill et al. (Nashville: Abingdon Press, 1971), 146-47.

27. This formulation was first suggested by Edmund Davison Soper, *The Philosophy of the Christian World Mission* (Nashville: Abingdon-Cokesbury Press, 1943), 225-27.

28. D. T. Niles, *The Preacher's Task and the Stone of Stumbling* (New York: Harper & Brothers, 1958), 33.

29. Reported and quoted in *Inside the Vatican*, February 1998, 17.

30. F. Dale Bruner, *Matthew, Volume 2, The Churchbook* (Dallas: Word Publishing, 1990), 742.

31. World Conference on Mission and Evangelism, "Report of Section 1: Turning to the Living God," *International Review of Mission* 78 (July/October 1989): 352.

32. Donald G. Dawe, "Christian Faith in a Religiously Plural World," *Christian Faith in a Religiously Plural World*, ed. Donald G. Dawe and John B. Carman (Maryknoll, N.Y.: Orbis Books, 1978), 31-32.

33. Eugene B. Borowitz, "A Jewish Response: The Lure and Limits of Universalizing Our Faith," *Christian Faith in a Religiously Plural World*, ed. Donald G. Dawe and John B. Carman (Maryknoll, N.Y.: Orbis Books, 1978), 66-67.

34. Ibid., 63-67.

CHAPTER TWO

God, Justice, and Religious Pluralism in the Old Testament

Elmer Martens

Religious pluralism, the competing claims to truth of rival religions, is hardly new. The Bible knows well this reality. In leaving Ur of the Chaldeans, Abraham left a Babylonian religion characterized by multiple deities. In Egypt, to which Abraham's descendants later moved, the religious environment was replete with gods such as Osiris and Isis.

The exodus took Israel to Canaan where, as we now know from archaeology, the pantheon of El, including Baal and Astarte, held sway. Later, Israel in exile was tossed back into the Chaldean cauldron of religious beliefs. Upon returning home, Israel was soon confronted and affronted by the Hellenizing Antiochus Epiphanes, who challenged the worship of one God by desecrating Jerusalem's temple. Still later, as a New Testament scholar notes, "The world in which the epistles were written was a world steeped in religious pluralism."[1]

Religious pluralism is biblical agenda. This essay investigates the portion of Scripture known as the Old Testament, or (in awareness of Jewish sensitivities) as the Hebrew Bible. It is also called the First Testament, to delineate its position on the issue of religious pluralism.

The purpose of this study is to give orientation to the twenty-first-century church, which is sharply challenged in its mission.[2] I will begin by identifying the point of entry for this study, then elaborate in turn on God's stance toward other so-called deities, toward other faith systems, and toward adherents of these faith systems. Finally, I will comment on Israel's interaction with other faiths.

46

A Controlling Viewpoint: Justice

At several nodal points in her history, Israel confronted with special sharpness the challenge of religious pluralism. At Israel's entry into the land of promise, Moses warned the people about entanglements with Canaanite religions. During Israel's monarchy era, Elijah encountered a state-established Baal cult under the auspices of Jezebel of Phoenicia (1 Kings 17–19). After Israel's exile the issue again loomed large, as Jerusalemites became fascinated with solar deities, Tammuz, and a wide spectrum of alien worship practices (Ezek. 8).

Scholars have followed different methods, but mostly methods of a historical cast, in examining the Old Testament for its teaching on pluralism.[3] This essay takes the approach of looking for a "control belief."[4]

One possible candidate for such a controlling viewpoint is the kingdom of God. This term is a major component in the New Testament material, and some scholars have also oriented the Old Testament around it.[5] This position poses a number of problems, however, including the relatively rare occurrence of the expression in the Old Testament.[6]

By contrast, the term "justice," along with its synonym "righteousness," is pervasive throughout the Old Testament. "Justice" (*mishpat*) appears more than 425 times in the Old Testament. Its importance as a major motif has been championed by R. P. Knierim.[7]

In the popular view, justice stands for fairness. The guilty are punished, the innocent are set free, the good are rewarded. The vocabulary of justice is legal, court-related. In the Old Testament the legal dimensions are certainly represented. But mishpat is better understood as practicing honorable relationships. This kind of justice reaches beyond the tribunal and the court to every conceivable human activity.

Justice is often coupled with righteousness (*sedaqa*). Righteousness is the disposition to do what is right according to an accepted standard. Biblically, righteousness is what God has declared correct and lawful.[8]

"Doing justice," the Hebrew idiom, is the implementation of divine norms, a "hands-on" righteousness. The emphasis on justice is an emphasis on conduct, behind which is the standard of righteousness.[9] The conduct in question occurs in the context of many relationships: person to person, spouse to spouse, teacher to pupil, citizen to nation, human to environment, and a host of others, including especially the relationship between a person and God.

Justice, in its popular Western definition, has a hard edge. Justice, as defined in the Bible, has a large component of compassion. The practice of daily life is characterized by love—love to God and love to neighbor. Justice, with its eye trained on the poor and disadvantaged, has a merciful tone. For a king to do justice may well include punishing the evildoer, but it also includes paying attention to the victim: "O house of David! Thus says the Lord: Execute justice in the morning, and deliver from the hand of the oppressor anyone who has been robbed. . ."(Jer. 21:12). Mercy and love are integral to justice and righteousness.

The God of Justice and the Plurality of Deities

In the Old Testament, religious pluralism took the form of polytheism. In the ancient Near East environment, the claim that there is but one true God was challenged. This challenge was met by asserting that Yahweh was the true God and by offering evidence, especially along the lines of justice, to support that claim.

Assertions of Yahweh's Uniqueness

The assertions about God's uniqueness, especially his incomparability, are found at those points noted at the beginning of this essay. Following the drama of the exodus experience, Israel confessed its faith by calling attention to the twin categories of holiness and power: "Who is like you, O Lord, among the gods?" (Exod. 15:11).[10]

During the era of the monarchy, Israel was confronted both inside its borders and beyond with the Canaanite baals. In the Psalms—many of which can be traced to this period—the refrain is frequent: Who is like God? (Ps. 35:10; 71:18-19; cf. Ps. 113:5-9). The question of who can be compared to Yahweh is answered in the statement: "Righteousness and justice are the foundation of your throne. . ." (Ps. 89:6, 14).[11]

If parts of Isaiah derive from the exile, as scholars sometimes claim, then statements there about God's greatness and incomparability may be intended to address the advances of Babylonian polytheistic claims. "Who is like me?" God asks (Isa. 44:7; cf. 46:9c). Labuschagne has demonstrated that the force of this question is not only to place Yahweh as the topmost figure in a hierarchical ranking but is idiomatic for placing Israel's God outside the category of "regular" deities altogether.[12] Yahweh, by reason of his justice and power, is in a class by himself.

Such assertions about God's incomparability fit logically with this assertion made at nodal points in Israel's history: Yahweh alone is God. It is a monotheistic claim that Israel hears in Moses' *shema*: "The Lord is our God, the Lord alone" (Deut. 6:4). Translators and interpreters give various renderings, such as "The Lord is one," for the final half of the confession.[13] Possibly both unity and uniqueness are intended in the shema. However nuanced, monotheism is implicit in the assertion.[14]

In the contest between Yahweh and Baal staged by Elijah on Mt. Carmel, the people render the verdict: "The Lord indeed is God; the Lord indeed is God" (1 Kings 18:39). That note about exclusiveness is heard again and again in Israel's later history, despite propagandists in Babylon favoring a multiplicity of deities. Isaiah, for one, is intransigent: "Thus says the Lord . . . I am the first and I am the last; besides me there is no god" (Isa. 44:6; cf. 44:8). "Before me no god was formed, nor shall there be any after me" (Isa. 43:10c). "I am God, and there is no other" (46:9b).

Isaiah insisted on the absoluteness of Yahwistic faith. It is to this belief about monotheism that Paul is heir when he states: "For there is one God. . ." (1 Tim. 2:5).

Evidences for Yahweh as Sole Deity

Scripture does more than baldly assert that there is one God: it supplies reasons for the assertion. Some of the verifications for God's exclusiveness and incomparability are rational (left brain) in appeal; others are more visionary and mystical (right brain).

Verification for the claim of Yahweh as the exclusively sovereign deity turns on several issues: power, the creation, divine engagement in history, and prediction. The story of Pharaoh's obstinacy in allowing enslaved Israel to leave his country, and the plagues that follow, makes a particular point: Egypt, and Israel too, are to acknowledge the greatness of Yahweh's power and position as the only God (Exod. 7:5, 17; 8:10, 22; 9:14; 10:2; 12:12; 14:4, 18; 16:12). The issue of power is also key in the contest with the prophets of Baal at Mt. Carmel (1 Kings 18:20-40).

A particular form of the argument for God's power is elaborated by Isaiah, whose apologetic for Yahweh is frequently based on creation. The rhetorical question, "To whom then will you compare me, or who is my equal?" is answered immediately by a reference to creation: "Lift up your eyes on high and see: Who created these?" (Isa. 40:25-26; cf. 48:12-13; 43:15; 44:24).

Another argument verifying God's sovereignty is his engagement on the plane of history.[15] Ezekiel's book, in which this is a key point, is distinguished by the so-called recognition formula, "And they/you shall know that I am Yahweh." This occurs more than 80 times. W. Zimmerli observes that it is not by speculation or philosophical reasoning that people will be persuaded about Yahweh but because of what has happened in history as a result of Yahweh's judgment and salvation.[16]

Isaiah's apologetic, related to history, focuses on prediction, the reality of prophecy and its fulfillment (Isa. 41:21-24). In contrast to other so-called deities, it is Yahweh who "has announced from of old the things to come" (44:7; cf. 46:8-11; 48:5).

Other arguments for Yahweh's supremacy and incomparability appeal to pictorial scenarios and visions. Psalm 82 draws on a mythology of divine councils and establishes the uniqueness of Yahweh as the sole divinity, with particular reference to justice. Hypothetically, so one is to read the psalm, a plurality of deities take their place in the divine council over which Yahweh holds court. At issue at once is the question of their administration of justice. "How long will you judge unjustly?" the gods are asked (82:2). The directive is clear-cut and expresses the passion of Yahweh: "Give justice to the weak and the orphan; maintain the right of the lowly and the destitute. Rescue the weak and the needy; deliver them from the hand of the wicked" (82:3-4). The gods are summarily deposed and cast to the earth as mortals. Thus God, so committed to justice, is to be feared in the councils of deities (Ps. 89:7, 14).[17]

Psalm 82 ends on a note of triumph with the supremacy of Yahweh clearly established, "Rise up, O God, judge the earth; for all the nations belong to you!" (82:8). It is by the criterion of justice that polytheism, a subset of pluralism, is to be addressed: "Justice, just rule, is that central activity by which God is God."[18]

Visions provide another apologetic for Yahweh's greatness. Note Moses at the burning bush (Exod. 3) and at Sinai (Exod. 32-34), as well as Elijah (1 Kings 19:11-18). More graphic and explicit are the depictions given by Isaiah (6:1-13) and Ezekiel (1:4–2:2). Ezekiel reports in great detail his vision of the chariot platform, the wheel, and the brilliance surrounding the one seated on the throne above the platform. The scene is spectacular; a summarizing word is *kabod* (glory, impressive, incredible), that quality that elicits worship. It is this God whom Ezekiel hears say: "I will feed them [Israel] with justice" (Ezek. 34:16). This extraordinary vision bears on religious pluralism, as is especially clear from the scene at the Jerusalem temple.

At the Jerusalem temple, where the kabod appears again, Ezekiel encounters a variety of other religious belief systems and practices (Ezek. 8-10). There in the temple is the image that provokes to jealousy—likely an asherah, a wooden pole representing the deity Astarte, dominant in Canaanite worship (8:5).[19]

In the temple inside a dark room are seventy Israelite leaders worshiping creatures, apparently according to the practices in Egypt (8:7-12). In the temple are worshipers of Tammuz, the dying and rising god of Assyria, with his counterpart Baal in Phoenecia (8:14). In the courtyard at the door of the temple are twenty-five males worshiping the solar deities, as was the custom in the ancient Near East generally (8:16). Talk about pluralism!

In the space of several hundred square yards in the temple court, Ezekiel is confronted with multiple religions. Inside this space there is also visible the glory of God, as Ezekiel had seen it in the inaugural vision (8:4). In the presence of Yahweh's awesome might and majesty, there is no need to debate the merits of these alternate deities and worship systems. Their illegitimacy is self-evident. No attempt is made to evaluate "from below" (from an anthropological stance) the rightness or wrongness of "other" religions. Seen "from above" (from a Yahwistic theology), all other religious preferences are a parody, a travesty.[20]

Some still claim that Israel never fully arrived at monotheism.[21] From the approach of a history of religion, that claim might be substantiated, but from the scriptural testimony there is no doubt about Israel's insistence on monotheism. Others have registered reservations that such a claim leads to intolerance, and that intolerance can lead to violence. But blame for violence cannot rightly be attributed to a belief in monotheism, for how one deals with competing claims or differences of viewpoints is a matter quite separate from the ideology at issue. To say that monotheistic belief contributes to world violence is to confuse cause and effect.[22]

Nevertheless, in the climate of postmodernism, the claim for monotheism is not always palatable. Regina A. Schwartz, for example, connects monotheism with notions of scarcity. She asks why God was stingy with his favors, so that only Abel's offering was acceptable. With the scarcity of divine favor, she claims, came murder and violence, and because of the emphasis on one God, one people, and one land, polarities and adversarial stances arose.[23]

In response, several points may be made. The first is to note that violence exists also where a plurality of gods are worshiped. Further, Schwartz's thesis is reductionistic. Violence, a complex phenomenon, has many sources—for example, greed and jealousy—so that an examination of human nature and fallibility might be more germane to her topic than the ideology of monotheism. More important still, her thesis quite overlooks and therefore fails to appreciate the nature of God's holiness as presented in the Bible. It is precisely God's righteousness and passion for justice which work against the negativity Schwartz attributes to the God of the Bible.

In summary, the Old Testament claim is that Yahweh, who is the God of Abraham, Isaac, and Israel, is also the God of the cosmos. He is so because he is the God of justice. All rival claims are empty, without warrant, weight, or ultimacy, because all other so-called gods are unjust (Ps. 82). Hence, claims by any other religion are met confrontationally with the verdict: "I am God, and there is no other" (Ps. 46:9b).

When it comes to pluralistic religions it is not tolerance but truth that is the issue. Christians confess in confidence that Yahweh, the God of Israel and the Father of Jesus Christ, is the sole deity and the only legitimate object of devotion and worship. There is no other god.[24]

God's Justice and Other Belief Systems

One conclusion about the Old Testament and religious pluralism is that Yahweh's claim to be God, uniquely and exclusively, is categorical. Yet it does not follow that the Old Testament takes an exclusive posture about other belief systems in the sense of judging them valueless.

The Old Testament allows for common ground between Yahwism and other religions, even if that common ground is not very extensive. Just as the effects of sin, though they touch every area in life, do not dictate that every dimension of life is altogether depraved, so also in the sphere of religions, while all claims to ultimacy stand under God's truth, not all that is related to other religions is thereby condemned. Moral and religious tenets in nonbiblical faith systems may in some instances be acceptable.

Three lines of investigation—from the prophets, from wisdom literature, and from the Torah—will show that there can be common ground between a non-Israelite religion and Yahwism. The nature of this common ground is important for our understanding of the Old Testament stance toward religious pluralism.

Amos is a prophetic book, the subject of which is often justice (see especially chapter 5). The opening eightfold woe against as many nations must be analyzed with the subject of justice in mind. Damascus is held accountable for cruelty to a neighboring population (1:3). Gaza is indicted for slave trade (1:6). Tyre is doubly accused, first for trafficking in the trade of human beings and secondly for treaty-breaking (1:9). Edom stands accused before Yahweh for its unrelenting hostility to its "brother," Israel (1:11). The people of Ammon in their craze to extend their borders committed gross evil by ripping open pregnant women (1:13). Moab is guilty for its insulting behavior in desecrating burial places (2:1).

Judah and Israel are also listed and indicted but on a different basis, namely their rejection of the divinely given Torah (Amos 2:4) and their breach of covenant with God. Neither of these criteria is apropos to the pagan nations. On what grounds then are these others accountable? On the grounds of common human decency. There are moral values such as honesty, consideration, and civility that are considered a given. Rudimentary ethical requirements are inbuilt, as it were.

An understanding of the basic requirements of justice exists among other peoples. Excessive cruelty, breaking of faith, and trading in human flesh are offensive and wrong and are recognized as such. Human beings are accountable to God quite apart from any specific revelation and will be judged by what they knew, as Paul also makes clear when he speaks about Gentiles having a law to themselves: "They [the Gentiles] show that what the law requires is written on their hearts, to which their own conscience also bears witness" (Rom. 2:15a).

The example from Amos 1–2 shows there are moral values in other cultures that can be affirmed as right. Moreover, while moral accountability is certainly heightened where there is knowledge of divine revelation, pleas for exemption from accountability because of an absence of specific divine revelation will not hold on the Day of the Big Audit. On the basis of Amos's prophetic text, one may extrapolate to say that there are positive moral and religious values in other cultures which can be affirmed from the standpoint of Yahwism.[25] One can also agree that "if as Master of the universe Yahweh holds exclusive rights to judge all nations . . . then the possibility of divine mercy is open to all who repent."[26]

That nonbiblical religions are not hopelessly depraved but incorporate convictions that correlate with Yahwism is demonstrated by the book of Proverbs. This book is about wisdom and the conduct of the wise; it sorts through behaviors, some of which are right and some wrong. These proverbs include sayings from regions outside Israel. The words of non-Hebrews Agur and Lemuel, both from Massa in Northern Arabia, are found in Proverbs 30 and 31.

A section of the Proverbs (22:17–24:22) contains material echoing proverbs from the Egyptian collection attributed to the Pharaoh Amenemopet.[27] One example must suffice. From Egypt comes the proverb: "Do not associate to thyself the heated man, nor visit him for conversation" (XI, 13F). The Bible states: "Make no friends with those given to anger, and do not associate with hotheads" (Prov. 22:24).

Proverbs is written so that readers will gain "instruction in wise dealing, righteousness, justice, and equity" (1:3). Wisdom announces: "I walk in the way of righteousness, along the paths of justice" (Prov. 8:20). Certain Egyptian precepts help define these "paths of justice."

Truth is not limited to what is divinely revealed; truth also derives from experience and from intuitive knowledge and so is not limited to

Israel's religious book. Thus, there is no warrant for a wholesale dispar-
agement of religious systems on the ground that they are not rooted in
Yahwism.[28]

From the Torah section of the Old Testament come further examples of overlaps between revealed faith and nonbiblical religions. Israel's judiciary system derives from Jethro, the Midianite (Exod.
18:19-27). Similarities exist between the so-called covenant code (Exod.
20:22–23:19) and the ancient Near East. Millard Lind notes these but
points also to the different orientation which marks the covenant code.[29]
Yet the similarity in content is not easily dismissed.

I cite these examples, not to argue that Mosaic legislation was necessarily dependent on other law codes,[30] though that conclusion is not
implausible, but to underscore the claim that biblically legitimate legislation is found in nonbiblical religions. Whatever the reason for this
overlap (whether a memory of an earlier divine revelation, or an inbuilt
sense of the right, or the pervasive ministry of the Spirit of God in the
world, or literary dependency of some sort), it follows that other belief
systems cannot be condemned wholesale. There is that in other cultures
which persons committed to the truth of the biblical material can affirm
and to which they can give approval.

But if divine justice will be the measure of what is legitimate, then it
is soon clear that many of the religious beliefs and practices of peoples
surrounding Israel come under divine judgment. A position statement
is given in Leviticus 18:3: "You shall not do as they do in the land of
Egypt, where you lived, and you shall not do as they do in the land of
Canaan, to which I am bringing you." The chapter continues with prohi-
bitions of incest, homosexuality, bestiality, and adultery, as well as child
sacrifice. "Do not defile yourself in any of these ways, for by all these
practices the nations I am casting out before you have defiled themselves" (Lev. 18:24).

That there is a fundamental clash of worldviews between Israel
and pagan religions—and that this is largely over what constitutes
justice—is illustrated in the Ahab–Naboth incident (1 Kings 21:1-27).
Ahab, King of Israel, wanted a choice vineyard which belonged to Naboth and offered to buy it. Naboth refused because land in Israel was not
to be sold, since in his tradition all land belonged to Yahweh, who had
apportioned it to families. Jezebel, Ahab's wife, believed that the god
Baal gave the land to the king, who then had an absolute right both to
distribute and to appropriate land. In the clash of these two worldviews
Naboth lost both his land and his life. Elijah insisted that Jezebel's actions were unjust.

In sum, where divine justice is the criterion, some beliefs and practices in other religions may accord with Yahwism, but others, perhaps most, will not. The prescriptions for conduct are not arbitrary but are determined by a Yahweh kind of justice.

God's Justice and Non-Yahwists

Our investigation so far has led us to two conclusions. First, because God is without equal, he stands in judgment over any and all other claimants to deity. Second, some values in belief systems outside Israel can be affirmed as legitimate, in accord with Yahweh's standard of justice, whereas others cannot.

These two conclusions still leave open the question of how God is disposed toward persons who live in the orbits of these non-Yahwistic faiths. On what basis can these people be saved?[31]

The answers, we must humbly admit, are largely inferential. As Christopher Seitz notes, "How God might deal with the nations in their own religious systems lies beyond the horizon of the Old Testament, precisely because of its understanding of the specificity of God's disclosure."[32]

God's election of Israel, to judge from the narratives, does not preclude the acceptance into his favor of persons from other faiths. Melchizedek, Jethro, Balaam, Job, and Rahab are God-fearers; none are Israelites. One could say that Jethro and Rahab had received witness to God through Israel (Exod. 18:1-12; Josh. 2:1-11). There is no indication of any such witness to Melchizedek, Balaam, or Job. All of them, however, appear in Scripture as receiving divine favor and acceptance. The questions then are: What is involved in being acceptable in God's sight? By what means are persons justified before God?

By posing the questions in this way, we have once again landed on the category of justice.

An answer which may at first seem oblique may be formulated by tracing in brief the Old Testament understanding of the means to salvation. The short answer is that persons are "saved" by embracing God. The longer answer entails recognition of several realities: (1) God is intent on reconciliation with humankind (Isa. 45:22). (2) God is Spirit; hence, "embracing God" is problematic. (3) God makes himself available through his gifts. (4) Specifically, these gifts are at least his promises, his Torah, and the person of Jesus. (5) As persons embrace these gifts by faith, God counts them righteous. (6) A faith response includes a behavioral change and entails a disposition of heart longing for purity.

Comment here must be limited to only a few of these assertions. God's gifts, a crucial component for human salvation, are wide-ranging. That the embrace of God's promise is the means to righteousness is stated forthrightly: "And he [Abraham] believed the Lord; and the Lord reckoned it to him as righteousness" (Gen. 15:6).

More controversial is the assertion that an embrace of the law in faith was sufficient before God to be counted by him as righteous.[33] Yet Moses (Lev. 18:5), Ezekiel (Ezek. 18:5-9), Jesus (Luke 10:28), and Paul (Rom. 9:31–10:5) all affirm that eternal life is made possible through an embrace of the law, God's gift of grace (John 1:16-17). The greatest gift of all is Jesus Christ; to embrace him in faith is to have eternal life (John 5:24). Through these three stages—promise, law, Jesus Christ—shines God's justice, a justice which remains consistent. Persons who respond to his gifts, whether promise (as Abraham), law including the sacrificial system (as Israel), or Jesus (as in the current dispensation), are counted righteous in God's sight.

This conclusion means that persons in the Old Testament are not condemned for not knowing about Jesus. Nor could the patriarchs be condemned for not embracing the Torah about which they were ignorant. It follows logically that persons living before Abraham or outside God's specific revelation could not in justice be held responsible for what they did not know (i.e., Sinaitic law). But this does not mean that they were not responsible, nor that they were without some access to God.

Abel offered a sacrifice that God accepted (Gen. 4:4). Noah is described as righteous: "[He] walked with God" (Gen. 6:9). The New Testament book of Hebrews declares that Abel "received approval as righteous" and that, by faith, Noah "became an heir to the righteousness that is in accordance with faith" (Heb. 11:4, 7). These two were not without a gift from God to embrace. The gift before them, we may infer, was the created world, a gift which pointed them to a Creator. Our inference is substantiated as correct by Paul: "What can be known about God is plain to them, because God has shown it to them. Ever since the creation of the world his eternal power and divine nature, invisible though they are, have been understood and seen through the things he has made" (Rom. 1:19-20; cf. Ps. 19).

Clendenin proposes three characteristics of persons who know God: *orthodoxy, orthopraxis, orthokardia*.[34] Orthodoxy, right belief, is exemplified by Abraham (Gen. 15:6; Rom. 4:3). Orthopraxis, right action, is illustrated by the pre-Abrahamic Abel. Orthokardia, a right heart (Deut. 6:4-5; 10:16) which the prophets described as a "circumcised" heart (Jer.

4:4; cf. Joel 2:12-13) and the Psalmist as a "contrite heart" (Ps. 51:16-17), is exemplified in pre-Abrahamic times by Enoch, who like Noah, walked with God (Gen. 5:24). All three characteristics are explicitly asserted of Job. As for orthodoxy, Job believed God (Job 19:25); as for orthopraxy, he practiced justice (Job 31); and as for orthokardia, he was "blameless and upright, and one who feared God and shunned evil" (Job 1:1).

It is not our task to decide the eternal fate of persons outside Yahweh's direct revelation. The tilt of Old Testament precedents, together with examination of God's *modus operandi* of justice, warrants concluding that persons could at least potentially respond in faith for salvation apart from special revelation (Scripture and Jesus Christ). In the New Testament, the Roman Cornelius may be cited as an example (Acts 10).[35]

It remains true that ontologically speaking, salvation is through Jesus Christ alone (John 14:6; Acts 4:12). Epistemologically speaking, however, persons apart from Jesus have at least the disclosure of creation and conscience. In short, persons have access to God through faith apart from knowledge about Jesus Christ.

On this issue of the eternal fate of persons in the orbit of other religions, our answer is that given by Abraham: "Shall not the Judge of all the earth do what is just?" (Gen. 18:25b; cf. Zeph. 3:5). The God of the Old Testament is a God of justice who will not act in caprice but in righteousness. Moreover, the eschatological scenarios include that of Egypt having an altar to the Lord in the center of its lands (Isa. 19:19). This elegant Isaiah text is described by Andre Feuillet as "the religious zenith of the Old Testament."[36] However, this passage should be compared to other texts that speak of the glorious prospect of nations coming to the light (Isa. 60:3; 45:23; Zeph. 3:9).

Justice, Israel, and the Nations

In summary, the God of Abraham, Isaac, and Israel is alone the true God. Peoples of different faiths have some knowledge of God, even if only minimal, which means that some of their beliefs and aspirations are to be affirmed. The God of justice will deal in righteousness with the eternal destiny of persons who live in the orbit of these religions. They cannot be censured or condemned for what they did not know; they, like we, will be justified if they wholeheartedly embrace the gift of God known to them. The more that is known about God, the more compelling is the call to embrace God.

Several passages from Isaiah, where "justice" and "nations" are prominent topics, point specifically to the way Israel was to function as God's agent. In Isaiah 49:17 the opening address is to the coastlands and "you peoples from far away" (49:1). The servant, here specified as Israel (49:3), has a mission both to (apostate) Israel and beyond. She is given "as a light to the nations, that my salvation may reach to the end of the earth" (49:6).

Whybray believes that "light" means enlightenment, but D. W. Van Winkle, drawing on the research of others, argues that the light is a figure for salvation (cf. 42:6, 16; 45:7; 49:6; 51:4).[37] The metaphor of light evokes images of a presence; one is not to think of evangelism, New Testament style. What should be noted in connection with our "controlling belief" is the mention of justice in the phrasing, "A teaching will go out from me, and my justice for a light to the peoples" (51:5).

Another passage, Isaiah 2:1-4, offers a complementary scenario to the "light" passages of 49:6 and 51:4. Again the world's people are in view. They are streaming up the mountain where the Lord's house is established, "the house of the God of Jacob," and they come for the purpose of being taught the ways of God. It is from Jerusalem that the word of the Lord will be given. It will be a radical word, given by one who "shall judge [exercise justice] between the nations" (2:4).

The three passages (49:6; 51:4; and 2:1-5) depict a scene in which Israel is an agent, but in the nature of an exhibit to which nations are drawn, though Israel shares the teaching of God when requested. In the Isaianic sense, to be a light does not entail messengers sent to make a verbal witness. Rather, it means remaining magnet-like, a trophy in "whom [God] will be glorified" (49:3) and to which peoples will be attracted.

If these three passages (49:6; 51:4; and 2:1-5) are primarily about an Israel in the mode of being, Isaiah 42:1-4, by contrast, depicts a mode of doing. Questions about the servant's identity miss the message of the text, which is to highlight the function, mode, and motive of an anonymous but ideal servant.

The nub points of the passage can be summarized as follows: The activities of the servant swirl around bringing justice (the word is mentioned three times in four verses). The goal is to persevere in this mission till justice reaches all the earth, even the coastlands (distant places). The mission is characterized by proclamation but not of the bombastic or self-advertising kind (42:2).

Moreover, the mode of mission is gentleness. The servant takes care not to snuff out the flickering wick or to break the bruised reed. God's servant is tender, yet also persistent and tough. The servant is highly motivated, for the servant is divinely endowed by an empowering Spirit.

To the extent that Israel qualifies as God's servant, her mission is unambiguous. It is to bring justice to the ends of the earth. Israel has a missionary responsibility to the nations, and that in two modes. In a largely passive mode, she is the showcase for what God's justice entails. In an active mode, she brings justice through proclamation.[38]

Concluding Theses

The foregoing discussion leads to the following conclusions about the Old Testament's word on pluralism, which in turn informs a believer's stance:

- Viewed from the biblical perspective of God's justice, the phenomenon of polytheism (a subset of religious pluralism) is both evil and false. God grounds his exclusivity in the passion for and exercise of justice. There is no god but Yahweh; that is, there is no other god that is just. Concerning the claim to monotheism, the believer is firm and uncompromising.

- Adjudicated on the basis of God's justice, other religions may include elements of moral truth. The fact that notions of justice in other religions are sometimes commensurate with God's revelation requires from the believer a respectful attitude toward other faiths and makes possible points of contact in interreligious dialogue.

- As to the possibility of salvation for adherents of other faiths who are without a knowledge of special revelation, the answer is best left to God, who proceeds justly. There is reason to hold, however, that non-Yahwists have access to God sufficient for their salvation apart from knowledge of salvation history and Jesus Christ. In God's economy it is the redemption by Jesus Christ on the cross that makes salvation possible at all for anyone. Epistemologically, however, knowledge of this event or other God-events in history, while compelling persons towards a faith commitment to God, is not "necessary." A faith commitment to God can be made, though perhaps is made only rarely, apart from knowledge of Christ's life and death. Believers do well to look and listen to discover how God is working.

- God's people, Israel and the church, are called to be exhibits of grace to the glory of God and proclaimers of God's justice. God's passion in bringing justice to the world far exceeds ours. Believers have reason to be bold and confident in this active witness to God's truth, irrespective of competing voices.

Notes

1. D. A. Carson, *The Gagging of God: Christianity Confronts Pluralism* (Grand Rapids, Mich.: Zondervan, 1996), 272. For Carson's definitions of pluralism, see pp. 13-22.

2. The nature of the challenge and the reason for a new awareness is discussed by Daniel B. Clendenin, *Many Gods, Many Lords: Christianity Encounters World Religion* (Grand Rapids, Mich.: Baker, 1995), 11-34.

3. Clendenin traces texts according to the "history of salvation" schema. "Old Testament Faith and the World Religions" (chapter 5), in *Many Gods, Many Lords.* A historical schema is also followed by John E. Goldingay and C. J. H. Wright, "'Yahweh our God Yahweh One': The Old Testament and Religious Pluralism," in *One God, One Lord in a World of Religious Pluralism*, ed. A. D. Clarke and B. W. Winter (Cambridge, England: Tyndale House, 1991), 34-52. A canonical schema is adopted in *Christianity and the Religions: A Biblical Theology of World Religions*, Evangelical Missiological Society, Series #2, ed. E. Rommen and H. Netland (Pasadena, Calif.: William Carey Library, 1995). In this book Ed Mathew deals with texts in the Pentateuch, Michael Pocock with Wisdom literature, and Robert B. Chisholm Jr. with prophetic literature. D. A. Carson stresses the plotline of the entire biblical story in *The Gagging of God*, 193-314.

4. The term is used by John Sanders to indicate the "givens" for an argument. See *No Other Name: An Investigation into the Destiny of the Unevangelized* (Grand Rapids, Mich.: Eerdmans, 1992), 32.

5. Cf. John Bright, *The Kingdom of God* (Nashville, Tenn.: Abingdon, 1953); J. L. Mays, *The Lord Reigns* (Louisville, Ky: Westminster/John Knox, 1994); M. Z. Brettler, "God is King: Understanding an Israelite Metaphor," *Journal for the Study of the Old Testament*, Supplement Series 76 (Sheffield, England: JSOT, 1989); George Ladd, *Jesus and the Kingdom* (New York: Harper & Row, 1964); and J. Gray, *The Biblical Doctrine of the Reign of God* (Edinburgh: T. & T. Clark, 1979). Cf. John Driver, "The Kingdom of God: Goal of Messianic Mission," in *The Transfiguration of Mission. Biblical, Theological & Historical Foundations*, ed. Wilbert Shenk (Scottdale, Pa.: Herald Press, 1993), 83-105.

6. In addition to its infrequent use, the term is problematic because of its reference to monarchy, which is not now a predominant political system; because of its gender identification, objectionable to some; and because of the secular definition of a kingdom as spatial.

7. *The Task of Old Testament Theology* (Grand Rapids, Mich.: Eerdmans, 1995), 120, esp. pp. 14, 17. Cf. J. Kraesovec, *La justice (sedaqa) de Dieu dans la Bible hebraique et l'interpretation juive et chretienne.* Oribs Biblicus et Orientalis 76 (Goettingen: Vandenhoeck und Reprecht, 1988); H. G. Reventlow and Y. Hoffman, eds., *Justice and Righteousness: Biblical Themes and Their Influence.* Festschrift for S. B. Uffenheimer. *Journal for the Study of Old Testament*, Supplement Series 137 (Sheffield, England: JSOT, 1992).

8. Cf. "*Sedaqa* is the quality of life displayed by those who live up to the norms inherent in a given relationship and thereby do right by the other person or persons involved." This quotation from James L. Mays is noted in a first-rate article on the subject by David Reimer in *New International Dictionary of Old Testament*

Theology and Exegesis, ed. W. A. Van Gemeren (Grand Rapids, Mich.: Zondervan, 1997) 3:744-69. The quotation appears on p. 763.

9. David Shenk cites Samuel Kibicho of Africa who has noted that "in Bantu languages the root word for justice is also the root for truth, wisdom, empowerment, win, or victory. All these gifts undergird the peace which sustains life." *Global Gods. Exploring the Role of Religions in Modern Societies* (Scottdale, Pa: Herald Press, 1995), 79. Shenk footnotes his source: Samuel G. Kibicho, "The Gikuyu Conception of God: His Continuity into the Christian Era and the Question it Raises for the Christian Idea of Revelation" (Ph.D. diss., Vanderbilt University, 1972), 33. Might there be convergences between Bantu and Hebrew on the meaning and importance of justice?

10. All Scripture references unless otherwise indicated are from the New Revised Standard Version.

11. For a more detailed discussion, see Robert B. Chisholm Jr., "'To Whom Shall You Compare Me?' Yahweh's Polemic Against Baal and the Babylonian Idol Gods in Prophetic Literature," *Christianity and the Religions,* 56-71.

12. C. J. Labuschagne, *The Incomparability of Yahweh in the Old Testament* (Leiden, Germany: E. J. Brill, 1966), 89-123, esp. p. 90.

13. So J. G. Janzen, "On the Most Important Word in the Shema," *Vetus Testamentum* 37, no. 3 (1987): 280-300. Cf. R. W. L. Moberly, "Yahweh is One: The Translation of the Shema," in *Studies in the Pentateuch.,* ed. J. A. Emerton (Supplements to *Vetus Testamentum.* Leiden, Germany: E. J. Brill, 1990). Patrick Miller holds that the ambiguity is irresolvable. *Deuteronomy. Interpretation: A Bible Commentary for Teaching and Preaching* (Louisville, Ky.: John Knox, 1990), 99. The New Testament quotation in Mark 12:32, "He (God) is one , and besides him there is no other," allows for both unity and exclusiveness.

14. D. Christensen, *Deuteronomy 1-11* Word Biblical Commentary (Waco, Tex.: Word, 1991), 145.

15. David W. Shenk singles out the two themes, creation and history, as the two arenas of God's self-disclosure and as the perspectives in the Jewish Christian understanding that impinge on his focal question of how the global gods affect the quality of life globally; *Global Gods,* 179-207.

16. W. Zimmerli, "Knowledge of God according to the Book of Ezekiel," in *I am Yahweh,* ed. W. Brueggemann, trans. D. W. Stott (Atlanta: John Knox, 1982).

17. W. Brueggemann concludes that the main force of the Mosaic revolution, "a theological *novum,*" is "to establish justice as the core focus of Yahweh's life in the world and Israel's life with Yahweh." *Old Testament Theology* (Minneapolis: Fortress Press, 1997), 735.

18. Patrick D. Miller Jr., *Interpreting the Psalms* (Philadelphia: Fortress, 1986), 124.

19. Cf. S. Hess, "Yahweh and His Asherah? Epigraphic Evidence for Religious Pluralism in Old Testament Times," in *One God, One Lord in a World of Religious Pluralism,* 533. Hess clarifies that for some Israelite rulers as well as for the populace at times, syncretism, along with a propensity toward the embrace of other religions, existed. My interest is not in a history of religions approach, but in a biblical theology approach where the canonical view, as represented by the

prophets, is definitive.

20. Further elaboration is given in my essay, "Ezekiel's Contribution to a Biblical Theology of Mission," in *Die Mission der Theologie. Festschrift für Hans Kasdorf zum 70. Geburtstag,* ed. Stephan Holthaus and Klaus W. Mueller (Bonn, Germany: Verlag für Kultur und Wissenschaft, 1998), 46-57.

21. E.g., James A. Sanders, "Adaptable for Life," in *From Sacred Text to Sacred Story: Canon as Paradigm* (Philadelphia: Fortress Press, 1987), 9-39.

22. There are other analyses of violence, e.g., "Human history is the relentless chronicle of violence that it is because when cultures fall apart they fall into violence, and when they revive themselves they do so violently." Gil Bailie, *Violence Unveiled. Humanity at the Crossroads* (New York: Crossroads, 1995), 6.

23. Regina M. Schwartz, *The Curse of Cain. The Violent Legacy of Monotheism* (Chicago: the University of Chicago Press, 1997). Her book should be compared with Gil Bailie, *Violence Unveiled. Humanity at the Crossroads* (New York: Crossroad, 1995). Bailie, leaning on the work of Rene Girard, shows how the biblical tradition, especially in the gospels, undermines systems of sacred violence.

24. D. A. Carson, in discussing the topic, "God is transcendent, sovereign, and personal," observes that "in the rising press of religious pluralism, this understanding of God [as transcendent and sovereign] is never allowed" (*The Gagging of God,* 223).

25. Terry C. Muck, "Is There Common Ground Among Religions?" *Journal of the Evangelical Theological Society* 40, no. 1 (1997): 99-112. He proceeds theologically to identify a threefold common ground: *logos spermatikos* (seed of wisdom), to which I would connect the Amos passage; *divinitatis sensum* (sense of the divine); and *imago Dei* (image of God).

26. R. Bryan Widbin, "Salvation for People Outside Israel's Covenant," in *Through No Fault of Their Own?* ed. W. V. Crockett and J. G. Sigountos (Grand Rapids, Mich.: Baker, 1991), 78.

27. The dating of the Egyptian papyrus manuscript is 7th-6th century, according to some. The proverbs themselves are almost certainly earlier. For a summary of the literary relationship between Egypt and the biblical Proverbs, see John Ruffle, "The Teaching of Amenemope and its Connection with the Book of Proverbs," *Tyndale Bulletin* 28 (1977): 29-68. Ruffle proposes a dependence, though indirect, of the biblical material on Egypt.

28. Further examples and discussion may be found in Andrew E. Hill and John H. Walton, *A Survey of the Old Testament* (Grand Rapids, Mich.: Zondervan, 1991). Cf. John H. Walton, *Ancient Israelite Literature in Its Cultural Context: A Survey of Parallels between Biblical and Ancient Near Eastern Texts.* Library of Biblical Interpretation (Grand Rapids, Mich.: Zondervan, 1989). Michael Pocock, "Selected Perspectives on World Religions from Wisdom Literature," in *Christianity and the Religions,* 45-55, acknowledges that literary forms from Israel and the ancient Near East are similar, and that even some content is similar, but insists on retaining an exclusivist stance.

29. "Law in the Old Testament," *Monotheism, Power, Justice. Collected Old Testament Essays,* Text Reader #3 (Elkhart, Ind.: Institute of Mennonite Studies, 1990), 61-81.

30. See H. J. Boecker, *Law and the Administration of Justice in the Old Testament and the Ancient East*, trans. Jerry Moiser (Minneapolis: Augsburg, 1980), 15-19.

31. Lesslie Newbigin states that to ask the question this way is to fatally flaw the debate. *The Gospel in a Pluralist Society* (Grand Rapids, Mich.: Wm. B. Eerdmans/Geneva: WCC Publications, 1989), 176. Salvation (and mission) includes other dimensions, such as community considerations and the glory of God, as he rightly states. But at some point the question of individual salvation does crystallize the issue of religious pluralism.

32. *Word without End. The Old Testament as Abiding Theological Witness* (Grand Rapids, Mich.: Eerdmans, 1998), 23.

33. For a more extended discussion, see my essay, "Embracing the Law: A Biblical Theological Perspective," *Bulletin for Biblical Research* 2 (1992): 128.

34. D. Clendenin, *Many Gods, Many Lords*, 137-39.

35. William J. Larkin Jr. is among those who hold that Cornelius "is not an appropriate model for today's non-Christian religions." "The Contribution of the Gospels and Acts to a Biblical Theology of Religions," in *Christianity and the Religions*, 72-91. The quote is from p. 81. So also Don Carson, *The Gagging of God*, 30-67.

36. Quoted in Lucien LeGrand, *Unity and Plurality. Mission in the Bible*, trans. R. R. Barr (Maryknoll, N.Y.: Orbis, 1990), 23.

37. D. W. Van Winkle, "The Relationship of the Nations to Yahweh and to Israel in Isaiah 40-55," *Vetus Testamentum* 35 (1985): 446-58. Cf. R. E. Clements, "A Light to the Nations: A Central Theme of the Book of Isaiah," in *Forming Prophetic Literature: Essays on Isaiah and the Twelve in Honor of John D. W. Watts*, Journal for the Study of Old Testament, Supplement Series 235, ed. J. W. Watts and Paul R. House (Sheffield, England: Sheffield Academic Press, 1996), 57-69. Clements, who examines three passages, Isa. 9:2; 2:6; and 60:13, sees them in conjunction with the royal Zion motif. R. F. Melugin observes that in Isa. 40-55 Israel was chosen for the sake of the *world* and that justice for Gentiles is central to God's purpose, but he thinks that these points are more forcefully made in Genesis. "Israel and the Nations in Isaiah 40-55," in *Problems in Biblical Theology: Essays in Honor of Rolf Knierim*, ed. Henry T. C. Sun, Keith L. Eades, J. M. Robinson, and G. I. Moller (Grand Rapids, Mich.: Eerdmans, 1997), 246-64.

38. "It is the task of the witnesses not only to attest the facts but also to convince the opposite side of the truth of them ([Isa] 41:21-24, 26; 43:9; 51:22; cf. Gen. 38:24-26)." A. A. Trites, *The New Testament Concept of Witness* (Cambridge, England: Cambridge University Press, 1977). John Oswalt's comment is puzzling: "Israel's function is that of witness as opposed to proselytizer." "The Mission of Israel to the Nations," in *Through No Fault of Their Own?* ed. W. V. Crockett and J. G. Sigountos (Grand Rapids, Mich.: Baker, 1991), 85-95. The quotation is from pp. 94-95.

CHAPTER THREE

Every Tongue
Shall Confess:
Truth and Pluralism
in the New Testament

J. Nelson Kraybill

New Testament authors interpreted the life, death, and resurrection of Jesus in the framework of a Jewish apocalyptic understanding of history. Thus, they defined salvation in terms so radically different from surrounding pagan religions as to make other claims to salvation seem irrelevant or utterly inadequate. Exploring implications of this radical understanding of salvation is the focus of this chapter.

"Obstinate" Christians in
Governor Pliny's Courtroom

Near the close of the New Testament era, in about 112 C.E., Governor Pliny from the Roman province of Bithynia wrote to Emperor Trajan asking advice on how the courts should deal with followers of Jesus. An unsigned placard had been placed in public, Pliny reported, accusing a "large number" of people of being Christians, and the named individuals were brought into the governor's courtroom.

Pliny wrote that his practice was simply to ask the defendants if they were Christians. Some denied it, and he set them free if they "invoked our gods according to the formula I gave them" and if they "offered sacrifices of wine and incense before [the image of the emperor] which I had brought in for this purpose along with the statues of our gods." Pliny also required defendants to "curse Christ," adding that he was told "real Christians cannot be forced to do any of these things."

If the accused admitted being Christians and did not abandon their faith, Pliny had them executed. "For whatever it is that they are actually advocating," Pliny wrote, "it seems to me that obstinacy and stubbornness must be punished in any case."

Pliny investigated the practices of Christians. He learned that

> on a specified day before sunrise they were accustomed to gather and sing an antiphonal hymn to Christ as their god and to pledge themselves by an oath not to engage in any crime, but to abstain from all thievery, assault, and adultery, not to break their word once they had given it, and not to refuse to pay their legal debts.

The governor had two Christian female slaves ("deaconesses") tortured and interrogated but "found nothing more than a vulgar, excessive superstition." Pliny rejoices in his letter that, after taking these decisive measures, the Christian "plague" receded. Surprisingly, people had been drawn into this new faith from "every age and class" and both sexes. But after a series of prosecutions,

> the [pagan] temples, almost deserted previously, are gradually gaining more and more visitors, and the long neglected sacred festivals are again regularly observed, and the sacrificial meat, for which buyers have been hard to find, is again being bought. From this one can easily see what an improvement can be made in the masses, when one gives room for repentance.[1]

Governor Pliny was baffled by the faith and practice of Christians whose faith contrasted so sharply with a pluralistic religious world. He also was troubled by the apparent missionary zeal and success of the Christians, who had drawn many people from pious pagan background into belief in Jesus. The requirements were fairly modest for Christians in Pliny's courtroom to save their lives, the principal expectation being that they would worship other deities (including traditional Greek and Roman gods and the deified emperor).

Emperor Trajan thought of himself as a tolerant and progressive ruler and replied that Pliny should not actively seek out Christians to punish them, nor should he admit anonymous testimony in court against them. Trajan agreed that properly accused Christians needed to be punished, "but only if they do not deny being Christians and demonstrate it by the appropriate act, i.e., the worship of our gods."[2]

The problem, in Trajan's view, was that Christians gave *exclusive* loyalty to Christ in a society that was pervasively pluralistic and syncretistic. Confessional exclusivism seemed narrow-minded and dangerous. What would happen to the empire if large numbers of subjects turned to a religion that disregarded the pantheon of traditional gods and rejected the divine status of the emperor? Cicero (first century B.C.E.) had warned that "the disappearance of piety towards the gods will entail the disappearance of loyalty and social union among [people] as well."[3]

The Pliny-Trajan correspondence gives a rare pagan perspective on how the earliest Christians engaged a pluralistic culture near the close of the New Testament era. Pliny understood that "real Christians" would not compromise their loyalty to Christ or accept the validity of other gods. Christians worshipped Christ "as a god," and their faith required them to live in honesty, integrity, and nonviolence.

The singular conviction and "excessive superstition" of Christians in Pliny's courtroom must have been rooted in writings that we call the New Testament. Although the New Testament canon would not reach its final shape for more than two centuries after Pliny wrote his famous letter, basic Christian texts in our Bibles would have been available to believers in Bithynia. Paul had done extensive mission work in Asia Minor, and his letters apparently were widely known (2 Peter 2:15). The author of 1 Peter seems to assume that readers in Bithynia knew the basic passion account of the Gospels (e.g., 1 Pet. 2:23-24), and the book of Revelation was addressed to believers in Asia Minor (Rev. 1:11).

Christian Identity Rooted in Apocalyptic Stream of Jewish History

Christians were not the first radical monotheists to come to the attention of Roman rulers, for Rome already had a centuries-old relationship with the Jews. During the time of the Maccabean Revolt (167-164 B.C.E.), the Romans were eager to strengthen their tenuous political foothold in the East by establishing a league of friendship with Jewish nationalists.[4] From this early friendship emerged an uneasy but enduring alliance between Jewish leaders in Palestine and pagan rulers in Rome. Most Roman rulers tolerated the fact that the Jews worshiped only one God, and even allowed *diaspora* Jews to send their annual "temple tax" to Jerusalem.[5]

When Christianity emerged and began to spread throughout the East in the middle of the first century, the Romans at first viewed the movement simply as a sect in Judaism. Gallio, proconsul of Achaia (c. 51 C.E.), treated the dispute between Jews and Christians at Corinth as a

Jewish internal affair (Acts 18:12-17). But the Romans gradually made a distinction between the two groups, as attested by Nero's targeted persecution of Christians after the great fire at Rome in 64 C.E.

What the Romans most feared from Judaism was not the sober practice of monotheistic Mosiac law, but rather a vibrant strain of apocalyptic eschatology that first spilled over into politics during the Maccabean Revolt. The book of Daniel seems to have emerged in its present form during that struggle and is the first of many Jewish literary works that divide history in two major eras: the present evil age of oppression and sin, and the age to come (the reign of God). Daniel anticipates that God will destroy the "beasts" of worldly powers (Dan. 7:11-12) and will send a "son of man," the Messiah, to usher in the Reign of God (Dan. 7:13-14).

At the time of the Maccabean Revolt, apocalyptic fervor fueled hatred against Greek rulers who controlled Palestine. When the Romans took possession of Palestine after 63 B.C.E., Jewish apocalyptic passions sometimes were directed against Rome. In both eras, apocalyptic writers viewed salvation as limited to those who gave exclusive allegiance to Yahweh.

Characteristics of Jewish Apocalyptic Thought

A small library of Jewish and Christian books (today called the *Pseudepigrapha*), from the centuries just before and after Jesus, share a paradigm of history that is similar to that found in Daniel 7-12. The Greek term "apocalyptic" ("unveiling," as in Rev. 1:1) came to be associated with this literary and theological movement because proponents sought to unveil the fact that God was firmly in control of history, even if pagan powers seemed to have triumphed. Klaus Koch outlines the typical Jewish apocalyptic world view with the following points:[6]

1. An urgent expectation of the impending overthrow of all earthly conditions in the immediate future.

2. The end appears as a vast cosmic catastrophe.

3. The time of this world is divided into two segments.

4. The introduction of an army of angels and demons to explain the course of historical events and the happenings of the end time.

5. Beyond the catastrophe a new salvation arises, paradisal in character and destined for the faithful remnant.

6. The transition from disaster to final redemption takes place by means of an act issuing from the throne of God, which means the visibility on earth of the kingdom of God.

7. The frequent introduction of a mediator with royal functions.

8. The catchword *glory* is used whenever the final state of affairs is set apart from the present and whenever a final amalgamation of the earthly and heavenly spheres is prophesied.

Jewish nationalists who fed on the apocalyptic movement saw no need to make accommodation of any kind to Roman power or to pagan religion. The end of the present age was at hand, God was about to send the Messiah, and every pagan political power would be destroyed. Various messianic pretenders during the first century (especially in Galilee) sought to throw off the yoke of pagan rule. The culmination of this movement took place in 66-70 C.E., when Jewish rebels briefly succeeded in ousting Roman armies from Palestine. The revolt ended in ghastly defeat and destruction, an event apparently marked by Jesus' words in Mark 13. After yet another disastrous rebellion and defeat in the second century (Bar Kochba, 132-35 C.E.), most Jews entirely abandoned apocalyptic eschatology.

New Testament Authors
Maintain a Modified Apocalyptic Framework

New Testament authors reflect most of the characteristics of Jewish apocalyptic thought outlined above by Koch but with one major difference: Even though the present evil age is not yet over in New Testament theology, the reign of God *already has begun* in the person and power of Jesus Christ. Whereas Jewish apocalyptic thought divided history neatly into two major segments (the present evil age and the reign of God in the future, with messianic intervention providing a transition between eras), Christian apocalyptic theology *overlaps* the two major eras.

The cross and resurrection of Jesus mark the beginning of the new era of the Reign of God, a reign that is real even though not recognized by much of humanity. The coming of Christ in victory (the *parousia*) will mark the end of the present age, the end of history as mortals know it. Jesus alone is God's appointed deliverer (Messiah), preparing the way for those who believe in him to enter the reign of God now in its present, preliminary form—and someday in its full glory.

Most New Testament authors expected the coming of Christ (parousia) to happen soon, and in light of this expectation, they took an exclusive attitude toward other religions. New Testament authors and missionaries could respect the sincerity and devotion of adherents to other religions, but it was inconceivable to them that other religions would be adequate to prepare anyone for divine judgment on the "Day of the Lord" (an Old Testament concept that Christians now equated with the parousia).[7]

Paul Knitter accurately concludes that, with such a mindset, "possibilities of other revelations or prophets were simply beyond one's consideration. There was no time." Even when the end of history was delayed, and Christians developed christologies that put less emphasis on the parousia, "Jewish eschatological convictions were preserved. Jesus was proclaimed as he who already achieved and anticipated what was to come, for all, at the end of history . . . the finality of the *end* shifted to the *center* of history."[8]

The entire New Testament rests on a belief that salvation from death or punishment at the time of the parousia is available to those who acknowledge the lordship of Jesus Christ now. Other religions are not necessarily evil but are fundamentally inadequate to the approaching crisis of history.

Fate and Salvation in
Pagan Religion of the Ancient World

How did New Testament understandings of truth and salvation differ from those of contemporary pagan religion? Traditional Greek and Roman religions may have been in decline during the New Testament era, but they still dominated the religious imagination of ancient peoples. The chief function of classic religion was to please and placate the gods, winning their favor with obedience and adulation in a fashion similar to how clients in the Roman patronage system won favors from their patrons.

Jupiter (Zeus) was father of gods and mortals, not in the sense of creator but in the sense that he was the protector and ruler of the human family.[9] Jupiter ruled the heavens, Neptune (Poseidon) ruled the ocean, and Pluto (Dis) ruled the underworld. Beyond these central deities was a bewildering host of gods and goddesses, each responsible for a particular realm or natural force: Iris was goddess of the rainbow, Mars the god of war, Venus the goddess of love, and so on. Gods lived much the same as humans, exhibiting the same virtues, vices, and whims.

Most in the Roman world believed every man had a *Genius* and every woman a *Juno*—a spirit that had given them being and who protected them throughout life. Mortals needed protection because both in this life and in the afterlife humans were subject to the whims of the goddess Fate (*Tyche*, or "fortune"). Fate could make mortals rich or poor, ill or well—and decided human destiny after death in the underworld.[10] There were differing levels of happiness in the underworld, ranging from *Tartaros* (a prison of punishment) to the Isle of the Blest.

The Romans were phenomenally successful at building empire because they were adept at integrating political, social, and religious ideas of subject peoples into their own fabric of society. Religion after religion from a far-flung empire found its way to Rome.[11] Many of these fall into the category of "mystery religions," meaning they offered adherents special powers and knowledge for admission to a place of blessing after death. Plato wrote that "whoever goes uninitiated and unsanctified to the other world will lie in the mire, but he who arrives there initiated and purified will dwell with the gods."[12]

Themistios (fourth century C.E.) further elaborates on a pagan view of the afterlife that made mystery religions attractive. When a human dies, he declared,

> At first one wanders and wearily hurries to and fro, and journeys with suspicion through the dark as one uninitiated; then come all the terrors before the final initiation, shuddering, trembling, sweating, amazement; then one is struck with a marvelous light, one is received into pure regions and meadows, with voices and dances and the majesty of holy sounds and shapes; among these he who has fulfilled initiation wanders free, and released and bearing his crown joins in the divine communion . . . beholding those who live here uninitiated, an uncleansed horde, trodden under foot of him and huddled together in mud and fog, abiding in their miseries. . . .[13]

With such a fearful visage of the afterlife, it is understandable that any religion promising secrets of spiritual initiation to the underworld would be popular. Members of a given mystery cult experienced secret rites of initiation, joined with other adherents in a common meal, and observed group rituals. From Egypt came the popular religion of Isis and Osiris/Sarapis, from Asia Minor came the Great Mother (*Magna Mater*) mysteries, and from the Far East came the secrets of Mithraism.

The latter religion included a gruesome ceremony in which the initiate (or perhaps a priest on the initiate's behalf) descended into a pit, over which a bull was slaughtered. Blood from the bull drenched the human subject, to salvific effect. Secrets imparted allowed the human soul to soar through celestial spheres, through the solar gate into the boundless beyond.[14]

The mystery religions, particularly Mithraism, were enormously popular in the first two centuries of the Christian era. Both classic pagan religion and the mystery cults offered strategies for manipulating fate and viewed salvation as a way to avoid misery after death. They did not begin to address the apocalyptic concerns of Jews and Christians who believed the end of history was at hand. Jews and Christians were monotheists, who believed that history was linear and in the firm control of a sovereign God. Ancient pagan religions either did not believe such a God existed or held that knowing the mind of such a deity was impossible.

New Testament Truth Claims in the Face of Religious Pluralism

Early Christians believed they had experienced a revelation of God in Jesus Christ that was singular in history. This revelation opened a way for mortals to enter into eternal life when the final judgment came in the *eschaton*.

The early church was profoundly outward looking, with believers urgently sharing good news they were certain no other religion could even remotely match. We have no record of the earliest believers engaging in dispassionate reflection on the relative merits of different religions. The Christ event was so unparalleled, and the implications of this revelation so universal, that the only worthy response of believers was to speak the good news as far and as quickly as possible.

The New Testament from start to finish is *confessional* and *apologetic* literature. These documents make no pretense of being unbiased; they are written by people whose lives were transformed by an existential encounter with the risen Jesus Christ. The joy and power of this encounter was so life-giving that Christians felt compelled to speak (Acts 4:20; 1 Cor. 9:16).

Any attempt to assess the attitude of early Christians toward other religions gravitates toward the book of Acts since it contains the only narrative record of missionary encounter with pagan people. There also are some clues about pluralism in the Gospel narratives of Jesus meeting people of pagan background.

New Testament writings reflect a new religious movement buffeted between the Jewish community (from which Christianity emerged) on the one hand and diverse pagan religions (from which many early believers came) on the other hand. In this environment of extreme pluralism, New Testament authors take the following positions:

1. Salvation for Jews (as for all people) hinges entirely on their willingness to confess Jesus as the Messiah.[15] Because early Christians saw

belief in Jesus as the only means of salvation in the approaching eschaton, they could not even affirm the faith of their Jewish contemporaries
who rejected Jesus as the Messiah. Paul took care to remind Gentile
Christians, however, that their theological roots were in Judaism: "remember that it is not you that support the root, but the root that supports
you" (Rom. 11:18).

Paul goes on immediately to state that the Jews were "broken off
[from salvation] because of their unbelief" (11:20). There is one hope,
however: if the Jews "do not persist in unbelief," they "will be grafted in,
for God has the power to graft them in again. . . . And so all Israel will be
saved" (11:23; 26). The Jews, in Paul's understanding, will be restored to
the Reign of God when they acknowledge Jesus as the Christ.[16]

Early Christian preaching to the Jews, as recorded by Luke, interprets the rejection and crucifixion of Jesus by his own people as an act
that puts them outside the law of God and probably outside salvation as
well (Acts 2:23). The apostle Peter, in his impromptu sermon at the temple, said Jews "acted in ignorance" and are called to repent,

> so that times of refreshing may come from the presence of the Lord,
> and that he may send the Messiah appointed for you, that is, Jesus,
> who must remain in heaven until the time of universal restoration that
> God announced long ago through his holy prophets. . . . And it will be
> that everyone who does not listen to that prophet [Jesus, in Luke's un-
> derstanding] will be utterly rooted out of the people. (Acts 3:20-23)

Salvation of the Jews is set in an apocalyptic context in Peter's sermon, and it is only through Jesus that the Jews will be restored in the
reign of God. A clear strain of anger toward the Jews comes through in
Stephen's sermon. He tells how Israelites in previous generations had
killed the prophets who foretold the coming of the "Righteous One"
(Jesus, in Luke's understanding), "and now you have become his be-
trayers and murderers" (Acts 7:51-52).

Anger toward Jews who reject Jesus is evident in the fourth Gospel,
in which the conspiracy to destroy Jesus is engineered generically by
"the Jews" (e.g., John 5:18). Despite the fact that many Jews rejected
Jesus, however, the New Testament documents a systematic attempt to
bring them the gospel. The book of Acts repeatedly portrays Paul going
first to the synagogue when he started preaching in a new city.[17] The
book of Revelation, despite hostile references to the "synagogue of
Satan" (Rev. 2:9; 3:9), nevertheless depicts salvation in profoundly Jewish terms: the 144,000 "sealed" servants of God are representatives of the
twelve tribes of Israel (Rev. 7:4-8).

2. The incarnation of God in Christ is an event without parallel in other religions. Nowhere is this conviction more evident than in the prologue to the fourth Gospel. The author of John has a missiological intent (John 20:31), and he directs his introduction to people who are accustomed to thinking in pagan philosophical terms: Christ is the visible manifestation of the *logos,* or "Word," of God.[18]

Greek philosophers held that every human (like every part of creation) is infused by at least some small portion of the divine logos (the *logos spermatikos*).[19] But the essence of God, in pagan thought, remained mysterious and hidden. The gods of Greek and Roman religion might give some clues to the nature of a transcendent God, and mystery religions might give esoteric knowledge for ascending into the sphere of the divine, but God himself was beyond knowing.

In the context of pagan agnosticism about a transcendent God, the author of the fourth Gospel constructs a startling syllogism that could be summarized as follows:

> The logos is the same as God (John 1:1).
> Jesus is the logos visible in the flesh (1:14).
> Therefore Jesus is God physically present among mortals (1:18).

Some early church writers understood John to mean that Jesus was simply the fullest revelation of a divine power and truth that already was pervasive in the universe, which led them to reflect on the meaning and merits of other religions. Justin Martyr (second century) went so far as to say that mortals who conformed to the nature of the logos could be considered Christians, if they did not know God as Jews and Christians know God.[20]

Justin believed that Greek mythology and philosophy pointed to Christ the logos just as surely as Moses did.[21] The Christ event remained unsurpassed in Justin's theology, however, because only in Christ was the "fullness" (John 1:16) of God revealed.

Despite the cosmic Christology in John's prologue, subsequent chapters dramatically narrow the way to salvation, so that it only is possible through Jesus. Having declared Jesus the Son to be a manifestation of the logos, the author then goes on to quote Jesus saying: "I am the way, and the truth, and the life. No one comes to the Father except through me" (14:6).

John is least apocalyptic of the four Gospels, sometimes presenting a realized eschatology of salvation benefits *in the present*, including an infusion of "eternal life" or "life of the age [to come]" here and now, and judgment on evil by the Holy Spirit apart from the parousia (16:7-11).

Yet even with this muted eschatology, the author of the fourth Gospel still casts salvation in recognizably apocalyptic terms. The incarnation of God in Christ prepares a way to salvation in face of the eschaton. Jesus says: "This indeed is the will of my Father, that all who see the Son and believe in him may have eternal life; and I will raise them up on the last day" (6:40); and, "I will come again and will take you to myself, so that where I am, there you may be also" (14:3).

3. Adherents of other religions worship worthless idols that will be of no value in the imminent eschatological crisis. This early Christian conviction is most evident in comments made to Gentiles who come to faith in Jesus Christ. In what probably is the earliest of New Testament writings, Paul reminds Christians at Thessalonica that they "turned to God from idols, to serve a true and living God, and to wait for his Son from heaven, whom he raised from the dead—Jesus, who rescues us from the wrath that is coming" (1 Thess. 1:9).

The gospel in Paul's understanding is not simply the story of Jesus' earthly ministry or a summary of Christian ethical teaching. The "good news" is that Jesus opened a way of salvation into the reign of God at the imminent end of time.

We do not know what religion the believers at Thessalonica held before they heard the gospel, but it is likely they came from a variety of religious backgrounds. Paul refers to their previous religious persuasion simply as "idolatry." Similarly, Peter writes to Gentile believers in Asia Minor, who were "ransomed from the futile ways inherited from your ancestors" (1 Pet. 1:18) and from "lawless idolatry" (4:3).

4. Those who adhere to other religions may be seeking God sincerely, and it is the Christian responsibility to point such seekers to the truth revealed in Christ. When Paul first visited Athens, he found the city center "full of idols" (images of gods and deified emperors). This left Paul "distressed" (Acts 17:16). Faithful to his Jewish roots, Paul began his missionary effort at Athens in a synagogue (17:17). In the marketplace he also addressed Epicurean and Stoic philosophers, with an emphasis on Jesus and the resurrection.

The resurrection was pivotal in early Christian theology because in apocalyptic thought resurrection from the dead signaled the arrival of God's reign (cf. Dan. 12:2). Jesus' resurrection was much more than corpse resuscitation; it was God's vindication of him as the Messiah and the beginning of many resurrections leading up to God's reign (what Paul calls the "first fruits of those who have died," 1 Cor. 15:20).

At Athens, Paul shows respect for the spiritual sincerity of his pagan hearers. He notes that they are "extremely religious" (Acts 17:22), that they are so devout that they even have an altar to the god they do not yet know. Seizing that observation as a point of entrance, Paul declares that the unknown God is the one revealed in Jesus Christ.

Paul indicates that the human search for God is innate: men and women are made so that they "search for God and perhaps grope for him and find him" (17:27). This captures Paul's (or Luke's) attitude toward other religions: they may represent sincere searching that brings people into some kind of genuine relationship with God.

Luke's respect for devout seekers who don't know Christ is evident in his telling of the encounter between Cornelius and Peter (Acts 10). As a centurion, Cornelius was thoroughly immersed in a pagan religious environment. The Roman army maintained a steady regime of worship, both of the deified emperor and of the traditional Roman gods.[22] Officers were required to officiate at sacrifices, and ordinary soldiers had to participate. Despite the fact that Cornelius functioned in such a context, Luke describes him as "a devout man who feared God with all his household; he gave alms generously to the people and prayed constantly to God" (Acts 10:2; cf. 10:22 and Luke 7:4).

God honored the prayer of this pious pagan and spoke to Cornelius through a vision (10:3-6). Peter also had a vision from God, which prepared him to speak the gospel to a Gentile centurion. When the centurion arrived at Peter's house and told of God's revelation to him, it brought a flash of insight to Peter:

> I truly understand that God shows no partiality, but in every nation anyone who fears him and does what is right is acceptable to him. You know the message he sent to the people of Israel, preaching peace by Jesus Christ—he is Lord of all. (Acts 10:34b-36)

Rather than dismissing other religions, Luke allows the possibility that "anyone who fears" God and "does what is right is acceptable (welcome or favorable) to him."[23] There is no indication here that Luke believed the pagan religion of Cornelius would ultimately convey salvation in the face of the parousia. Rather, the devout searching for God that was evident in Cornelius prepared the way for him to hear the gospel of Jesus Christ. God honored the centurion's prayer and brought him to someone who could speak the good news of Jesus Christ, who is "Lord of all." The essential understanding for salvation focuses on two main apocalyptic points: God raised Jesus from the dead (10:39-40), and Christ will come "as judge of the living and the dead" (10:42).

5. The plight of people in pagan religions, before they hear the gospel, can best be described as "ignorance." In his sermon at Athens, Paul

implies that people who have not yet heard of the good news of Jesus live in (almost) excusable ignorance. Arguably, those who bow down to "gold, or silver, or stone" (Acts 17:29) foolishly misunderstand the nature of a transcendent deity. God has been tolerant and merciful toward such people, but now a new age of divine revelation has come that requires a decisive response from mortals:

> While God has overlooked the times of human ignorance, now he commands all people everywhere to repent, because he has fixed a day on which he will have the world judged in righteousness by a man whom he has appointed, and of this he has given assurance to all by raising him from the dead. (Acts 17:30-31)

This presentation of other religious perspectives as "ignorance" already is familiar in the book of Acts. When Peter first preaches the gospel in the Jewish temple at Jerusalem, he tells his fellow Jews that they "killed the Author of life" when they crucified Jesus (3:15). But Peter allows that the Jews "acted in ignorance" and that God now opens the way to repentance and "times of refreshing" for all who call on the name of Jesus. There is an approaching "time of universal restoration" (3:21), an apparent reference to the parousia. An apocalyptic framework of history provides the context for considering other religions, and the resurrection of Jesus is the reality on which salvation hinges.

The theme of ignorance appears again when Paul and Barnabas heal a crippled man at Lystra. The crowds are so amazed that they take the two apostles to be the gods Zeus (Jupiter) and Hermes (Mars). A priest of Zeus brings flowers and prepares to make a sacrifice to the two Christian missionaries. Distraught, the missionaries tear their clothes and stop the ritual with the announcement that "we bring you good news, that you should turn from these worthless things to the living God." In past generations, this God

> allowed all the nations to follow their own ways; yet he has not left himself without a witness in doing good—giving you rains from heaven and fruitful seasons, and filling you with food and your hearts with joy. (Acts 14:16-17)

The response of Paul and Barnabas contains an implicit apocalyptic message. Although in the past God was lenient in tolerating pagan religion, allowing nations "to follow their own ways," now a new (and final) chapter of history has begun with the good news of Jesus Christ (14:21).

6. Other religions may have elements of truth in them, in part derived from what can be seen about God in creation. Paul's description at

Lystra of God's (past) tolerance toward other religions (Acts 14) seems to imply that devout pagans might discover some truth about God simply through the witness of creation. God's character is evident because God sends rain and supplies mortals with food and joy.

But if Paul had believed that this natural revelation would give enough knowledge of God for mortals to face the eschatological crisis, he would not have risked his life to preach the gospel. Instead, he dismissed the pagan rituals of his hearers as "worthless things" (Acts 14:15). Paul then apparently spoke his usual apocalyptic, messianic message about Jesus—and nearly died from being stoned (14:19). Later Paul put that brutal experience in apocalyptic context: "It is through many persecutions that we must enter the kingdom of God" (14:22).

Luke seems to give an accurate portrayal of Paul rejecting natural revelation and pagan religion. In his letter to Christians at Rome, Paul discusses the (eschatological) "wrath of God" and says that

> Ever since the creation of the world [God's] eternal power and divine nature . . . have been understood and seen through the things that he has made. So [humans] are without excuse, for though they knew God, they did not honor him as God . . . and they exchanged the glory of the immortal God for images. . . . (Rom. 1:20–23)

7. The approaching eschaton is a cataclysmic event in which only a minority of humanity will be saved by baptism into Jesus Christ. From the perspective of a tiny, persecuted flock of Christians in a hostile pagan environment, the author of 1 Peter anticipates the approaching liberation at Christ's coming. "The end of all things is near," he tells his readers (1 Pet. 4:7). He compares his situation in history to the circumstances of Noah, when God was about to destroy the earth with a flood. In that holocaust,

> a few, that is, eight persons, were saved through water. And baptism, which this prefigured, now saves you—not as a removal of dirt from the body, but as an appeal to God for a good conscience, though the resurrection of Jesus Christ, who has gone into heaven and is at the right hand of God, with angels, authorities, and powers made subject to him. (1 Pet. 3:20)

Christian baptism, in Peter's understanding, is parallel to the ark of Noah—a singular vehicle of salvation in an otherwise lost world. Similarly, Paul seems to view Israelite deliverance at the Red Sea as a parallel to Christian baptism (1 Cor. 10:1-5).

8. No amount of syncretism is acceptable for followers of Jesus Christ. Paul's Corinthian correspondence contains lengthy discussion of

Christian involvement in other religions. At issue was the question of whether followers of Jesus should eat meat offered to idols or worship in pagan temples (1 Cor. 8-10). This was a serious question for many early believers, since trade guilds and other political, social, and economic associations typically incorporated pagan religious rituals into their gatherings.[24] Paul repeats the Christian (and Jewish) understanding that there in fact *are* no other gods—or at least no gods that Christians will acknowledge (8:4-6).

Fortified with this monotheistic conviction, apparently some believers at Corinth were inclined to be present at certain pagan shrines and rituals (8:9-12). Paul considers the logic of this stance but moves on to a definitive rejection of any participation in pagan religion. He tells his readers to "flee from the worship of idols. . . . I do not want you to be partners with demons. . . . You cannot partake of the table of the Lord and the table of demons" (1 Cor. 10:14, 20-21).

9. The gospel of Jesus Christ is for the entire world, and God's people function as a welcoming, communal agent of hospitality, reconciliation, and salvation to people of other religious persuasions. The canonical New Testament begins and ends with strangers from other religious backgrounds worshipping Christ.

The Gospel of Matthew begins with an account of wise men who come from the East to worship the infant Jesus (Matt. 2:1-12). These were pagan astrologers (perhaps Mithraic priests). The same Gospel ends with Jesus commanding his disciples, "Go therefore and make disciples of all nations. . . . And remember, I am with you always, to the end of the age." Mission happens in an apocalyptic framework of anticipating the eschaton.

The book of Revelation ends with salvation depicted poetically in the form of a New Jerusalem in which the "temple is the Lord God the Almighty and the Lamb." Nations "will walk by its light, and the kings of the earth will bring their glory into it. Its gates will never be shut by day—and there will be no night there" (Rev. 21:23-25).

It is startling that the "kings of the earth" are included in this salvation, because they are the villains of the Apocalypse, pagan rulers who "fornicated" with the "great whore" of Rome (Rev. 18:9). This New Jerusalem saving community is *on earth*, not in heaven. It perhaps is a figurative representation of Jesus' prayer, "your will be done, on earth as it is in heaven" (Matt. 6:10).

Both Matthew and Revelation give hints of salvation being very inclusive, a theme echoed elsewhere in the New Testament. Paul looks forward to a time when "every knee should bend, in heaven and on earth and under the earth, and every tongue should confess that Jesus Christ is Lord. . ." (Phil. 2:10-11). Early Christians believed God to be merciful, "not wanting any to perish, but all to come to repentance" (2 Pet. 3:9).

Conclusion

New Testament authors believed an end-of-the-age crisis was imminent and were certain that life in the approaching reign of God would only be through faith in the risen Christ. The Old Testament had anticipated a blessing for all of humankind through Abraham, and now that promise was coming to fulfillment in Jesus (Gal. 3:14). New Testament proclamation of this message was full of confidence, perhaps even immodest certainty.

In the first-century church, the method of sharing this faith was always through noncoercive witness and invitation. Many early believers, including Paul, were prepared to lay down their lives to share the gospel. Christians were eager to relate to nonbelievers (1 Cor. 5:9, 10; 1 Pet. 3:15) and sometimes acknowledged the sincerity of those who earnestly sought God but did not yet know Jesus. Several New Testament authors seem to anticipate a broad salvation that incorporates people of all nations. The canonical texts, however, allow no compromise with pagan religion by incorporating either pagan practices or pagan beliefs into the church (e.g., 1 Cor. 5:11; 1 John 2:18-24; 4:1-6; Rev. 2:20-23).

Despite uncompromising confessional boundaries, early believers related with love and hospitality toward people of other religions. Jesus had healed the servant of a Roman centurion (Luke 7:1-10) and the daughter of a Syrophoenician woman (Mark 7:24-30)—both of whom probably belonged to other religions. The early church seems to have continued the tradition of respect and sensitivity toward adherents of other faiths.[25]

The pagan emperor Julian complained in a letter (362 C.E.) to a pagan high priest at Galatia that recent growth in the Christian church was caused by the Christians' "moral character, even if pretended." To another pagan priest Julian observed that "The impious Galileans support not only their poor, but ours as well."[26] Confessional exclusivism did not mean Christians shut themselves off from caring relationships with people of other religious persuasions.

The early church did not waver in confessing Christ alone as Lord, but the church avoided becoming an exclusive group. The door was open to all who believed and earnestly wanted to follow Jesus. Early witnesses invited spiritually hungry people to a living community of forgiveness, belonging, and service—a community that is a foretaste of the reign of God that some day will embrace all of creation.[27]

Notes

1. Pliny the Younger, *Letters* 10.96; trans. M. Eugene Boring, *Revelation,* Interpretation Commentary Series (Louisville, Ky.: John Knox Press, 1989), 14-15.

2. Pliny, *Letters* 10.97.

3. Cicero, *De Natura Deorum* 2.3.8.

4. Josephus, *War* 1.1.4 (38); 1 Macc. 8.17-30; 12.1-4.

5. Josephus, *Antiquities* 16.6.2 (163); cf. Matt. 17:24.

6. These points are summarized by J. Christiaan Beker in *Paul the Apostle: The Triumph of God in Life and Thought* (Philadelphia: Fortress Press, 1980), 136.

7. In the NT, see 1 Thess. 5:2, 4; 1 Cor. 1:8; 3:13; Rom. 2:5, 16; Phil. 1:6, 10; Heb. 10:25; 2 Tim. 1:12, 18; 4:8; and in the OT see Joel 1:15; 2:1-11; Amos 5:18-20; 8:9-14; Zeph. 1:7-18; 3:8-13.

8. Paul F. Knitter, *No Other Name: A Critical Survey of Christian Attitudes Toward the World Religions* (Maryknoll, N.Y.: Orbis Books, 1985), 183.

9. Jack Finegan, *Myth and Mystery: An Introduction to the Pagan Religions of the Biblical World* (Grand Rapids, Mich.: Baker Book House, 1989), 160.

10. Among the exceptions were the deified emperors, who ascended to the place of the gods after death. Upon his death in 14 C.E., witnesses gave sworn testimony that they saw the soul of Caesar Augustus rise to the heavens.

11. There were, however, periodic attempts to cleanse Rome of foreign religions and reestablish classic religious beliefs. Emperor Tiberius (14-37 C.E.), for example, tried to banish all foreign religions (including Judaism) from Rome—but his successor Caligula welcomed most religions back into the capital. Suetonius, *Tiberius* 36.1. Emperor Claudius (41-54 C.E.) expelled all Jews from Rome (Acts 18:2).

12. *Phaedo* 69c, cited by Finegan, 171.

13. August Meineke, *Ioannis Stobaei Florilegium* 4.107-8, cited in Finegan, 176.

14. Finegan, 211.

15. For a full discussion of this exclusive Christology, see Clark H. Pinnock, *A Wideness in God's Mercy: The Finality of Jesus Christ in a World of Religions* (Grand Rapids, Mich.: Zondervan, 1992), 49-80.

16. Paul understands the "Deliverer" of Rom. 11:26 to be Jesus.

17. Acts 13:14; 14:1; 17:1, 10; 18:4, 19, 26; 19:8.

18. See Calvin E. Shenk, *Who Do You Say That I Am?* (Scottdale, Pa.: Herald Press, 1997), 98-100.

19. See Carl E. Braaten, *No Other Gospel! Christianity Among the World's Religions* (Minneapolis: Fortress Press, 1992), 95-97.

20. 1 Apology 46.

21. 1 Apology 20-21.

22. See J. Helgeland, "Roman Army Religion," in ANRW II, 16.2 (1978), pp. 1470-1505; also, G. R. Watson, *The Roman Soldier* (Ithaca, N.Y.: Cornell University Press, 1969).

23. See Shenk, *Who Do You Say*, 102-104.

24. See J. Nelson Kraybill, *Imperial Cult and Commerce in John's Apocalypse* (Sheffield, England: Sheffield Academic Press, 1996), 109-141.

25. There seems to have been more tolerance in the church toward people of other faiths than there was toward apostate Christians (cf. 1 Cor. 5:9-13).

26. Rodney Stark, *The Rise of Christianity* (San Francisco: Harper Collins, 1997), 76-94.

27. For a provocative discussion of missiology as radical alternative community, see Alan Kreider, *Worship and Evangelism in Pre-Christendom* (Cambridge, England: Grove Books Ltd., 1995).

CHAPTER FOUR

Anabaptist Missions and the Critique of Christendom

John D. Roth

Introduction

On the night of March 21, 1526, a group of Anabaptists in Zurich broke through a window in the New Tower and escaped their prison cell by lowering themselves to the moat below. Two weeks earlier the city council of Zurich had sentenced the nineteen prisoners—among them five women and the three most prominent leaders of the Anabaptist movement in Switzerland: Felix Manz, Conrad Grebel, and George Blaurock—to life imprisonment for "disobedience, to the injury of public order and authority and the subversion of the common interest and true Christian conduct."[1]

According to the testimony of Wilhelm Exell, who was captured almost immediately, the group was undecided about where to go once they had made their way outside the city wall. "One said he would go here, and another there," reported Exell, but others joked among themselves and said they would go to the red Indians across the sea.[2]

We know where many of the escapees went. Grebel traveled eastward to Maienfeld, where he died of an illness in August 1526. Manz went to Embach, where he taught and baptized until he was recaptured and executed by Zurich authorities in January 1527. And Blaurock embarked on a remarkable three-year missionary career in the Tirol before he too was captured and burned at the stake in September 1529.

Apparently no one in the group ever made it to "the red Indians across the sea." But this comment, made no doubt in jest, offers a poignant entree into the topic of missions and the Anabaptist critique of European Christendom. For the history of Anabaptist missions in the heartland of Europe coincides almost exactly with a renewed interest in Catholic missions sparked by the voyages of overseas expansion.[3]

Christendom and the "Inner Logic" of Spanish Missions to the New World

Both historians of Anabaptism and contemporary Mennonite theologians tend to describe Christendom disparagingly, in a kind of shorthand caricature. Christendom was that monolithic, theocratic fusion of politics, religion, and culture, invented by the Emperor Constantine shortly after his alleged conversion in 314, which marked the fall of the apostolic church. Contrary to the teachings of Christ, Christendom's defenders extended religious convictions with the sharp edge of the sword; they sanctified political aggrandizement with appeals to divine favor; and they perpetuated this unholy alliance by baptizing infants into territorial churches and by a system of sacraments which turned salvation into a commodity controlled by the church which could be bought, sold, and bartered.[4]

Like all caricatures, there is an element of truth to each of these points. But in our hurry to defend religious voluntarism or the genius of the Anabaptist separation of church and state, we often overlook the appeal of Christendom as a means of ordering medieval society. We fail to appreciate how deeply engrained and self-evident Christendom's presence was in the lives of most Europeans during the late Middle Ages.

In its barest outlines, the logic of Christendom ran something like this: Before the resurrected Christ ascended to heaven, he passed his spiritual authority on to the apostles and, by extension, to the newly established church which spread out from Jerusalem. The church thus became the living "body" of Christ on earth. Like Christ, it had a physical, temporal form, but its spiritual authority, like Christ's, was literally universal (hence the term Catholic). At no place on earth did the authority of the Catholic Church lack presence, albeit in latent form.

In its temporal expression, the church reflected the divine hierarchical order of creation. At its head was the pope—the vicar of Christ—who in the master's absence wielded the full authority of the absent lord. Under the pope a vast hierarchy of spiritually endowed offices—known as the *sacerdotum*—extended from the cardinals and archbishops down to the parish priest, a hierarchy which preserved clear lines of accountability and authority.

Contrary to popular opinion in the sixteenth century, the primary purpose of this ecclesiastical hierarchy was not to collect tithes. Rather, the sole purpose of the church—in theory, at least—was to administer the sacraments. More specifically, the church existed to make it possible for ordinary people to enter into the living presence of God.

The most common sacrament, of course, was communion. Once the priest consecrated the wafer and the wine, commoners could, at least for a moment, literally become one with God. It is crucial to note here that the sacraments were efficacious only if administered by a priest who had been duly invested with this spiritual authority by the hierarchy of the church. In other words, there was no legitimate sacrament (and therefore no salvation) apart from the mediation of the church.

The authority of the church was not only universal, it was also ubiquitous. Its sacred presence was woven inextricably into the secular fabric of daily life. The church's monasteries were the centers of cultural transmission, its universities the arbiters of knowledge, its cathedrals the standard of architectural style and aesthetic taste.

In the village, the church's spire dominated the visual horizon. Its bells announced baptisms, weddings, and funerals and brought divine protection against hail or floods. Saint's days and religious festivals punctuated the daily calendar. At planting and harvest time, the village priest blessed the fields with incense and prayers. And the natural world of daily life, no less than the Bible, told the story of God's intentions and purposes. Starry skies at night were full of divine portents. A bountiful harvest was the sure measure of God's favor, while plague, famine, and Turkish incursions were equally clear signs of divine displeasure.

In many respects, the essence of Christendom was the way in which religious realities intersected deeply and self-evidently with political power. Indeed, even though much of medieval history can be described in terms of the titanic struggle between the spiritual authority of the papacy on the one hand, and the temporal authority of feudal lords and kings on the other, there was never a question as to whether the cross and the sword belonged together. The debate focused rather on the question of who would take the lead role in this tempestuous marriage. In any event, kings and princes in the Holy Roman Empire received a papal blessing at their coronations; they, in turn, had a significant voice in the internal affairs of the Catholic Church.

The specific points at which the interests of the church intersected with those of feudal lords were numerous. I will highlight two—the oath and infant baptism—because they serve to underscore the shocking and audacious nature of the Anabaptist movement and its critique.

In a feudal society of unstable political alliances, personal allegiances were almost always sealed with an oath: a formal ceremonial promise to fulfill specific obligations, with the threat of divine retaliation if those promises were broken. By their explicit appeal to the transcendent authority of God, oaths guaranteed political alliances of all sorts; they were the glue that held medieval society together. To be sure, oaths could be broken or ignored, but no one doubted they were an essential—and divinely sanctioned—feature of medieval life.

A second crucial point of intersection between the spiritual and political order of Christendom was infant baptism. Since at least the fifth century, it had been standard practice in the Catholic Church to baptize infants. Saint Augustine had provided the most systematic theological rationale. He argued that the presence of original sin in the newborn demanded that divine grace be mediated through the sacrament of baptism, to spare the infant from eternal damnation if it should die an untimely death. Salvation was a gift initiated by God and mediated through the institution of the church via the sacrament of baptism.

But baptism had a political dimension as well. Given the fact that since the late fourth century everyone in the Roman Empire (soon to be called the Holy Roman Empire) was to be a Christian under penalty of law, there was also a kind of "functional" logic to infant baptism. The ritual marked not only the entrance of the child into a spiritual communion of saints, but also its passage into the civil community of the local village and territory. By the Middle Ages, baptism was the moment when a newborn child took on a political identity, officially entered into the tax rolls as a Christian subject of the local feudal lord.

These, then, were the essential features of Christendom: a church with universal and exclusive spiritual authority, woven into the cultural fabric of medieval society and welded firmly to the political interests of feudal lords and the early modern state. Odd though it may seem to us, a German peasant in the sixteenth century assumed that the church—as the body of Christ—was indivisible and that spiritual and temporal matters were inherently intertwined. The calling of the individual, baptized at birth, was not to choose from a smorgasbord of religious or political options but to submit to Christendom's divinely established order.

Christendom and Catholic Missions to the "New World"

Not surprisingly, Catholic mission efforts in early modern Europe reflected these general assumptions. On the one hand, there was very little call for home missions in Christendom since everyone in the Holy Roman Empire—apart from the stray Jew or Muslim who happened to wander into the community—had already been baptized as an infant and was therefore already a part of the kingdom of God. Foreign missions, on the other hand—whether in the form of the Crusades or as an extension of overseas exploration and territorial expansion—would, inevitably, reflect an amalgam of religious and political interests.

Here the story of Catholic missions to the "red Indians across the sea" becomes very instructive.[5] From the very beginning, the interests of the church and the interests of Spanish or Portuguese monarchs were inextricably intertwined in mission efforts in the New World. Among the directives given by the Spanish monarchs to Christopher Columbus had been an explicit order to "learn their [the Indians'] disposition and the proper method of conveying them to our holy faith."

Columbus named the first island he encountered San Salvador, in honor of Jesus, and the second Santa Maria de la Concepcion, in honor of the Virgin Mary. The Indians he brought back in chains were baptized with great fanfare, with the King and Prince John serving as godfathers.

In three short decades, the Spanish had completed their conquest of Mexico and Central America. And as the Spanish armies advanced, so too did the interests of the Catholic Church. In his diary describing Hernan Cortes's campaign into Mexico, Bernal Diaz del Castillo graphically depicted the venture as a divine mission blessed by God at every step. The campaign followed a pattern: first the men would destroy local temples and idols, then they would set up a cross and altar, and finally they would forcibly baptize Indian women, who were then distributed among the men, including Cortes, as concubines.[6]

Following Cortes's decisive victory over the Aztecs in 1521, Spanish mission efforts began to assume an expanded and more systematic form. In the spring of 1526—only a few weeks before the Anabaptists' escape from the New Tower in Zurich—Emperor Charles V, Europe's most powerful political lord, sent 120 Franciscans, seventy Dominicans, and ten Hieronymites to the New World and charged them with the task of baptizing the native populations into the Catholic Church. The success of their efforts was astounding. In 1529, Peter of Ghent declared that he and one of his colleagues had often baptized 14,000 people in a single day during one campaign, and calculated his personal total to be somewhere around 200,000 baptisms. Two years later, only a decade after the conquest of the Aztecs, Zumarrage reported that the Franciscans alone had baptized more than 1 million persons. Another source from 1536 puts the figure at 4-9 million.[7]

Between 1524 and 1535—a period which coincides precisely with the spread of Anabaptism in Europe—Spanish conquistadors subdued the Incas in Peru and soon thereafter took control over much of the West Indies, all of Central America, and what are now the southernmost parts of the United States. By the end of the sixteenth century, the large majority of the human population south of the Rio Grande had become members of Christendom by virtue of baptism.

Modern Christians—especially Anabaptists—recoil at such accounts of physical and cultural violence, of coerced baptisms, of missions carried out by the sharp tip of the sword. Yet nothing in the logic of Christendom itself would find it odd to extend the gospel or the authority of the Catholic Church by collaborating with military force or the political interests of a Christian monarch.

It is worth noting, for example, that when Columbus or Cortes or any of the other conquistadors landed in the New World, they planted the flag of the Catholic Church but formally claimed the territory only for the King of Spain. There was no need to claim it for the church since the territory *already* was under sovereignty of the universal church. Thus in a significant sense Catholic missions in the sixteenth century could be understood as a procedure by which the church formally claimed what already rightfully belonged to it. Mission was merely the "mechanics" of asserting the independent reality of the church's universal authority through the means of baptism and catechism. As with infant baptism, individual consent in the matter was simply not a highly relevant point.

Clearly, this bare overview does not begin to tell the full story of Catholic missions in the New World. A more complete version of that story would need to place the mission effort in a broader economic and political context. It would explore evolving strategies for communicating the catechism to natives, and it would need to include more gruesome details of torture and violence, as well as the accounts of missionaries like Batholome de las Casas who protested vigorously against the dehumanization of Indians that accompanied the Spanish conquest.[8]

But even if that story were told in its full detail, most moderns would react with dismay and disapproval. Most of us raised in a post-Enlightenment culture simply assume that the sacred and the secular occupy two distinct realms of reality. Most of us are reflexively opposed to a blind fusion of religious zeal and political power; the idea of using physical violence or coercion for spiritual ends strikes most of us as almost incomprehensible.

This brings us to the Anabaptist critique of Christendom. For at the same historical moment that Europe's most powerful kings and prelates were setting their sights across the sea, small groups of itinerant, often unlettered, Anabaptist missioners had begun preaching a radical new version of the gospel to the villagers and burghers of central Europe. Their critique of Christendom helped to bring about its eventual demise. At the same time, paradoxically, that critique gave rise to some of the vexing questions of religious pluralism.

The Anabaptist Critique

Mission, by its very nature, implies a challenge to the basic premises of the dominant culture. Such was the character of the Anabaptist movement. From the moment of the first adult baptism in January 1525, Anabaptism represented a revolutionary alternative that challenged Christendom's most fundamental assumptions.

The critique did not go unnoticed. Within a year of the movement's inception, political and religious leaders had come to regard the Anabaptist critique as so threatening to public order that they responded violently with imprisonment, interrogations, torture, and even death. By 1529, an imperial edict granted every ruler in the Holy Roman Empire the right to execute without a trial anyone who publicly challenged the sacrament of infant baptism.

Surely part of this concern must be attributed to the rapid growth of the Anabaptist movement. Almost immediately following the establishment of the first congregation at Zollikon in January 1525, Anabaptism spread into Bern, Basel, Strasbourg, and Alsace, northward into Baden and Swabia, along the Neckar river into Württemberg, and eastward to Appenzell, St. Gall, Chur, the Tirol, and far beyond to Moravia, where, by 1527, there were an estimated 2,000 Anabaptists living in the town of Nickolsberg alone. During the four years between 1525 and his execution at the stake in 1529, Georg Blaurock baptized at least 1,000 people. The confirmed baptisms of other early itinerant preachers such as Hans Hut, Leonard Schiemer, and Michael Kürschner all number well over 100 each.

From Strasbourg, Anabaptism spread down the Rhine River, where it found popular reception in the Low Countries.[9] By the middle of the sixteenth century, Hutterite communities in Moravia had developed a regular pattern of spring and fall mission campaigns that sent teams into South German territories.[10]

It is difficult to determine with absolute precision the quantitative success of the Anabaptist mission outreach, but it is reasonable to estimate that at its height the movement included between 15,000 and 20,000 people.

To be sure, this is not an astoundingly large figure. Thirty years ago, social historian Claus-Peter Clasen argued in an empirical survey of Anabaptism that since its adherents never numbered than one percent of the total population, it should be considered a "minor episode" in the history of the Reformation.[11] But judging by the vehemence of their response, contemporary authorities certainly did not consider the Anabaptist mission movement to be a minor episode. And ideas, once unleashed, can have an impact far more powerful than a statistical survey can fully convey.

What was the nature of the Anabaptist critique? Why did European princes and bishops find it so offensive? And behind the critique, what were the positive elements of the Anabaptist message that attracted such an enthusiastic response, especially in the face of draconian threats, the loss of property, imprisonment, torture, and even death? The answers to these questions all intersect in Anabaptist missions.

The Missionary Message

The Authority of Scripture

At the heart of the Anabaptist mission movement—fueling its appeal and credibility at the popular level—was a fresh reading of Scripture, especially the New Testament, and the emerging conviction that the early church of Acts differed in crucial ways from the institutional church of Rome. The centrality of Scripture—the primacy of the Word— was a general Reformation theme, of course. Yet Anabaptist missioners brought several distinctive convictions to Scripture that set them at odds with the defenders of Christendom, both Catholic and Protestant alike.

Though they differed significantly on how the Bible was to be interpreted, Catholics and Protestants both assumed that the task of biblical interpretation ultimately rested in the hands of those trained and ordained to that role. In other words, biblical interpretation should be controlled by ecclesiastical authorities. What possible good could come from common, unlettered peasants—ignorant of the biblical languages and the rich theological tradition of the church fathers—debating the meaning of the Scriptures? Allowing untrained lay people to interpret Scripture invited a kind of hermeneutical anarchy. In the words of Thomas More, it simply "granted to every individual the freedom to chart their own path to Hell."

The Anabaptists directly challenged this assumption. Scripture, they argued, should not only be accessible to everyone—either through the vernacular written word or by memorization—but it should be read, interpreted, and heeded by ordinary people gathered under the authority of the Holy Spirit to discern the will of God. In their view, the presence of the Holy Spirit and a genuine desire to understand—both things accessible to *all* people—were more crucial to proper biblical interpretation than formal training or an appointment to ecclesiastical office.

Even more radically, the Anabaptists insisted that Scripture— especially the teachings of Christ in the New Testament—was a living text. It was to be studied as the standard for daily Christian life, even if its teachings—such as those in the Sermon on the Mount—seemed to violate natural reason, ecclesiastical tradition, and political self-interest. Part of the Anabaptist suspicion of the so-called *Schriftgelehrten* (academic theologians) was their strong tendency to develop sophisticated arguments for avoiding the plain and simple meaning of the text. According to the Anabaptists, the Bible was not given by God to be debated but to be lived.

In recent years, historians have rightly qualified this "heroic" description of Anabaptists as absolute biblical literalists who resolutely and consistently lived out the teachings of Jesus. We know that the Anabaptist movement had a social context, charged with peasant unrest, anticlericalism, and apocalyptic expectations. We also know that the Anabaptists did not read Scripture in the complete absence of a hermeneutic tradition. But Anabaptist missioners invariably made their initial appeal on the basis of a new understanding of Scripture that challenged old assumptions: everyone, regardless of training or office, should have access to the Bible; its meaning, though not always unambiguous, could be understood by the gathered believers with the illuminating presence of the Holy Spirit; and its message was authoritative for daily life in a clear, plain, direct sense.

To argue, as did the Anabaptists, that Jesus' words in Scripture were to be understood and practiced literally was profoundly unsettling. It challenged the authority of the sacerdotum, it portrayed the institutions of Christendom as corrupt and hypocritical, and it opened the door to radical New Testament notions on economics and power which could serve—as in the case of the Twelve Articles of the Peasants' War of 1525—as the blueprint for a social revolution.

Salvation as Conversion

The study of Scripture, however, was not an end in itself. With Luther, the Anabaptists insisted that the whole point of Scripture was to proclaim the good news of salvation. But they understood salvation in a very distinctive way. For Catholics, the primary focus of salvation was found in the sacraments, particularly the sacraments of baptism and communion. For the newly established Protestant groups, salvation was an inward transaction by which human sinfulness was forgiven through the divine grace of God. But in both cases—whether via the sacraments or the predestined gift of grace—the drama of salvation was an event that occurred independently of the attitude or personal convictions of the recipient.

The Anabaptists, by contrast, understood salvation in terms of a process, and they insisted that the individual decision was a crucial step. For them, salvation began with the desire for repentance. It included God's gracious forgiveness of sin, and, significantly, it extended to a genuine conversion in the life of the believer—that is, a qualitative change of character through the empowering grace of God, which became evident in concrete behavior. In countless interrogation records, Anabaptists reported that they joined the movement because of "powerful preaching" that called them to repent from sin, to yield themselves fully to the Spirit, to be baptized into the new community of faith, to study the Scripture, and to live a life modeled after that of Christ.[12]

Thus, salvation for Anabaptist missioners was not primarily a sacramental act or the inner, personal experience of grace. Rather, it was a conversion: a fundamental reshaping of attitude and priorities, symbolized by voluntary baptism, which marked the beginning of a new life under the lordship of Christ.

For the defenders of Christendom, this view of salvation— premised on the voluntary choice of an individual and resulting in a transformed moral character—was profoundly disturbing. It not only replaced the millennium-old tradition of infant baptism with adult voluntary baptism, it undermined the church's authority as the sole spiritual intermediary between humans and God. It implied that the great majority of people in Christendom had not experienced true conversion, were not living according to the precepts of Christ, and had been deceived by the false claims of the Catholic Church that the sacraments would indeed save them.

The Community of the Redeemed

Ultimately, neither Scripture nor salvation could be fully understood apart from a third key feature of the Anabaptist missionary message: the church as a visible, disciplined community separated by the quality of its Christian life from the fallen order around it. Catholic Christendom assumed that the church embraced and blessed *all* of society and culture; Luther and the reformers, on the other hand, argued that the true church—made up of those to whom God had granted the gift of grace—was invisible.

The Anabaptists challenged both of these understandings. If Christian faith involved a voluntary choice, and if that choice resulted—necessarily and inevitably—in a new way of life, then the community formed by these individuals would be a clearly defined, visible minority in the dominant culture. It would be an alternative society, composed of members whose determination to follow the costly teachings of Christ would led them inevitably into conflict with the defenders of the old order.

This gathered community, at least in its ideal form, provided a communal context for reading and discerning the meaning of Scripture. It was this gathered community that nurtured the new convert in the faith: sustaining, challenging, and disciplining the disciple in the high calling of following the way of Christ. It was this gathered community—not the state, the institutional church, the family, nor the self—that was the primary focus of God's saving acts in history. Anabaptist congregations disavowed all forms of violence, even those of self-defense; they rejected civil offices and the swearing of oaths in faithfulness to Christ's teaching in the Sermon on the Mount; and they called on their members to share freely of their economic possessions.

All this was intolerable to the defenders of Christendom. The missionary message of the gathered community challenged the seamless unity of the Catholic Church and seemed to threaten the stability of the political order. By suggesting that all of life—culture, politics, faith, economics—should be judged according to the standard of the New Testament, it drove a drove a wedge into the fusion of Christianity and culture that had been a defining feature of Christendom. Not surprisingly, political and religious authorities—Catholic and Protestant alike—denounced the Anabaptists as seditious anarchists who were destroying the foundations of European society.

Missionary Method and Rationale

The Anabaptist movement of the first generation was deeply defined by its missionary character. Yet surprisingly enough, Anabaptists seem to have given relatively little attention to mission strategies. At the most, they seem to have sought a common mind on certain key theological themes, made some ad hoc provisions for the economic support of itinerant preachers, and sought general understandings regarding a division of missionary labor in specific territories.[13]

Intense persecution and the congregational character of early Anabaptist polity seem to have discouraged theoretical reflection about missions or the development of a highly centralized approach to missionary outreach. Nevertheless, several overarching themes in regard to missionary methods quickly emerged.

Centrality of the Great Commission

Modern Protestants tend to assume that the admonition of Christ in Matthew 28 to "Go therefore and make disciples of all nations . . ." has always been the foundation of Christian missions. But throughout most of the Middle Ages, what we now call the "great commission" attracted attention in the church only because the command to baptize "in the name of the Father and of the Son and of the Holy Spirit" served as a crucial proof text for defending the Trinity.

Following Erasmus, the Anabaptists were the first to recover this text (and its parallel in Mark 16) as the *locus classicus* for Christian missions.[14] "Our faith stands on nothing other," wrote Hans Schlaffer, "than the command of Christ in Matthew 28 and Mark 16. For Christ did not say to his disciples: Go forth and celebrate the Mass, but go forth and preach the Gospel."[15]

For the Anabaptists, the great commission provided biblical authority for the following: the lay apostolate (Christ's command applied to all Christians, not just those ordained to a special office); an itinerant ministry in a culture where wandering strangers were regarded with deep suspicion ("go into all the world"); and, perhaps most importantly, a precise theological statement about the proper sequence of conversion (believe and be baptized). Although Hubmaier and others developed a much more systematic theological defense of adult baptism, many Anabaptist missioners were content to quote Matthew 28 or Mark 16 as the only word necessary on the subject.

"Firstly," explained Hans Hut in language reminiscent of other Anabaptist testimony, "Christ said, go forth into the whole world, preach the Gospel to every creature. Secondly, he said, whosoever believes, thirdly—and is baptized—the same shall be saved. This order must be maintained if a true Christianity is to be erected. . . ."[16]

"The Earth Is the Lord's"

For the Anabaptists, the proper arena of missionary activity was the entire world, not the artificial boundaries of a political territory. In part, this expansive view of the "mission field" was imposed on them from the outside since persecution virtually compelled the Anabaptist to become mobile to survive. Harassed or exiled from their homes, Anabaptist refugees—men and women alike—fanned out into neighboring towns and territories in search of more hospitable reception. And wherever they went, they shared their understanding of the gospel. Menno Simons, the great leader of the Dutch Anabaptists, described the circumstances vividly:

> Therefore, we preach, as much as possible, both by day and by night, in houses and in fields, in forests and wastes, hither and yon, at home or abroad, in prisons and in dungeons, in water and in fire, on the scaffold and on the wheel. . . . For we feel His living fruit and moving power in our hearts. . . . We could wish that we might save all mankind from the jaws of hell, free them from the chains of their sins, and by the gracious help of God add them to Christ by the Gospel of His peace.[17]

As refugees they met with suspicion and resistance almost everywhere they went. Wandering strangers were rarely welcomed in early modern European villages, and the church closely guarded its hold on the office of preaching. Repeatedly, court officials referred to Anabaptist lay preachers as *Schleicher und Winkelprediger* (sneaks and corner preachers) who had no authority to expound on the word of God. And Anabaptists were frequently exiled from a particular region with dire threats if they should return. Almost as frequently, Anabaptists defied the court's right to exclude them from a region and defended their recalcitrance with a quote from Psalms 24: "The earth is the Lord's and all that is in it."

The Importance of Oral Communication

Since Anabaptist leaders had very limited access to formal means of communication, such as pulpits and printing presses, the spread of the movement relied almost exclusively on oral communication and face-to-face contacts. Not surprisingly, these contacts focused initially on family networks, friendship groups, and occupational circles. An itinerant preacher might go to the home of someone sympathetic to the Anabaptists, read and expound on Scripture to the friends and relatives of the household, and baptize those who were ready to commit themselves to the movement. Rarely were these meetings larger than fifteen or twenty persons.

Historian Arnold Snider has given a graphic description of one such missioner, a needle-seller named Hans Nadler.[18] As he traveled from city to city, Nadler would strike up conversations with people and, according to the court testimony, "whenever he met goodhearted persons in inns or on the street . . . he would give instruction from the Word of God." If a listener was open to hearing about suffering and persecution and was ready to "abstain from the joys of the world," Nadler would outline how the hearer could "receive the Word of God like a child and . . . be born anew."

Remarkably, Nadler was illiterate. But he developed a system of preaching and instruction based on line-by-line expositions of the Lord's Prayer and the Apostles' Creed that could be understood by virtually everyone, educated and uneducated alike.[19] Nadler is not noted today as a fiery evangelist or someone who baptized hundreds of people. Yet his simple, direct approach to missions—somewhat akin to what we today might call "friendship evangelism"—was typical of Anabaptist missions. Ironically, the one formal attempt by the Anabaptists to organize their mission outreach in a more systematic way—at a gathering of leaders in Augsburg in 1527—is remembered not as a mission conference but as the "Martyrs Synod" because so many of the participants were killed within the year.

The Outcome of Anabaptist Mission

New Creatures in Christ

The intended outcomes or goals of Anabaptist mission were implicit in their message. Missions should lead, in the first place, to a changed life—what the Anabaptists described as a "new creature in Christ." The "new creature" was transformed not only by the inner work of God's forgiving grace but also by an outward change in daily behavior, made possible by God's empowering grace. Wherever they went, Anabaptists quickly gained the reputation of being noticeably more virtuous—more moral, more honest, more trustworthy—than their neighbors, a fact which authorities alternatively admired, resented, or denounced as a new form of monasticism. The changed lives of Anabaptist converts—a point noted by friends and foes alike—was an integral part of Anabaptist mission and a festering point of irritation to Catholics and reformers alike.

Redeemed Communities

A second outcome of missions was the creation of new congregations, voluntary gatherings of believers who were intent on restoring the apostolic church. These congregations sought, by the exercise of church discipline in accordance with Christ's teachings in Matthew 18, to create a church "without spot or wrinkle," a church worthy of being the bride of Christ.

Herein lay the power—and the threat—of Anabaptist communities: in their insistence on the absolute authority of Christ they "desacralized," or relativized, the institutions of Christendom. Anabaptist congregations were no longer dependent on the Catholic Church as the mediator of salvation through the sacraments of infant baptism or the eucharist. They refused to take up the sword or kill on behalf of the state or its interests. They rejected the oath in accordance with Christ's teaching in the Sermon on the Mount. And they denied familial bonds of affection when these conflicted with the call to follow Christ unto death. In a society premised on the universal authority of the church and the divine sanction on the given cultural, political, and economic order, it is not surprising that the Anabaptists' separatist communities created a fear completely out of proportion to their actual threat to European society.

Persecution and Martyrdom

Thus, a third outcome of Anabaptist missions was persecution and martyrdom. It is, of course, a recurring paradox in the history of the church that efforts to eliminate a movement by violence frequently serve as one of the most effective strategies for mission. If the Anabaptists of the first generation had tempered their critique of Christendom and had retreated into spiritualism, they might have escaped persecution. But their persistent determination to speak, teach, and preach their understanding of the gospel ultimately led to the martyrdom of some 3,000 Anabaptists and the imprisonment of countless more.

To be sure, there were some Anabaptist who in the face of prison or torture recanted their position. But the many stories of those who remained firm to the end make it clear that the steadfast consciously regarded their executions as a form of witness, as a graphic testimony both to the inherent violence of Christendom and the power of Christ's nonresistant love in the face of death. Many of the accounts collected in the *Martyrs Mirror* highlight the moving sermons preached by the condemned prisoner to the crowd gathered for the execution. They describe in detail the hymns sung, the prayers offered, the letters written, and the words of encouragement given as a final testimony to their faith.

Authorities often tried to prevent these opportunities for public witness by cutting out the condemned person's tongue or affixing a tongue-screw to impose silence. But in the end, the stories of faithfulness unto death could not be silenced; the martyr's death offered a more powerful and eloquent testimony to the Anabaptist understanding of the gospel than any sermon they ever preached. Over time, a "theology of martyrdom" emerged, at least among some Anabaptists, which suggested that persecution, torture, suffering, and death were all concrete evidence of God's presence in a sinful and fallen world. Seen in continuity with Christ, Stephen, the apostles, and the early church, martyrdom became a seal of God's approval of a Christian life well-lived, a crown of glory and life.

At no other point does the contrast between Anabaptism and Christendom become more graphic. As Catholic missionaries in the New World were extending the kingdom through mass baptisms, with the cross in one hand and the sword in the other, Anabaptist martyrs at home were testifying to an alternative, nonviolent kingdom through the sacrifice of their lives.

Conclusion: Relevance of the Anabaptist Critique

On the surface, it may seem that the Anabaptist mission movement offers few resources for addressing a pluralistic, modern world. The questions contemporary missionaries ask are deeply informed by post-Enlightenment doubts regarding the universal nature of truth, by a modern awareness of cross-cultural pluralism, by concerns about cultural arrogance shaped by the nineteenth- and twentieth-century missionary movements. The Anabaptists, on the other hand, gave little thought to the epistemological questions of postmodernity and were only barely aware of religious possibilities beyond the Christian faith. Their mission efforts—directed toward fellow Christians who shared their own language, cultural heritage, and religious texts—were not explicitly "cross cultural."

Yet in a very real sense, the theological wedge that Anabaptism drove into Christendom was a prelude to many of the questions that we ask today. Their challenge to the universal authority of the church—through their insistence on the right of the laity to read and interpret Scripture; their understanding of salvation as a process which required the free choice of the individual and resulted in a transformed moral character; their view of the church as an voluntary gathering, a visible subculture in society, independent of the state; their rejection of violence; and their appeal to the literal teachings of Christ—all opened a host of new questions which sixteenth-century Anabaptists never could have anticipated. I want to highlight only three of these themes in the hope that they can suggest some points of continuity between the reforms of the sixteenth century and our own day.

The Paradox of Freedom

There is a historiographical tradition that depicts the Anabaptists as harbingers of modernity. Their insistence on believers baptism and the separation of church and state freed the individual conscience from the tyranny of collective institutions; it provided the foundation for modern notions of religious freedom and the autonomous individual.

There is an element of truth to this argument, yet it is only a partial truth. For the Anabaptists' notion of individual freedom in matters of religion was inseparably bound to their understanding of the disciplined church. The individual was not free in the modern sense of radical autonomy; rather, individual freedom was understood in the context of an absolute—though uncoerced—commitment to a new social order, the community of believers. Paradoxically, the practice of church discipline—something moderns tend to regard as an infringement on freedom—actually ensured that the individual who committed to the group continued to make that commitment as a free and voluntary choice. Without the practice of church discipline, choices regarding allegiance are meaningless, but the noncoercive nature of the discipline guarantees that the choice is indeed genuine.

Verbal Witness as Inseparable from Witness of Deed

An emphasis on individual choice can easily lead to a view of evangelism which is focused on language, on the rational arguments that persuade the individual to join the movement. And indeed, as I have suggested above, the Anabaptists believed strongly in the power of face-to-face communication and in the authority of the spoken word in preaching and teaching. Yet they would have found the Enlightenment confidence in persuasive speech—a mode of witness which has come to characterize much of modern evangelical mission work—strange and incomplete. Words about faith only took on a depth of meaning insofar as they became embodied in deed.

The Anabaptists had little patience for Protestant congregations filled with people who had responded to the Word of God in their hearts but showed no outward evidence of it in their behavior. Grace apart from a transformed life was ineffectual grace. In a postmodern context, the Anabaptist message may be to balance our preoccupation with linguistic "truth claims" with frank questions about holy living. In other words, it makes no sense to debate the epistemology of precepts if there is no corresponding commitment to actual practice; indeed, it is often in the practice that the salience of the precept emerges with greatest clarity.

Confrontational Nonviolence

In light of our modern sensibilities to cultural pluralism and our awareness of the pitfalls of cultural arrogance, the Anabaptist mission style can seem needlessly confrontational, audacious, and even offensive. The Anabaptists openly defied the symbols of ecclesiastical authority (e.g., disrupting the sermon of the local priest or refusing to baptize their infants), and they stubbornly challenged some of the most basic assumptions of their culture (e.g., that a Christian could not wield the sword, swear an oath, or hold a public office, and that the sacerdotum was irrelevant to matters of faith). To be sure, they did so on the basis of a shared Scripture, but they brooked no compromise in their arguments and they persisted in spreading their ideas even when the host culture was deeply offended and sought every available means to silence them. Today we would likely describe them as culturally insensitive.

Yet in the midst of their utter self-confidence, one can consistently hear a clear note of humility in Anabaptist theology that guards against a confusion of human interests—no matter how noble—with the will of God. In sharp contrast to the missionary methods of Christendom, persuasion—not coercion or manipulation—was the only acceptable means of witnessing to God's love and grace. And the community of faith which extended the invitation did so without making any prior claims or demands in regards to cultural loyalties, political self-interest, or racial identity.

Though Anabaptists have not always managed to maintain these ideals in actual practice, their strongest critique of Christendom—yesterday as well as today—has been the quality of their own life in community, a life lived by the grace of God in obedience to Christ as a light to the world.

Notes

1. *The Sources of Swiss Anabaptism,* Leland Harder, ed. (Scottdale, Pa.: Herald Press, 1985), 448.

2. Ibid., 451.

3. It is important to note from the outset that I am not claiming to chart any new scholarly territory here in terms of primary source research into either Catholic or Anabaptist missions. A good overview of the scholarship on the topic of Anabaptists and missions can be found in the thirteen essays gathered together in *Anabaptism and Mission*, Mennonite Missionary Study Series 10, Wilbert R. Shenk, ed. (Scottdale, Pa.: Herald Press, 1984); Wolfgang Schäufele, *Das missionarische Bewußtsein und Wirken der Täufer* (Neukirchen-Vluyn: Neukirchener Verlag des Erziehungsvereins, 1966) offers the most comprehensive study of Anabaptist mis-

sion understandings and practice; Franklin H. Littell, *The Anabaptist View of the Church: A Study in the Origins of Sectarian Protestantism* (Boston: American Society of Church History, 1952), puts Anabaptist missions in the broader context of ecclesiology; and Ray C. Gingerich, *The Mission Impulse of Early Swiss and South German-Austrian Anabaptism* (Ph.D. diss., Vanderbilt University, 1980), offers a careful analysis of the substance and appeal of Anabaptist missions. For an important new line of inquiry into oral culture and the transmission of ideas, see Arnold C. Snyder, "Orality, Literacy and the Study of Anabaptists," *MQR* (October 1991), 371-92; "Communication and the People: The Case of Reformation St. Gall," *MQR* 67 (April 1993), 152-73; and his *Anabaptist History and Theology: An Introduction* (Waterloo, Ont.: Pandora Press, 1995), 101-113.

4. The most perceptive and persistent critic of Christendom within the Anabaptist tradition has been John Howard Yoder, whose voluminous writings on ethics and theology almost always take the claims of Christendom as a point of departure. For a good introduction to Yoder's critique, see the essays in *The Priestly Kingdom: Social Ethics as Gospel* (Notre Dame, Ind.: University of Notre Dame Press, 1984), especially "The Constantinian Sources of Western Ethics," 135-147.

5. Kenneth Scott Latourette, *A History of The Expansion of Christianity, Vol. 3: Three Centuries of Advance* (London: Eyre and Spottiswoode, 1944), esp. 83-122.

6. Bernal Diaz del Castillo, *The Discovery and Conquest of Mexico, 1517-1521*, ed. and trans. Irving A. Leonard (New York: Farrar, Straus and Cudahy, 1956).

7. Latourette, *Three Centuries of Advance*, 113. In 1541, Bishop Julian Garces of Tlaxcala wrote that he was baptizing at least 300 persons every week.

8. For a scorching account of this broader story, see George E. Tinker, *Missionary Conquest: The Gospel and Native American Cultural Genocide* (Minneapolis: Augsburg Fortress, 1993) and the more general, but no less critical, history by Kirkpatrick Sale, *The Conquest of Paradise: Christopher Columbus and the Columbian Legacy* (New York: Alfred A. Knopf, 1990).

9. For these figures, see Hans Kasdorf, "The Anabaptist Approach to Mission," in *Anabaptism and Mission*, 66.

10. For more on Hutterian missions, see Leonard Gross, *The Golden Years of the Hutterites* (Scottdale, Pa.: Herald Press, 1980), 42-55, and Claus-Peter Clasen, *Die Wiedertäufer im Herzogtum Württemberg und in benachbarten Herrschaften* (Stuttgart, Germany: W. Kohlhammer, 1965), 180-86.

11. Claus-Peter Clasen, *Anabaptism: A Social History, 1525-1618* (Ithaca, N.Y.: Cornell University Press, 1972), 30-48.

12. See, for example, the references to Hubmaier on this point cited by Gingerich, *Mission Impulse*, 77-83; for other sources, see Franklin Littell, "The Anabaptist Theology of Mission," in *Anabaptism and Mission*, 18-23.

13. For an excellent summary of early Anabaptist mission strategy, such as it was, see Wolfgang Schäufele, "The Missionary Vision and Activity of the Anabaptist Laity," *MQR* 36 (April 1962), 99-115.

14. Abraham Friesen has developed this argument systematically in his *Integrating Christianity: Erasmus, the Anabaptists and the Great Commission* (Grand Rapids, Mich.: Eerdmans, 1998).

15. Quoted in Littell, "The Anabaptist Theology of Missions," 19.

16. Ibid.

17. Quoted in C. J. Dyck, "The Anabaptist Understanding of the Good News," in *Anabaptism and Mission*, 35.

18. Snider, *Anabaptist History and Theology*, 106-7.

19. For more on Nadler's remarkable system, see Russel Snider-Penner, Hans Nadler's "Oral Exposition of the Lord's Prayer," *MQR* 65 (October 1991), 393-406.

CHAPTER FIVE

Contemporary Global Pluralism: The Approach of Hinduism

Lawrence M. Yoder

A Brief Introduction to Hinduism

The idea of a religion called Hinduism is not originally Indian. It was apparently generated first of all by Persians, who thought it fitting to label the whole range of religious beliefs and practices of the peoples dwelling along the great river of northwestern India with a single name, a name taken from the name of that river—Sindhu (the Indus). The idea stuck. To this day not only do outsiders call the main streams of traditional religion in India Hinduism, but so do many Indians, especially when they are outside India and communicating in a European language.

The name "India" itself derives from the same source and usage.[1] But the Indian name for the religion of India is *dharma,* the law or way.[2]

Today there are large numbers of Hindus in Pakistan, Nepal, and Indonesia and growing numbers in many other countries, apart from India itself. The spread of Hinduism has occurred by migration and conversion, but also by the spreading influence of Hindu ideas about the world.

The Republic of India defines a Hindu as an Indian who is not a Muslim, a Christian, a Parsi, or a Jew.[3] We might also add Buddhists, Jains, and Sikhs to the list of Indians who are not Hindus, plus all the non-Indians who have not joined a Hindu religious movement.

Hinduism so defined has no founder, no creed, and no single book acknowledged as canon or holy Scripture for all Hindus. This religion of

India is immensely diverse, incorporating a wide range of beliefs, practices, perspectives, and social groupings that developed over thousands of years.

Modern Hinduism has two ancient sources, Indian religion going back to the third millennium B.C.E. and Aryan religion brought into India through the invasion of Aryan peoples from the northwest around 1500 B.C.E. Ancient Indian religion flourished in an urban society based on highly developed agriculture. The "River" (Indus and Ganges) was the source of fertility and water. Ritual purity was crucial. It was achieved and maintained through ablutions and bathing in the river.

The state itself was sacral. Male and female deities provided a means for expressing special interest in the fertility so crucial for this agriculture-based society. The female goddesses embodied the *sakti*, which was regarded as the strength or power of the male. The male god (who may have been Shiva in an earlier form) had three faces. At least the germ of the concepts of karma and reincarnation was present, along with some elemental concept of the practice of yoga (meditation). These accompany the symbols of male and female sex organs, the *lingam* and the *yoni*.

The invading Aryans from Persia did not displace the older culture and religion but rather integrated much of it into the beliefs and practices they brought with them. Sanskrit, which developed as a language in this context with its many Indo-European root words, is symbolic of the intermingling of Indian and European religion and culture in this new civilization. The Vedas, the Rig Veda being the oldest, are our link with early Aryan religion. These hymns to the Aryan gods are considered the revelations of Brahman—the ultimate source—by way of inspired sages (*rishi*).

The Caste System

The invasion of light-skinned Aryans into the northern plains of India eventually produced a situation where it was felt necessary to prevent the further racial intermingling and intermarriage between them and the dark-skinned native Dasas, whom they had conquered. And so emerged the concept of four distinct social groupings called *varnas*, which literally means colors ("castes" in English).[4]

The varna with the highest status and influence were the Brahmins, the priestly caste. Next came the *Kshatrya varna*, the ruling or warrior caste. Then came the *Vaisya varna*, the common merchant, artisan caste, including many of mixed Aryan-Dasa descent. Finally came the *Sudra varna*, presumably the remaining unmixed Dasa population. Here, in the insistence of the Brahmins that the Aryan population isolate themselves from the native Dasa populace and rule over them, we have a clear manifestation of racism, the belief that people of one race or skin color are inherently more worthy and noble than other races.

The varna-caste system is given ontological, one might say ontocratic, foundation in the myth that the four castes were formed out of the body of the original cosmic Man, Purusha, who allowed the gods to sacrifice him. Out of his mouth the gods made the Brahmin, and of his arms the Kshatrya (or *Rajanya*). From his thighs were formed the Vaisya, and from his feet came the Sudra, the lowest varna.

More than anything else, it is the caste system that came to separate Hindus into virtually mutually exclusive social groupings with widely divergent religious practices. The Brahmins developed their increasingly elaborate speculations in the origin and nature of the universe, which came to center in the rock-firm belief that the essence or core of all reality was something called Brahman or *Atman*, which pervades or encompasses all things.[5] This was accompanied by the growing belief that all apparent reality is mere *maya*, a deceptive veil from which humanity must seek liberation.

Devotion to one or another of the major gods of Hinduism and participation in an array of cults and rites centering on such deities characterize the religious belief and practice of the lower classes and are the source of much more diversity. In addition to the great gods of Hinduism whose names many of us would recognize, there are millions of gods associated with particular places, ritual practices, and groups of people. Thus, a Hindu might well be a pantheist, a polytheist, a monotheist, or even an atheist. He might be a dualist, a pluralist, or a monist.

This leaves us with the impression that Hinduism is thoroughly pluralistic, that any belief is tolerated and accepted—as long as a person remains loyal to the rites and requirements of his or her caste. It is simply inconceivable that a person might try to leave the caste or marry a person from another caste. Such violation of the system would make the person who did it an outcast, a nobody. Indeed, many Hindu religious leaders and reformers make precisely these claims, while at the same time decrying the understanding Muslims and Christians hold in common: that the community of faith—the *ummah* or the church—should call and gather people from all segments, castes, and levels of society.

Some of the variety of Hinduism can be described through statements like these:

- Most Hindus believe in God in one way or another—though some do not.

- Some are vegetarians out of their respect for life; others practice much animal sacrifice including sacrificial meals.
- Some worship Shiva, others Vishnu, his incarnations Rama or Krishna (like the Hare Krishna), or goddesses such as Durga.
- Worship in India's myriad villages differs in many ways.
- God, the ultimate or absolute being, is conceived of in either personal, monotheistic terms involving intense personal devotion to the deity, or in completely impersonal (even atheistic) terms.

Unifying Themes in Hinduism

Amid this apparent pluralism, there are some overarching themes that unite, or at least provide some commonality to, the wide range of beliefs and practices we have spoken of. One major unifying theme in Hinduism is India itself—Mother India, the source of life.

Mother India nurtures her many peoples from her fertile plains. She is identified with the soil, the earth. In contrapuntal relationship to this nurturing mother are the forests and mountains, which are the abode of powers which are understood to oppose human endeavor.

Traditionally, the idea of adoption into the Hindu family by religious conversion is a completely alien concept. One is either a child of India in one of its castes, or one is not. However, we must note that from ancient times to modern, Hinduism has been transplanted into many other geographical contexts, both by migration and "mission." The "Brahmin mission" from the early centuries of the Common Era exported not a revealed message of salvation, but rather the priestly caste's ability to help the "ritualistic and bureaucratic subjugation" and organization of the newly entered region. Beginning in Southern India, but expanding as far as Java in Indonesia, indigenous kings called on Brahmins trained in writing, administration, and ritualized bureaucracy to assist them "in the formal organization, in the Hindu matter, of [their] patrimonial bureaucratic rule and status structure and to consecrate them as the legitimate Raja or Maharaja in the sense of the Hindu Dharmashastras, Brahmanas, and Puranas."[6]

A second main theme of Hinduism is "the River," the symbol of life flowing in an unending stream. The River is a place to go to bathe in a purifying, life-giving stream. It is the source of purifying waters to drink. At death, ashes left after cremation are scattered on its waters.

A third element common to all Hindus is the caste system described above. All Hindus are members of one caste or another and are obligated to fulfill the social, religious, and ritual demands of their caste.

There is no way to move from the caste into which one is born and remain an acceptable member of Hindu society. The discounting or ignoring of the caste system by missionaries and converts creates a basic challenge to Hinduism.

A fourth basic Hindu commonality is the pervasive concept of reincarnation, the flow of life through many existences. These existences include all animal and human life. Part and parcel of the doctrine of reincarnation is the law of karma. This is essentially the understanding that even as one's present level of existence is the result of accumulated good or evil deeds performed in past existence, so one's deeds in this life together with their consequences flow on into one's next life, determining whether one is born in a higher or lower state of existence.

While a given lifetime offers no possibility of the improvement of one's present estate or caste, it does offer the possibility that, by means of diligent performances of the requirements of one's caste, devotion to deity, and/or meditation (yoga), one can be reincarnated on a higher plane, a higher caste. A good goat on dying might be born into a new existence as an outcast human.

The obverse is also true. Poor performance of the requirements and rites of one's caste assure that in one's next existence one will be born in a lower caste, as an outcast, or as any one of the whole hierarchy of animals. (It must be noted that there is virtually no link of consciousness between one existence and the next. One does not know what happened in one's past life that brought about the present state of affairs.)

Samsara (suffering) is the term used to describe the cycle of birth, life, death, and rebirth. Life cycles of suffering are endless unless through perseverance over many lifetimes one arrives at *moksha*, the state of blissful oneness with Brahman and release from the cycle. The deterministic explanation about one's present circumstances in life is balanced by the opportunity to improve one's state in the next life by choosing rightly in the present one.

The fifth element common to virtually all of Hinduism, advocated as it is by the Brahmin caste, is that the things apprehended through ordinary human perception, such as human experience as individuals, are mere maya, pure deception, and the source of all suffering. Behind this veil is the reality of Atman-Brahman, the essence of the ultimate.

Salvation in Hinduism

Hindus themselves speak of three great paths to salvation in Hinduism. The first and oldest path is the way of works. It might also be called the way of ritual, primarily domestic ritual.

Most people of India follow this path. It is easy to understand, and it is practical. It consists basically of the hopeful performance of duties, rites, and ceremonies that add to one's store of merit. This accumulated merit assures that in one's next life one will be born in a higher state, perhaps as a Brahmin.

The most important kind of good work is the performance of sacrifices. To his seer and guru a man owes the study of the Veda, the most ancient sacred books. To his ancestors he owes offspring, and to his fellow humans he owes hospitality. Later law codes laid heavy emphasis on rites of passage. The way of works for women is summed up in their duty to meekly serve their men—father, husband, and sons.[7]

The second path to salvation is the way of knowledge. This path has its foundation in the Upanishads.

The basic premise of this way is that the cause of human misery is ignorance. Not knowing the truth about things is the basic human problem that must be overcome. The best-known school of thought in this way of knowledge is that evil arises out of persistent human belief that humans, in and of themselves, amount to something, while in point of fact—according to Indian monism—only one thing exists, and that is the Brahman-Atman. Belief that anything else exists is delusion and the source of untold suffering.

In the context of a research project I was doing in California some years ago, I attended many services of a congregation of the Self Realization Fellowship, one of the many Hindu religious communities that have gained a following in the West over the last 30 years. The founder of this group was Paramahansa Yogananda, whose best-known work is *Autobiography of a Yogi.*[8] The chant used most frequently over the time of my visits with them included lines like these:

I am the bubble, make me the sea;
I am the bubble, make me the sea.
Wave of the sea be lost in the sea;
wave of the sea be lost in the sea.
I am the bubble, make me the sea.[9]

The vision represented in these lines is that all that has real existence is the sea, the ocean of cosmic consciousness, to use a phrase these people commonly use to represent the Absolute. Any apparent individuality has as much substance or permanence as a bubble in the surf, or whitecaps on a wave. Such bubbles in the surf are like a momentary disturbance in the cosmic order of things. Well-being for the individual comes when he or she dissolves in the sea and his or her atman becomes one again with the Atman-Brahman of the ocean of cosmic consciousness.

This is at the heart of the religion of the Brahmins. It involves serious study of the sacred texts, through which the true nature of reality becomes more clear. It involves also the expectation that as one becomes older—after one's sons have their own sons—one should become a hermit, and finally, as one becomes aged, a mendicant holy man. The goal is to attain the experience of union with the eternal Brahman before death. This Brahmin vision is the framework for the developing practice of meditation (*samadhi*) and yoga in Hinduism, including the repeated uttering of the mystical syllable *om,* understood to be a means of getting in touch with the deepest vibrations of the universe, the Brahman.

The third way to salvation is that of *bhakti,* or devotion to any one or more of Hinduism's multitude of gods and goddesses. This path involves cultivated practices of passionate love and devotion to a chosen deity, which draws one into hopeful and deeply felt interaction with him or her. This is the path which brought with it the construction of many elaborate temples and shrines for the performance of various rites of devotion. The best known literary representation of this form of Hinduism is *Bhagavad Gita,* or Song of the Blessed Lord.

Anyone witnessing the corporate worship practice, or *puja,* of the Hare Krishna, the International Society for Krishna Consciousness, may have sensed the kind of rapture this "sacrifice" is intended to produce. This puja consists of dancing up and down while chanting the names of the deity:

> Hare Krsna, Hare Krsna,
> Krsna Krsna, Hare Hare,
> Hare Rama, Hare Rama,
> Rama Rama, Hare Hare.[10]

Preparation for such corporate ritual includes careful bathing of the images of the deities and offering them carefully prepared delicacies. Continued chanting dance of this nature can bring one to a point of entrancement and a sense of intimate contact with the deity.

The Hindu Approach to Pluralism

The worship place of the Self-Realization Fellowship referred to above was a building that would pass for a Christian meetinghouse in most any town in the United States. When I entered the narthex, two things immediately caught my attention. The first of these illustrates the virtually universal Hindu attitude to non-Hindu religions.

Displayed in three large panels across the front of the worship area were large portraits of six saints or avatars venerated by this sect of Hinduism. One of the figures was Paramahansa Yogananda, the founder of the Self-Realization Fellowship. Another was Sri Yukteswar, one of Paramahansa's mentors. And in their midst was a portrait of Jesus, apparently a reproduction of Solomon's head of Christ.

Clearly, the figure of Jesus Christ had been incorporated into the frame of reference and worldview of Hinduism. Paramahansa Yogananda gives ample documentation as to how he incorporated Jesus into his framework as one more great incarnation of the deity.[11] This incorporation is accomplished by means of the assumed belief that all religions are in essence identical, that they are intended to bring about human union with the ultimate Essence of the universe. The apparent unique elements of various religions are merely accidental.

In the mid-seventies, Soehadiweko Djojodihardjo, my mentor and friend during my sojourn as a teacher in Java, repeatedly said in my hearing that the most serious challenge facing the Christian church in Java was the monism which characterized the Javanese worldview. Java was historically the center of a whole series of Hindu and later Hindu-Buddhist kingdoms from about the seventh to the fourteenth centuries. Mojopahit, the most powerful of these, encompassed nearly all of southeast Asia.

The observation Djojodihardjo was making was that the pervasive monistic ethos of the religion of Java, profoundly influenced at the worldview level through the "Brahmin mission" referred to above, had been able to absorb and domesticate the Islam that came after it, bending the external forms and practices of Islam to fundamental impulses of "Brahminized" Javanese religion. Djojodihardjo's concern, to which I dedicated my dissertation, was whether the same process would absorb and domesticate Christian faith, bending it to the basic framework of the "Brahminized" religion of Java.[12]

It took me some time to grasp the basic issues Djojodihardjo was concerned about. But as I became more of a student of the communication and expression of the Christian faith in the world of Java, I came to understand the issues more clearly. As I pursued my study, I developed an illustration through which I tried to communicate how Islam has been domesticated, so to speak, and incorporated into the worldview of the religion of Java. In terms of the vernacular Javanese people use to speak of Atman-Brahman, which is the ultimate essence of all reality, the Javanese speak of *Tuhan yang Maha Esa*, which translates as something like "the Lord which is the Ultimate Essence." I pictured this reality as a large circle with a heavy line.

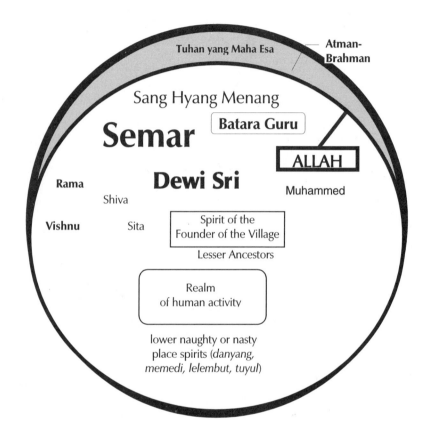

A perception of Hindu-Javanese reality[13]

In this circle I pictured various Hindu and native Javanese deities, such as Sang Yang Menang, Semar (the ancestor of the Javanese), and Dewi Sri (the goddess of fertility). In the upper part of the circle appeared Allah, the God of Islam (who is linked to "the Lord who is the Ultimate Essence"), as well as Mohammed, his prophet. In the center, I placed various human ancestral heroes and living humanity. Lower in the picture I placed all sorts of lesser deities and spirits of place.

The key to the picture was that Allah, the one and only God of Islam, appeared in the graphic as one of a whole group of divine beings in the framework of the Ultimate Essence of reality identified as the encompassing circle or sphere. In fact, Indonesian Muslims routinely identify Allah as "Yang Maha Esa" (the One who is the Ultimate Essence). There also appears the purely human figure of Mohammed, who has become a lesser, semidivine figure, something like an avatar in the same pantheon.

How did this happen? The issue in this case was that the missionaries who carried Islam to Java brought merely the beliefs and practices of Islam as they were expressed in the original context and failed to communicate essential Islamic understandings about what the world is like, what and who God is, and who and what humans are in the world. The most basic remedy for whatever goes wrong in this "Muslim" world of Java is to practice *samedi* (meditation) in various ways, by means of which one gets back in touch with the Essence of Reality, which in my illustration is the sphere that encompasses and relativizes all else.[14]

Each new belief or religion that enters the world of Hinduism is in danger of being swallowed up, the new beliefs coming to be regarded as additional manifestations of the unknowable divine that encompasses all. Unless the new religion or belief system effectively engages the deep knowledge and assumptions of the Hindu-Javanese worldview, it is in danger of being assimilated.

The all-encompassing worldview of Hinduism is powerfully reinforced by the caste system. The immigrant groups of new religions are simply given space as additional sub-castes, or *jati*. The ontocratic philosophy of what is, readily provides space for one more group like the tens of thousands of jatis that already exist. A message that challenges the ontocratic philosophy and its social structure in the form of the caste system is intolerable.[15]

The caste system plays a key role in enforcing or supporting Hinduism's monistic or monolithic worldview in a country where Hinduism is the majority religion. At the same time, the many successful efforts of Hindus to migrate and plant communities in other societies show that Hindu conceptions of reality are themselves powerful. Although some Hindu immigrant communities try to carry with them their corporate caste behavior, the philosophy of Brahmanism has had a powerful effect on communities and groups outside the Hindu homelands.

On the Indonesian islands of Bali and Java, only remnants of the caste system remain. But the beliefs that undergird it, Brahmin philosophy and theosophy, continue to have a powerful influence, even on large segments of the Muslim population which makes up the majority of Java's 100 million people. The many *kebatinan* (mystical) groups that flourish in Java are ample evidence of this.

The following is a Javanese mystical analysis of the human makeup. The chart shows the power of Brahministic philosophy among these people.

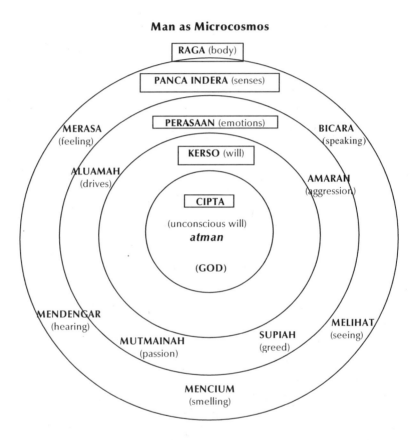

Man as Microcosmos

A Javanese analysis of the human makeup from the perspective of a mystic[16]

Djojodihardjo kept a diagram like this in his front room. He frequently used it to explain the monistic essence of Hindu-Javanese psychology and philosophy.

A human is a microcosm, a sort of revelation of the entire cosmos. Individuality has to do with one's body, senses, emotions, and will. But in one's innermost being, each person is atman (*cipta*) and identical to atman in every other human being. Each person is also identical with Atman-Brahman, the ultimate essence of all reality.

The problem with humans, in this view, is that they do not know that they are in fact one with all other humans and the cosmos. What they need is insight into, and experience of, that fact. Such insight and experience comes through meditation, yoga, and mystical practice. Human maturation and refinement is a process of losing one's individuality in the monistic reality that encompasses all.[17] One might also add that the ruling monarch is the highest and most powerful representation of this reality.

In this kind of framework one person cannot be enlightened and simultaneously be in conflict with any other person, or the order of the cosmos. Calling into question the order that exists is inconceivable. To act in conflict with that order is to regress to a level of subhumanity, or infancy. Through this monistic model of human experience in the world, pluralism (any other religious practice) is allowed as another way (in terms of method or intensity) maturation or refinement can be pursued. Peasant villagers, for instance, are not likely to be schooled in the refinements of this vision of the human as micro-cosmos. However, their relatively lower position in the scheme of things is clearly understood by all. Authority is in the hands of the governing class. Open confrontation with that ruling class violates the order of things.

The question for Christians (and Muslims) is, how does a Christian (or Muslim) understanding of God and humans and their place in the world engage and challenge this worldview? When Islam and Christianity are true to their own visions of God and humanity, they cannot but challenge this monistic worldview and its claims to a pluralistic perspective of toleration toward other religions.

Reform Hinduism as a Missionary Faith

Over the past 40 years, many Hindu teachers have carried on more or less successful missions. They have communicated not only the Hindu understanding of what is wrong in the world but also their various Hindu ways of salvation, particularly the path of personal devotional to various Hindu deities and the path of meditation (yoga). Inevitably these teachers cast their particular approach to religion as essentially the same in intent as Christianity or any other religion it encounters—but a little more effective.

This perspective is in diametric opposition to that of the world's missionary religions—Buddhism, Christianity, and Islam. Almost two thousand years ago, Buddhist rejection of the caste system contributed to the demise of Buddhism in the land of its birth. For both Christianity and Islam the community of believers—the ummah and the church—

must transcend all caste distinctions and separations. If and when Hinduism succeeds in defining a new religious group as a caste or jati, then any further conversions from any other caste are inconceivable and impossible to tolerate.

Clearly, both Islam and Christianity carry built-in assumptions about the world and the place of humans in it that conflict with Hindu views. While recent reformers of Hinduism claim that the Hindu way offers open tolerance to all other religions, they still retain monistic assumptions about the nature of the world and the place of God and humans in it. These assumptions are fundamentally antipluralistic and unaccepting of Muslim and Christian visions of the world.

Conversely, a missionary vision like that of Islam and Christianity, as well as Buddhism in many of its forms, assumes and asserts a level of pluralism that at least theoretically allows persons to choose another way. Conversion from one belief system to another is at least a possibility, though often vigorously resisted.

Hindu and Western Worldviews

With regard to pluralism, we may observe dynamics in the West that are very parallel to those of Hinduism. Western societies are assumed to be thoroughly pluralistic. But one of the foundational assumptions of modern and postmodern Western pluralism is that all religions are in essence the same. As in the case of Hinduism, modern or postmodern views tend to assert that one path is as good as the next. Taking no religious path is also acceptable, providing one fulfills one's community obligations. No religion is fundamentally better than another in this view.

A basic corollary is that it is inappropriate to make an issue of one's particular beliefs and practices. Certainly one is not to seek to recruit a person from one community of religious practice to another. The absolute law in Hinduism is that birth determines a person's religious path. In modern Western secularism the first commandment appears to be, "Thou shalt not hold to exclusive religious convictions." And the second is like unto it: "Thou shalt not seek to convince other people of thy religious convictions."

Conclusion

The conclusion regarding the Hindu approach to religious pluralism and that of the modern and postmodern West may be the same. Both appear to be fundamentally pluralistic, but at a deep level both hold to monolithic or antipluralistic assumptions. The Christian church must learn to identify these assumptions and engage them directly.

Notes

1. C. George Fry, James R. King, Eugene R. Swanger, and Herbert C. Wolf, *Great Asian Religions* (Grand Rapids, Mich.: Baker Book House, 1984), 33.

2. John B. Noss, *Man's Religions* (New York: Macmillan Publishing Company, 1980), 72.

3. Geoffrey Parrinder, ed., *World Religions, From Ancient History to the Present* (New York: Facts on File Publications, 1971), 192.

4. The Malay and Indonesian word for color, *warna,* comes from the Sanskrit *varna.*

5. Surendranath Dasgupta, in his *A History of Indian Philosophy*, states it this way: "The sum and substance of the Upanishad teaching is involved in the equation Atman=Brahman.... The word Atman was used in the Rig Veda to denote on the one hand the ultimate essence of the universe, and on the other the vital breath in man. Later in the Upanishads we see that the word Brahman is generally used in the former sense, while the word Atman is reserved to denote the inmost essence in man, and the Upanishads are emphatic in their declaration that the two are one and the same." (London: Cambridge University Press, 1932), vol. 1, 45-46.

6. Max Weber, "The Hindu Social System," in *Indonesian Trade and Society*, ed J. C. van Leur (Bandung, Indonesia: Sumur Bandung, 1960), 79.

7. Parrinder, ed., 179-181.

8. Paramahansa Yogananda, *Autobiography of a Yogi* (Los Angeles: Self-Realization Fellowship, 1977).

9. Booklet of Chants supplied to participants.

10. A. C. Bhaktivedanta Swami Prabhupada, *Bhagavad-Gita As It Is* (Los Angeles: The Bhaktivedanta Book Trust, 1984), 377.

11. Paramahansa Yogananda, *Autobiography*, 561f.

12. Lawrence McCulloh Yoder, "The Introduction and Expression of Islam and Christianity in the Cultural Context of North Central Java" (Ph.D. diss., Fuller Theological Seminary, 1987), 1-3.

13. Ibid., 228-236; the chart is copyright © 1987 by Lawrence Yoder.

14. Clifford Geertz, *The Religion of Java* (Glencoe, Ill.: The Free Press, 1960), 99.

15. David W. Shenk, *Global Gods, Exploring the Role of Religion in Modern Societies* (Scottdale, Pa.: Herald Press, 1995), 100.

16. From a chart displayed by Soehadiweko Djojodihardjo on the wall of his house. He used this with other charts to teach the engagement of Christian faith with the Hindu-Javanese worldview.

17. Yoder, "The Introduction and Expression of Islam," 219-226.

CHAPTER SIX

The Muslim Ummah and Global Pluralism

David W. Shenk

"Islam is the truth!" the imam of a Philadelphia mosque declared.

The imam and I were leading a dialogue between Christians and Muslims. His homeland was Sudan; he had a doctorate in religious studies and Islamics from Temple University and had been a resident in the United States for a decade.

"Would you consider contacting the President and Chief Khadhi of Sudan," I asked, "to encourage them to give Christians the same freedoms in Sudan that Muslims enjoy in the United States?"

The imam's response was curt. "I would never consider writing such a letter," he said. "Wherever the Muslim *ummah* [community] can acquire political control, it must circumscribe the church to protect and advance the truth of Islam."

Ten years of residency in Philadelphia and a doctorate from a secular American university had not planted seeds of doubt in the imam's soul concerning the use of political power to protect and advance Islam.

In an Islamic view, writes New York University Islamist Bernard Lewis, "The body politic and the sovereign power in it are ordained by God himself to promote his faith and to maintain and extend his law."[1] Further, Lewis says:

> The principal function of government is to enable the individual Muslim to lead a good Muslim life. This is, in the last analysis, the purpose of the state, for which alone it is established by God, and for which alone statesmen are given authority over others. The worth of the state, and the good and evil deeds of statesmen are measured by the extent to which this purpose is accomplished.[2]

116

In Sudan the Muslim ummah viewed a growing church as a threat to the integrity of Islam. Therefore, the Islamic government had to act decisively. A failure to act would make the government illegitimate, for the primary role of political authority is to protect the integrity of the ummah.

Yet the issues of Islam in global pluralistic culture are more complex than theological formulations might suggest. There is also a long history of confrontation between Western "Christianized" societies and peoples governed by Muslim authority.

For example, in the mosque that night in Philadelphia, the imam expressed deep personal wounds that surely influenced his theology and his views of the church.

"I am offended by what Christian governments have done to my people," the imam said. "My grandfather was treacherously killed in the Battle of Omdurman by the Christian General, Gordon Pasha. I, my family, and my people can never forget that treachery and that injustice."

To understand the attitudes of Muslims toward non-Islamic ideologies or religions, we must recognize the wounds of Muslims such as the imam. A comprehensive understanding would require us to consider the legacy of the Crusades, Western colonialism, the emergence of the state of Israel, and the periodic confrontations between Western powers and Islamic powers.

An example of the clash is the August 1998 bombing of the U.S. embassies in Kenya and Tanzania and the retaliatory American bombing of a pharmaceutical plant in Khartoum and military base camps in Afghanistan. The legacy of history and current political, cultural, and economic ferment do influence Muslim responses to non-Muslim faiths and ideologies.

We recognize that, in practice, Muslims take diverse stances in regard to the real-life issues of pluralism. Yet in my many conversations with Muslims in Asia, Africa, North America, and Europe, I observe remarkable similarity in their theological positions in relationship to pluralistic culture. It is the root historical experiences and the theological stance that relate to pluralism that this essay explores.

The Hijrah

Muhammad and his companions migrated from Mecca to Medina in A.D. 622. This is the *Hijrah*, or the migration. The Hijrah is the beginning of the Muslim era, just as the birth of Christ marks the beginning of the Christian era.

The Muslim era does not commence with the birth of Muhammad in 570. It has no relation to 610 when Muslims believe that the Angel Gabriel brought the first Qur'anic revelation to Muhammad. The era does not begin with the Qur'anic description of Abraham who with his son Ishmael established the faith of Islam in Mecca. Rather, the Muslim era begins with Muhammad's secret flight to Medina.

Why is the flight so central in Muslim self understanding? This question takes us to the core issues of commitment to the truth in a world of multiple claims to truth. The question introduces the vexing issues of the sovereignty of God and human freedom.

For twelve years Muhammad had preached in Mecca. His message was not well received. He and his disciples were persecuted; sometimes their lives were under threat. On one occasion most of his followers fled Mecca to Ethiopia, where they lived as refugees under the protection of that Christian regime. Muhammad's preaching and persuasion could not break the back of the strongholds of idol worship and paganism that permeated Meccan society.

Muhammad was troubled with self-doubt. If he was indeed a prophet of God, why was he unable to establish a viable community of Muslim faith in Mecca? If God was sovereign, how could it be that a prophet of God suffers? It was in the midst of this theological and personal crisis that the Medinans invited Muhammad to come to their city as their governor.

In Medina Muhammad became both a prophet and a statesman. With the instruments of political and military power, Muhammad established the Muslim ummah. This was the supreme evidence that he was indeed a prophet of God. Under his generalship, Muslim armies achieved victories on the battlefield against the enemies of the ummah. Within ten years most of Arabia, including Mecca, had come under Muslim authority.

It is noteworthy that six centuries earlier the Galileans had invited Jesus to become king. He refused that invitation. Instead he "set his face" to go to Jerusalem, where he told his disciples he would be crucified. At the time of his arrest, he said that he could call on twelve legions of angels to protect him; he did not. Instead he was nailed to a cross and died between two crucified criminals. Christians confess that this Christ crucified is the power of God.

It is evident that Islam and the gospel take us in quite different directions in our understandings of the kingdom of God. Muslims find the cross incomprehensible; if God is sovereign, the Messiah could not suffer. Just as God rescued Muhammad from ignominy in Mecca, so also

God would have rescued Jesus the Messiah from the ignominy of the cross. Islam, therefore, denies that Jesus was crucified. The cross reveals vulnerability. That is impossible, for the truth of God must triumph, never suffer.

The Region of Peace and the Region of War

Political and military control empowered Muhammad to establish the *Dar Al-Salaam,* the region of peace. Islam is established as the authority throughout the Dar Al-Salaam. All territory under the authority of the Muslim ummah is the region of peace; all regions outside that rule are the region of war, *Dar Al-Harb.* These regions are yet to be brought under Islamic rule. The world is divided between these two communities, the region of peace and the region of war.

As Kenneth Cragg writes, there is a

> consciousness of "otherness" deep in the Muslim mind and soul, whatever precise political or cultural form is chosen to implement it. Dar Al-Salam and Dar Al-Harb is a fundamental distinction running through all humanity: the household of submission to God and the household of non-Islam still to be brought into such submission.[3]

Of course, communities of Muslims might exist in the Dar Al-Harb. They are islands of peace in the region of no peace. But these islands of peace are incomplete expressions of the ummah. Completeness requires political control; it requires incorporation into the region of peace.

For this reason all Muslim communities yearn for the completion that is only possible in the Dar Al-Salaam. The quest for political control is a universal characteristic of Islam. Kenneth Cragg describes Islam as "the most resolute and unperturbed of all faiths in placing trust, and finding pride, in political religion."[4]

The Muslim mission is, therefore, twofold. *Dawlah* is the quest for political control over territory. This is one of the primary energizing forces for the war in southern Sudan. The Muslim ummah has sought to establish the rule of Islam over those regions of southern Sudan that have not yet been incorporated into the Dar Al-Salaam.

Daawah is the invitation to Muslim faith. Muslims give witness: *La Ilaha Illa'llah Muhammadan Rasulu'llah* (There is but one God, Allah, and Muhammad is the apostle of God). Muslims invite people to submit to that confession and all that the confession implies.

The Muslim ummah is only complete when Dawlah (political control) and Daawah (witness and invitation) proceed together. That was the nature of Muhammad's rule in Medina, and it is the best model for a Muslim political system.

The Constitution of Medina

In Medina, Muhammad established the ideal model for the Muslim state. He developed a constitution. Procedures for dealing with minorities, such as Christian or Jewish communities, were developed.

The Constitution of Medina was committed to establishing brotherhood, justice, and consensus. It did not establish a democracy. Political freedom and individual rights were not included in this model government. The rights of the community superseded the rights of the person.[5] For thirteen centuries, that ethos has permeated the Muslim ummah.

This principle, of community rights superseding individual rights, was applied to the challenge that Jews in Medina presented to Muhammad. Although the Jews were respected as a people of the Book (Torah and Psalms), there was intolerance toward anyone who threatened the integrity of the ummah. When members of the Jewish community in Medina were suspected of being traitors to the ummah, they were put to death.

Human Rights

In modern times the Muslim World League has developed an Islamic Declaration of Human Rights as a Muslim response to the United Nations Declaration of Human Rights. The Muslim statement reveals areas of tension between the principles embraced by the United Nations and those of the global ummah. The Islamic declaration emphasizes the rights and integrity of the community, while the United Nations is committed to the rights and freedoms of the person.

The uproar that followed the 1989 publication of Salman Rushdie's *The Satanic Verses* is an example of the collision between the commitment to individual freedom in a liberal democracy and the Islamic mission to preserve the integrity of the community of faith. Muslims viewed Rushdie's book as blasphemy, an affront against God and Islam.

Protest riots touched many Muslim communities. The Iranian Muslim authorities at the time determined that Rushdie was guilty of blasphemy and must die.

Devout Muslims could not comprehend how any responsible society would condone blasphemy in the interest of personal freedom. Western democratic leaders, on the other hand, were appalled that a death sentence would be pronounced for writing an offensive book. Rushdie was a British citizen. In protest of the death sentence against him, the United Kingdom recalled its ambassador from Iran and had no ambassadorial representative there for the next nine years. (In 1998, the Iranian government withdrew its support for Rushdie's sentence.)

Conversion

The protection of the integrity of the Muslim community and the truth of Islam is a core value in the Muslim ummah. This is the reason it is well-nigh impossible for responsible Muslim religious or political leaders to accede to the right of a Muslim to convert away from Islam and embrace another faith.

In 1979 I participated in a consultation on the Christian church and the Muslim ummah sponsored by the World Council of Churches. About one hundred participants from several dozen countries were present at this Mombasa, Kenya, meeting. At that time John Taylor directed the Christian–Muslim dialogue section of the World Council of Churches.

Taylor was elated by a major breakthrough. After many years of conversations with a few Muslim decision makers, these professional Muslim and Christian participants in dialogue had finally come to agreement that every person has the "right to convert and be converted." Despite the elation about this breakthrough, we were all aware that the decisions of these elite theologians did not influence opinion where Christians met Muslims in the local village.

Lamin Sanneh points out that whenever the national or regional Dar Al-Salaam fails to fulfill its responsibilities, the local Muslim communities function as complete Muslim political systems. This is to say that Muslim theologians dialoguing with Christians in Geneva, legislation in the U.S. Congress about religious persecution, or decisions by the Egyptian parliament affirming the rights of minorities have little effect on the commitment of local Muslim communities to protect the integrity of the ummah and the truth of Islam.[6]

It is also true that at the village level relations between Muslims and Christians are often most congenial. Nevertheless, that congeniality would be severely tested if a Muslim were to decide to become a Christian.

The Muslim ummah has the obligation to preserve truth and protect believers. For this reason, early on, apostasy from Islam was punishable by death. The integrity of the ummah and the preservation of the truth of Islam had to be preserved by any means necessary. In modern times, however, many Muslim societies are hesitant to implement the full force of the law of apostasy. More often various forms of ostracism are used, such as exclusion from one's family.

Hypocrites

Hypocrites, *munafiqun*, are considered to be especially pernicious in the Dar Al-Salaam.[7] These are people who masquerade as Muslims, but whose hearts are not sincerely Muslim. Partly because of this, some Christian missionary efforts to contextualize the church so that it converges with Islamic culture can be quite offensive to Muslims.

Muslims often prefer that people of other faiths behave like outsiders, not like Muslims. In Malaysia, for example, Christians are forbidden to use Muslim terms such as Allah in written or oral communication. In some communities Christians are permitted to worship on Sunday, but not on Friday, when Muslims gather for their weekly preaching assembly. Those who are not Muslims should function in a manner that keeps the religious boundaries clear.

Dhimmis

Ideally, non-Muslim communities are allowed to worship quite freely. These groups are called the *dhimmis*, meaning the protected ones.

Wherever Islam has exerted its political control over a region for an extended period of time, the dhimmis cluster into respective island-like communities known as *millets*. Consequently, throughout the Middle East today there are Christian villages scattered in the cultural and religious sea of Islam.

The dhimmis provide space in the Dar Al-Salaam for Christians, Jews, and Zoroastrians. However, there has always been ambivalence on how the Muslim authorities should relate to atheists or polytheists. Several Qur'anic injunctions command coercive confrontation against such infidels.[8] These commands are counterbalanced by the command against the use of any "compulsion in religion."[9]

In the Dar Al-Salaam, the dhimmis system assures the integrity of the Muslim ummah. The non-Muslim communities are subjected to certain hardships that are intended to encourage conversions to Islam. Typically the dhimmis have been required to pay *jizya*, a quite heavy tribute for the privilege of being protected.

Muslim men may marry women from the dhimmis; children born to such marriages have to be Muslim. But no man from the dhimmis can marry a Muslim woman. Any church or synagogue building or renovation requires approval by the Muslim authorities. Ideally, only Muslims should hold policy-level positions in a society governed by Islam.

The Community of Truth

Restrictions such as those mentioned above have varied from era to era and from region to region. Nevertheless, the Muslim ummah everywhere carries in its soul the conviction that it is the steward of the final and definitive truth for all humankind. Therefore, the political order should be formed in a manner that forthrightly encourages all alternative communities and individuals to move towards the truth, Islam. All non-Islamic truth claims should wither away.

The ummah is the middle community of faith and serves as a light to all nations. It does not embrace the legalism of Judaism or the impractical ethical ideals of Christianity. Rather it is well-balanced.

The Qur'an proclaims:

Thus have we made of you
An *unmat* [community] justly balanced,
That ye might be witnesses
over the nations.[10]
Elsewhere we read,

Ye are the best of Peoples,
Evolved for mankind,
Enjoining what is right,
Forbidding what is wrong.[11]

Tanzil

The Qur'an is the rule that guides the Dar Al-Salaam and the ummah in being a "witness over the nations." This revelation is *tanzil*, meaning it has been sent down. The Qur'an is the criterion of truth; it divides believers from nonbelievers.

God sent down the first revelation to Adam and Eve. He provided them with guidance, instructing them in the beliefs and practices of Islam. They were the first Muslims. However, humans strayed from God's guidance. So God sent guidance down in the form of books, so that the guidance would be preserved from generation to generation.

In his mercy, God has sent down five books:
- The Suhuf (Scrolls) through the Prophet Abraham. (They have been lost.)

- The Taurat (Torah) through the Prophet Moses.
- The Zabur (Psalms) through the Prophet David.
- The Injil (Gospel) through Jesus the Messiah.
- The Qur'an (Recitation) through the Prophet Muhammad.

Islam is the content of all these books of revelation. The Qur'an, which is the last book, contains nothing new; it is a clarification and summary of the previous books. The final revelation is in Arabic and is the exact replication of a portion of the eternal Mother of Books in the heavens. Therefore the Qur'an cannot be translated. It is an Arabic Qur'an.[12]

Christians are the People of the Book who possess the former Scriptures. Although all Muslims must believe that these former Scriptures are sent-down revelation, most are convinced that these Scriptures are corrupt. They embrace this notion even though the Qur'an has high regard for the former Scriptures and counsels Muslims to go to those who have them for clarification on the meaning of the Qur'an!

The Nature of Revelation

Biblical Scripture and the Qur'an have different understandings of the nature of revelation and truth. Muslims receive the Qur'an as a sent-down revelation that transcends human history and culture. By contrast, Muslims observe, the Bible is fundamentally a history book.

While the Qur'an might refer to historical events as parables to illustrate truth, it is in essence a book of teaching and instruction. Muslims preserve the history of the life of Muhammad and the early Muslim community in their *hadith* (traditions). By contrast, in the biblical writings, history is hopelessly interwoven with the Word of God. Muslims are perplexed; corruption seems to be the only way to explain this messy mixing of history and revelation.

In biblical revelation, the acts of God in history are the essence of revelation. In Islam God sends down guidance; in biblical faith God meets us personally in our historical and cultural circumstances. In Islam revelation is sent down; in biblical faith revelation is incarnational, and supremely so in Jesus Christ. The incarnation of God in Christ means that God has become fully present among us in Jesus of Nazareth.

Scripture and Culture

Incarnation or tanzil—these divergent understandings of revelation profoundly affect the respective approaches to cultural pluralism in biblical faith and Islam. In biblical, incarnational revelation, God encounters us, dialogues with us, and enters our history and culture with us and among us. God loves us, suffers for us, and redeems us. In Qur'anic tanzil revelation, God has mercy on us and therefore sends his guidance down to us. He sends prophets to guide us. God reveals his will. However, God himself does not encounter us.

The implications of these two understandings of revelation for cultural pluralism are significant. For example, the church in mission gives very high priority to translating the Scriptures into languages everywhere. In contrast, the Muslim ummah in mission establishes Arabic language schools wherever people desire to become Muslim, so that they can learn to recite the Arabic Qur'an.

Lamin Sanneh comments on the profound divergence between tanzil and incarnation in respect to African cultures. Sanneh grew up in a Muslim home in Gambia and converted to the Christian faith in his early adult years. He is now professor of missions at Yale Divinity School.

In his book, *Translating the Message, the Missionary Impact on Culture*, Sanneh demonstrates that the Christian missionary vocation of translating the Bible into local vernaculars empowered the local cultures to critique the cultural imperialism of the Western missionaries. As the Christian faith became incarnated in local culture and idiom, the churches were empowered to critique evils in their local cultures as well. The Christian movement across the African continent empowers, celebrates, embraces, and transforms local cultures.[13]

The energizing center of this astonishing empowerment phenomenon is the presence of the Bible in the local languages. In a world of globalization of culture, the Bible in local idiom is a potent gift inviting the preservation of local culture.

Sanneh notes, however, that the Arabic Qur'an cannot be translated. Thus the Muslim movement has no corrective to the tug towards the Arabization of culture. In fact, Islam pulls cultures in that direction. The most influential leaders are usually natives of Arabic-speaking countries; it must be so, for only they know Arabic well enough to properly interpret the Qur'an.

Consequently, Muslim theologians in Africa call for the de-Africanization of Muslim culture. By contrast, the Christian theologians call for the cultural Africanization of the Christian movement.

There are about a billion Muslims worldwide. Their mosques are found in cities and towns around the globe; they speak many of the several thousand languages of humankind. Yet in worship all Muslims pray the same Arabic prayers with all facing a Meccan shrine, the

Ka'bah. By contrast, the diversity of Christian worship is astounding and dramatic.

Is revelation sent down (Islam), or does it occur through incarnation (the gospel)? This divergence has major implications.

Tawhid

God is one and has no associates: this is the doctrine of *tawhid*. The most damnable sin a person can commit is ascribing associates to God. That is *shirkh*.

In contrast to Christian faith, the nature of the unity of God in Islam provides no possibility for diversity. The conversation in God that Christian trinitarian theology embraces is impossible in Islam's unitary monotheism. However, the church that is nurtured by trinitarian theology participates in the paradox of unity in astounding diversity. Christian denominations are one expression of that diversity. But the Muslim ummah views Christian diversity as evidence of false religion.

Just as God is one, so his will is also one. The Iranian sociologist, Ali Shari'ati, has developed a modernist approach to the political order and national identity that is committed to tawhid on earth, just as in heaven. He was the theological genius behind the Iranian Islamic revolution.[14]

Tawhid requires the submission of every area of life to the unitary will of God, Islam. Ali Shari'ati argues that any divergence from the unitary will of God is also shirkh, just as pernicious as ascribing associates to God. The political, economic, cultural, domestic, private, and public domains need to express tawhid.

Nation-states are an abominable aberration of tawhid, for nations bring diabolical division into the ummah. There is only one Muslim ummah, not many. Tragically, nation-states frequently force divided loyalties on the ummah. This is shirkh and must be resisted and corrected. A goal of the Iranian revolution was and is to bring all Muslims together in a united ummah that transcends nations.

Bidah

Innovation is *bidah*; it is prohibited. Islam is the primal, middle, and final faith of humankind, without innovation or change.

God first revealed Islam to Adam and Eve. They worshiped at the Ka'bah in Mecca.

Abraham and Ishmael were the middle prophets, who revived the true religion of Islam at the Ka'bah in Mecca. They worshipped God at the Ka'bah, just as Adam and Eve had worshipped.

Muhammad is the final prophet, through whom the Qur'an was revealed. He renewed the true worship of God at the Ka'bah. The Qur'an introduced nothing new; it was and is the final clarification of Islam.

History hangs, suspended as it were, in the parenthesis of a changeless Islam. This is the reason Muslim scholars have developed Islamic Law (*Shari'ah*) in an attempt to define the universal changeless will of God for human conduct.

Five times daily, Muslims bow in prayer and submission to the will of God. They always face the Ka'bah in Mecca when they pray. In their bowing toward Mecca, Muslims everywhere proclaim that there is no change or innovation in God's will. They are facing not only the place, but also the manner of worship and practice of Adam, Abraham and Ishmael, and Muhammad.

How can Muslims embrace a changeless Islam in a changing, pluralistic world? That is the arena of increasingly intense debate and conflict in the local and global ummah.

Islam in a changing world is the issue the Pakistani Islamic scholar Fazlur Rahman addressed in the mid-1960s when he wrote his book *Islam*.[15] Rahman lamented that Muslim theologians were not calling for a reinterpretation and adaptation of Islam for modern times. In his book he sought to pioneer a way forward. That book earned him an exit from Pakistan; he subsequently taught Islamics at the University of Chicago.

The difficulty of developing a theology of pilgrimage towards a changing future contributes to a crisis in many areas of the global ummah.

For example, the secularist Muslims in Turkey are considering banning all Islamic schools. The Islamist political party has been banned. Turkey is in a bind. The government wants admission into the European Union, but the tough repression of the antidemocratic Islamist party is not applauded by European liberal democracies.

Algeria, likewise, struggles with endemic civil war after the military canceled the 1991 elections won by the Islamist parties. In both Turkey and Algeria, the officials who ban Islamist parties are secularized Muslims. However, they well know that Islamic orthodoxy does not nurture democratic pluralism and personal freedoms. For those aspirations, they must drink from other spiritual or philosophical streams. They repress the Islamist parties because an Iranian kind of Islamic revolution is not their vision of the future.

While the political leaders fret, in mosques from Jakarta to New York, the Friday sermons consistently remind the congregations that shirkh is the worst sin and bidah the second worst sin a person can commit. Therefore, the clerics warn, submit every aspect of life under the eternal unchangeable guidance of Islam.

The reform movements in the ummah all struggle with the issues of shirkh and bidah in a pluralistic world. Some like Fazlur Rahman have encouraged a path of faithfulness to the spirit of Islam that is adaptable to the pluralistic contexts wherein Muslims live. Others like S. Abdul Ala Maududi have pled for a recreation of the model community Muhammad established in Medina. All seek the path of faithfulness to Islam.

Natural Muslims

Muslim means *believer*. Islam teaches that Adam and Eve were the first Muslims. As children of these first parents of humankind, we are, therefore, all naturally Muslims. Every child is born a Muslim and will grow up as one, if not directed away from the truth of Islam.

The Qur'an declares that Islam is the "standard religion." It is "the pattern on which he [God] has made mankind."[16]

Throughout the ages God has sent numerous prophets to encourage peoples everywhere to submit to Islam. The biblical prophets were part of that train of messengers. However, there have been prophets for every people, not just the Jewish prophets of biblical faith. Muslim tradition estimates that there have been 124,000 prophets![17]

The Qur'an states, "For we assuredly sent amongst every People an apostle, [with the command], 'Serve God, and eschew Evil.'"[18]

Thus the Muslim ummah is confident of the finality of Islam. Those who have not yet submitted to Islam are, nevertheless, naturally Muslim. They were born Muslim, but other traditions have turned them away. As the Muslim witness is proclaimed from minarets around the world, Islam will eventually penetrate the deceptions that draw people away from their natural inclination.

The Story of a Family

My wife, Grace, and I were invited to a gracious dinner in the home of a Muslim husband and Christian wife. They were in distress and sought counsel. I shall call them Nur and Jane.

They had two young sons. Nur permitted his wife to go to church. However, he prohibited her from saying anything to their sons about her church experience. Jane was not permitted to pray with the boys or tell them anything about her faith. She wept inside, for her faith was precious to her.

Nur explained that their sons were born Muslim, and it was his responsibility to be sure that they would not be enticed away from Islam.

Both were righteous and faithful parents. Yet their home was at an impasse. That family was a microcosm of the arenas where Christian faith and Islam meet in a world of many faiths.

The issues of faith and freedom in a pluralistic world are tough stuff. What is truth? How shall truth prevail? Islam and the gospel nurture different responses to those questions.

Notes

All quotations from the Qur'an are from the Abdullah Yusuf Ali interpretation, *The Holy Koran* (Beirut: Dar Al Arabia, 1968).

1. Bernard Lewis, *The Political Language of Islam* (Chicago: Chicago University Press, 1988), 25.

2. Ibid., 29.

3. Kenneth Cragg, *The Call of the Minaret*, 2nd. ed. (New York: Orbis Books, 1985), 189.

4. Kenneth Cragg, *Muhammad and the Christian* (Maryknoll, N.Y.: Orbis, 1984), 32.

5. George W. Braswell Jr., *Islam, Its Prophet, Peoples, Politics and Power* (Nashville, Tenn.: Broadman and Holman Publishers, 1996), 127.

6. Lamin Sanneh, *Piety and Power, Muslims and Christians in West Africa* (Maryknoll, N.Y.: Orbis, 1996), 85-145.

7. *Qur'an*, Women: 4:88-89.

8. Ibid., Repentance: 9:5; Victory 48:16.

9. Ibid., The Heifer: 2:256.

10. Ibid., The Family of 'Imran: 3:110.

11. Ibid.

12. Ibid., Joseph: 12:2.13; Yunus: 10:64, 94.

13. Lamin Sanneh, *Translating the Message, The Missionary Impact on Culture* (Maryknoll, N.Y.: Orbis, 1989).

14. Ali Shari'ati, *On the Sociology of Islam*, trans. Hamid Algar, (Berkeley: Mizan Press, 1979).

15. Fazlur Rahman, *Islam* (Chicago: University of Chicago Press, 1966).

16. *Qur'an*, The Roman Empire: 30:30.

17. Badru D. Kateregga and David W. Shenk, *A Muslim and a Christian in Dialogue* (Scottdale, Pa.: Herald Press, 1997), 64.

18. *Qur'an*, The Bee: 16:36.

CHAPTER SEVEN

The Aporetic Witness

Susan Biesecker-Mast

Introduction

I do not think that we live in a pluralistic world, if by that we mean a global context in which every difference is valued the same as every other. On the contrary, in our world white is better off than black, the West encroaches on the East, Microsoft beat Apple, and the logic of capitalism governs all circuits of exchange that matter.

Of course, today's differences are not the same as yesterday's differences. Whereas yesterday's differences tended to be viewed as natural, given, and immutable, today's differences tend to be seen as cultural, historical, and contingent. But even if today's differences are considered contingent and thus more easily changed, they are ranked and compared nonetheless. Even the constantly changing differences (or products) of consumer capitalism are valued and organized.

To test this point, try to convince an adolescent that a pair of Nike athletic shoes is just as cool as a pair of Airwalk athletic shoes. The very logic that makes it possible to sell the latest anything—be it a shoe, a minivan, a computer—presumes that "newer" is better, even if what is "newer" these days looks like something from the fifties. In short, ours is a world that turns on the better and worse, not the different but equal.

If differences are hierarchized, then they are ordering our world so that some people, things, and styles are valued while others are devalued. But if differences are not immutable, then we may be able to change them and, thereby, alter what is considered true and untrue, worthy and unworthy, wise and unwise. Hence, to use the shoe example again, although it is unlikely that you will succeed in convincing the adolescent that one brand of shoe is just as good as another, it is possible.

As Anabaptists we have known throughout our history that the current order is never the same as God's reign. Until the reign of God is

130

fully realized there will always be a very big difference between God's way and the ways we human beings make sense out of differences.

But while the chasm between our world and the reign of God has not changed over time, what may be different for us now is that postmodernity—this context of hierarchized but changing differences—may be an opportunity for our witness to make a difference. Whereas in the recent past we attempted to differ from a world that was largely unwilling to alter its course known as "progress," today we may find ourselves witnessing to a world that, though still hierarchized in troubling ways, finds new plausibility in our alternative.

The opportunity that this shift from modernity to postmodernity may have opened for faith to speak to reason has not gone unnoticed by theologians. Indeed a number of what we might call postmodern theologians have advocated various ways that Christians ought to witness in their contemporary context. However, because these theologians have tended to mistake our postmodern world for a pluralistic world, they also have tended to write theologies that promote cultural security over faithful witness.

Three Theological Responses to Postmodernity

The Communitarian Response

The communitarian response (also known as postliberal theology) is perhaps the postmodern theology that takes most seriously the proposition that we live in a pluralistic world.[1] According to communitarians, religions do not consist of God's singular truth or express some core Christian experience. Instead, they are cultural-linguistic constructs. They are culturally specific, since each is constituted by the particular place and moment out of which it emerges, and linguistic, since each is governed by a set of rules or doctrines with which any particular utterance (whether sermon or ritual) must comply. Taken together, then, religions are differently born and governed—pluralistic.

Although, for communitarians, religions will consist of versions that differ according to their culture and time, those versions can be comparatively evaluated. Versions that are more internally coherent or more consistent with the ancient doctrines of the faith should be evaluated more favorably. Thus, a version whose theology is most rational and whose utterances conform best to the idiom of classic Christianity should be considered "unsurpassable" compared to the rest.[2]

Communitarians argue, then, both that we live in a pluralistic world and that we should rank religions as better or worse. I agree that we should evaluate religions as better or worse, though I am not clear on their rationale for doing so, given their presumption that our world is pluralistic. In any case, I disagree with their criteria, which insist that a religion conform to the Enlightenment's standards of reason and require that a version of a religion reiterate the oldest doctrines of its faith.

The first criterion is troubling because it obliges us to fully subject religion to reason. Although Christianity may make compelling and logical arguments, as a discourse of faith, Christianity ought also to be allowed to outstrip reason.

The second criterion presumes that versions that abide by the oldest doctrines are the best. For an eschatological religion like Christianity such a criterion seems ill-suited since it will always prefer those versions of Christianity that reflect what Christianity has been as opposed to what it is called to become. Taken together, these two modes of evaluation appear to work against Christianity since they favor a conservative version of a decidedly utopian discourse.

The Triumphalistic Response

Like the communitarian response, the triumphalistic response assumes that we live in a pluralistic world. Unlike communitarians, triumphalists do not consider this change in context to be an occasion to think of Christianity as particular to the culture or cultures out of which it emerges.[3] Instead, triumphalists take postmodernity to be an occasion to spread the word more widely.

With the end of modernity and its accompanying confidence in reason, triumphalists argue, comes an opportunity for God to become relevant again. People are ready, they say, to consider that God may have a role in the universe, that religion may be important for a moral society, that God is central for hope, and that God may help human beings resist the excesses of science.

For triumphalists, the end of modernity represents the liberation of God from philosophic and scientific assumptions that had rendered religion irrelevant. Such liberation enables Christians to make their case that God is central to life. Christians should not squander such an opportunity, triumphalists argue, but instead should seek to penetrate the whole world with Christian questions, values, and answers. Thus Christians will remake the world for God. Triumph indeed.

For Anabaptist Christians whose spiritual ancestors were executed by an imperial Christendom, such a response should be disturbing. Triumphalists take our postmodern world only as an opportunity to exert all available influence so as to make our world over into their own particular Christian likeness. Their disturbing call ignores democratic politics, which are our inheritance from modernity and which were invented largely to protect freedom of religion. Indeed, the triumphalist response seems to be an attempt, however unwitting, to return to the days before modern democratic politics—that is, before discourses of freedom, conscience, and choice had sway.

In short, the triumphalist response is a call for a return to Christendom. As such it is an imperialistic call that responds to today's diversity with an attempt to make all others the same.

The Constructionist Response

Somewhere between the communitarian response, which is as culturally isolating as it is conservative, and the triumphalistic response, which sends the Christian out into the world but only to dominate it, we find the constructionist response.[4] Like communitarians and triumphalists, constructionists accept the proposition that ours is a pluralistic world characterized by culturally specific and ultimately foundationless differences. Unlike communitarians, however, constructionists do not theorize themselves into a culturally isolating corner. On the contrary, constructionists argue that Christians must leave their communities and meet the other because others are similar to God insofar as they are, like God, a mystery.

As constructionists seek to move beyond the borders of their communities, they do not aim, as triumphalists do, to dominate the rest of the world. Instead of trying to make every other into their own image, constructionists want to engage the other in a manner that respects difference. One way to characterize constructionists, then, would be as communitarians pursuing a culturally sensitive public theology.

Of the three postmodern theological responses to our supposed pluralistic condition, the constructionist response is the most promising, because it takes seriously the culturally constructed character of any version of any religion without retreating to cultural isolation. It seeks to be an outward-looking yet nondominating theology as it calls us to converse with and be converted by the other. Indeed, these are well-made aims for these times in which our recognition of difference and our love of neighbor call us to seek the other out without also seeking to make the other over into an image of our self. But can these claims give full account of the deathly danger inherent to a concrete Christian witness? I do not think so.

I agree with constructionists that God and the stranger are mysteries. I also agree that we are obliged as Christians to seek out both. And I agree, as constructionists further argue, that doing so is risky. Yet I cannot understand why we should expect, as Scott Holland has argued, that contact with the other will always be an enriching experience.

In an essay in which Holland advances a constructionist theology vis-à-vis the work of David Tracy, he says that the Christian theologian will venture out because "she has counted the cost. She is convinced that a deepened self-consciousness, God-consciousness, and cosmic consciousness comes only through a creative hermeneutics of genuine conversation with the other. . . ."[5]

If counting the cost means that the outcome can be calculated in advance, then again I fail to see the risk. If I know beforehand that no matter who or what the other is, no matter what our conversation yields, I will be better off, then I have really ventured nothing at all.

As I said, I agree that the other is really other. But that being so, I do not think we can ever know in advance what the outcome of any interaction will be and whether, when we are done, we will be better or worse off. The cost of discipleship is, as Jesus insists, a self-denying, enemy love that surpasses all calculation of gain or loss.

Derrida's Religious Turn

As Anabaptists, we should seek a mode of Christian witness that is radical, defenseless, and gutsy for these times. To pursue such a witness, I suggest we consider the work of a postmodern philosopher who is usually passed over by postmodern Christian theologians but whose recent turn toward religion may teach us much about how we Anabaptists may give a confident witness in postmodernity.[6] I am referring to Jacques Derrida and his recent reading of Kierkegaard's interpretation of the story of Abraham and Isaac in his book, *The Gift of Death*.

Derrida is poststructuralist. This means that he takes structuralism so seriously as to push it to its own limits. Structuralists argue that signs have meaning only in relation to other signs and that their meaning is not a more or less accurate reflection of reality but, instead, a human construct and social convention. Thus, "cat" is "cat" only insofar as it is not "dog," and not because it refers to something like cat-ness per se.

Structuralists also argue that although meaning is not an effect of reality, it is nonetheless regular. Since a sign signifies in relation to other signs, its meaning will remain fixed by those very relations. In other words, signs work in structures of relations among signs that keep their meaning constant. Thus the name "structuralism."[7]

Derrida, however, stretches structuralism to its limits and, in the opinion of many, opens up some fascinating and surprising avenues of thought. According to John D. Caputo, one of Derrida's most informed commentators and explicators, Derrida makes at least two crucial contributions to structuralism that have the effect of constituting poststructuralism.

The first is Derrida's claim that although meaning is governed by the logic or system of relations that allows any sign to signify, meaning is no more determined by that logic than it is by reality. As Caputo explains it,

> Derrida argues that, though rule-bound up to a point . . . the play of traces [or gaps between signs that are their "quasi" condition of possibility] is not a "closed system" but ultimately an open-ended play. He argues against the "closure" of the play and holds that the effects of which "iterability," the code of repeatability, is capable cannot in principle be contained, programmed, or predicted. It always [is] possible, in principle, as a "structural" matter, to repeat differently; that is built right into the very idea of "iterability" or "repetition."[8]

In other words, Derrida argues not only that we make meaning of the world by way of binary structures, rather than by way of a correspondence between word and thing, but also that these structures are not universal, trans-historical, or determining, as structuralism has held. Thus, although structures shape our utterances, so too may our utterances work on our structures.

Derrida's second contribution, according to Caputo, is to notice that language is not unique in these attributes. Whether we are talking about commercials, paintings, commodities, or people, meaning or order is made all the time by this operation of signs set in relation to other signs according to some one or another logic. Again, Caputo:

> In addition to arguing against closure, Derrida also generalizes what was originally a linguistic model . . . so that *différance* [or how signs signify by differing from other signs and also deferring the meaning of other signs] is not restricted to language but leaves its "mark" on everything—institutions, sexuality, the worldwide web, the body, whatever you need or want. This does not amount to arguing that these things are all linguistic. . . . Rather he is arguing that, *like* a language, all these structures are marked by the play of differences, by the "spacing" of which *différance* is one of the names.[9]

Thus, structuralism is stretched beyond its limits to all modes of making meaning. The rules of grammar and the rule-breaking potential of every utterance apply equally as well to every sphere of human activity. So, for instance, punk dress disrupted the economy of fashion as it fetishized the old in a system utterly dependent on "the newest."

Let me highlight two aspects of Derrida's thought that are particularly crucial and often misunderstood. First, Derrida's poststructuralist theory is antiessentialist but not relativist. To be sure, Derrida does say that signs are discontinuous with reality. But he does not say that they are all the same or that they are all valued the same. On the contrary, for Derrida, signs are products of differences that matter. In order for any one sign to signify, it must be set in relation to other signs according to which some signs are valued more than others. Some historical examples include the privileging of white over black in racism, man over woman in patriarchy, and profit over gift in capitalism.

Second, Derrida's thought is critical but not nihilistic. Derrida's work often involves interrogating the meanings, orders, and hierarchies that we have produced. Yet he does so, I think, not to rid of us meaning or order per se but, instead, to put us on the track of what has not yet been.

As human beings we cannot but make meaning and, in doing so, to set up hierarchies and to privilege some things over other things. For Derrida, however, the fact that we must make meaning—that we do not have the choice but to say this is better than that—does not absolve us of the responsibility to examine what systems of privilege we make or reproduce. So whenever we make meaning we are obliged, according to Derrida, to look out for what must have been put aside in the act of meaning-making. When we do that, says Derrida, we set out on the track of how our world might be otherwise than we have made it. In this way Derrida's thought is hopeful and creative, not nihilistic and destructive.

I believe that Derrida's thought may be well-suited to our nonfoundationalist and nonpluralistic times. Enlightenment groundings have slipped out from under us, but meanings and hierarchies have not disappeared. Derrida's work may help us to appreciate these twin contemporary conditions and, more importantly, may guide us toward making our world otherwise. But can Derrida help us remain faithful to Christianity and, more specifically, to our Anabaptist heritage?

As mentioned above, Derrida has recently turned to religious discourses and specifically Christianity. Indeed in *The Gift of Death*, Derrida offers readings of a number of texts including Kierkegaard's interpretation of the story of Abraham and Isaac[10] to give us a genealogy of the ethical subject that points us toward a new kind of ethical subjectivity, one that is, according to Derrida, decidedly Christian.[11]

Derrida's attention to religious discourse, I believe, may teach us much about right relations and confident witness because Derrida's ethical subject is constituted in and by certain difficult relations with others. To flesh out all too briefly Derrida's ethical subject, I will seek to describe it in relationship to three others that are crucial for ethics, history, and sociality. These others are God, the future, and other people.

One of the lessons we can draw from Derrida's reading of the Old Testament story of Abraham and Isaac, in which Abraham is asked by God to sacrifice his beloved son, is that God is utterly incomprehensible to us mortals. We cannot begin to understand how our God could ask such a thing of Abraham. There is no reason we can conjure to rationalize the demand of such a deed. And yet God asks it.

This is a God, Derrida suggests, that is beyond us or who might be described as the *tout autre*, the altogether other. Yet the Bible teaches us, Derrida points out, that this is a God of infinite goodness too. This is a God of unfathomable creativity, generosity, and forgiveness. Indeed, God's infinite goodness is every bit a part of God's otherness. Unlike us fallen beings, who break our promises, sell our souls, and betray our loved ones, God is goodness through and through.

Such goodness is not an object (as the Good was an object[12] in Plato's philosophy) that we might possess by holding it in our sight or comprehending it with our reason. Rather, it is an other. This, Derrida argues, is the particular brilliance of Christianity:

> A personal gaze, that is, a face, a figure, and not a sun [as in Plato's philosophy]. The Good becomes personal Goodness, a gaze that sees me without my seeing it.

Not as a thing but rather as an other, such goodness is available for relation. We can be in relation to it. Indeed, argues Derrida, the Christian subject is one who has taken up a relation with goodness, with God.

God as goodness, then, is not something Christians can ever get their heads all the way around. Such goodness eludes us even as we are in relation to it. It is beyond us, as that which sees and knows us all of the time and that which we know is nearby but which we cannot see. As Derrida puts it, "God sees without being seen."

Knowing as much, we interiorize God's goodness in God's watchfulness. Whatever we do, we never can it do entirely in secret since God is with us all the time. These are the beginnings, then, of the ethical subject, argues Derrida: one, who in being in relation to the God of goodness and the God of all knowing, knows her works do matter as good or bad in God's eyes.

The second lesson we may learn from Derrida's engagement with Christianity is that the future is open. Of course, our modes of making sense of our world, all the structures of language and order we have built, will constrain us. We will tend toward the reiteration of what has already been the case. That is the historical burden of the world we humans have made in all its materiality.

And yet, the future is not determined by what we have already done. Rather, its outlines and logic elude us too. In this sense, Derrida argues, history is a problem because we cannot bring it under control:

> The moment the problem [of history] were to be resolved that same totalizing closure would determine the end of history: it would bring in the verdict of nonhistoricity itself. History can be neither a decidable object nor a totality capable of being mastered. . . .[13]

History itself, Derrida is arguing, presumes the open-endedness of a future we cannot predict since history is the opening up of one moment to another that is other. No narrative of progress, no story of revolution, no relation of dialectical terms can anticipate or contain the transformation of the present into its other, the future.

That this is so, says Derrida, is downright scary:

> We tremble in that strange repetition that ties an irrefutable past . . . to a future that cannot be anticipated; anticipated but unpredictable; *apprehended*, but, and this is why there is a future, apprehended precisely as unforeseeable, unpredictable; approached as unapproachable. Even if one thinks one knows what is going to happen, the new instant of that happening remains untouched, still unaccessible, in fact unlivable.[14]

Yet in that fear of what we cannot know in advance lies the possibility of the impossible. In the undecidability of the future is the possibility that the truly impossible, say, perhaps the reign of God, may indeed come to pass.

The third lesson of Derrida's turn to religion and, in particular, to Christianity is that just as God is other, so too is every person also other. There can be, says Derrida, no substitute of one of us for the other—not really, anyway. One of us might sometime sacrifice ourselves so that an other may be spared. Even so that other one will never be spared death for good. One day death will come. Each of us is concrete, particular, and finite:

> Because I cannot take death away from the other who can no more take it from me in return, it remains for everyone to take his own death *on himself*. Everyone must assume his own death, that is to say

the one thing in the world that no one else can *either give or take*: therein resides freedom and responsibility.[15]

What mortality means, according to Derrida, is not that we are each unique individuals according to an ideology of individualism but, rather, that we are each singular. We may be like one another as, say Americans, but we are irreplaceable to one another. This is crucial, argues Derrida, for in that singularity is not only the possibility but also the obligation that we be responsible for ourselves. Since none other can live or die as any other, then each of us must take it on ourselves to do our deeds and to be held accountable for them.

Moreover, argues Derrida, our singularity is of God. Since God is wholly other, then everything that is also other is also of God. Thus, just as I cannot really apprehend God, so too I cannot really understand any other human being. Every other person is always, in the final instance and despite any similarities, a mystery to me. Hence, I can neither fully comprehend her, nor generalize to her, nor predict her. She outstrips my power to understand, as I do hers.

Free to Choose and Responsible to Choose Well

As Derrida shows in his reading of the story of Abraham and Isaac, Abraham hears clearly God's command that he sacrifice his son but cannot possibly imagine what God means to be done. What can God as infinite goodness have in mind in this abhorrent command? God's will eludes Abraham; still he must choose whether to obey or to defy.

Therein lies a beginning for Abraham's ethical subjectivity: he has a choice insofar as he faces both goodness in God and the unknowability of God's will. As one who is in God's gaze and is of God, he seeks to choose well. Further, this choice is his responsibility. He will be accountable for it. Abraham cannot pass the responsibility of his choice on to God, even though it is God's command, because only Abraham and no one else, not even God, is in the position of choosing whether or not he will put the knife to Isaac's throat.

Thus our relation to God as wholly other gives us our freedom to choose in the face of goodness and our burden of responsibility to choose well. If God were not wholly other, if we could know in advance precisely what God would have us do, then we would have no choice at all. It is the being held accountable (in God's gaze) and the not knowing (God's will) that forms what Derrida calls the *aporia*, or impossibility, of responsibility that is the condition of possibility for ethics.

The undecidability that constitutes an action as a choice and that is an effect of the subject's relation to God is closely related to an effect of the second relation—that is, between the subject and the future. As I explained above, Derrida theorizes history as open-ended, capable of anything. This means that what we do in the here and now is of the utmost importance. Since the future is not over-determined by the past, it remains sufficiently open that our actions may have the power to shape the as-not-yet.

In short, the future is our responsibility. By that I do not mean that Derrida's ethical subject is saturated with a power to make the world into whatever she or he desires. Derrida is not resurrecting the modern subject who is entirely the agent of her own destiny. The burden of history is great. But in that burden are the traces of all the choices we did not make or that we sought to eschew and that, thereby, remain latent and available. The world might have been otherwise; thus it can yet be otherwise. What it will be, this new ethical subject cannot say. Still it is her responsibility in the face of the infinite goodness of God to endeavor to make the choices and take the actions to make it better. That this responsibility before God and the future is as biblical as it is terrifying, Derrida makes abundantly clear:

> In the Epistle to the Philippians 2:12, the disciples are asked to work towards their salvation in fear and trembling. They will have to work for their salvation knowing all along that it is God who decides: the other has no reason to give to us and nothing to settle in our favor, no reason to share his reasons with us. We fear and tremble because we are already in the hands of God, although free to work, but in the hands and under the gaze of God, whom we don't see and whose will we cannot know, no more than the decisions he will hand down, nor his reasons for wanting this or that, our life or death, our salvation or perdition. We fear and tremble before the inaccessible secret of a God who decides for us although we remain responsible, that is, free to decide, to work, to assume our life and our death.[16]

Finally, as I have said, Derrida constitutes this new ethical subject not only in relation to God who is wholly other and to a future that is other than the past, but also to every other person. This ethical subject is to act toward goodness and a better future always through relation to an other.

This is an impossible responsibility. It is impossible because we cannot really know the other. How are we to be good to the other when we cannot fully understand that person's needs, desires, experiences, motives, and deeds? It is impossible because whenever the subject seeks to be good to another, she or he is by necessity neglecting some other other. There is no getting around such limits. Insofar as each of us is singular, finite, and irreplaceable, we can only make one response at a time.

Abraham is acutely aware of this aspect of being an ethical subject. Abraham can only serve God, the wholly other, at the expense of another other, his beloved son Isaac. He cannot be good to both. In fact, he can only serve the one, in this case, by doing a terrible thing to the other. That is not merely an ethical dilemma. This is the very crux of being an ethical subject: that in choosing to do well by someone, the subject is by necessity slighting another.

For Derrida, then, there can be no purity, no comfort, and no self-righteousness in ethical action. Every good deed is at least a deferring of some other goodness left undone. If we are to be ethical subjects, Derrida is saying, we must bear the burden of all the options we did not take.

Now, of course, God spared Abraham the evil deed, in the final moment. But, says Derrida, he did not spare Abraham the act of choosing. When God removes the command, Derrida argues, he only does so after Abraham has already made his son a gift of sacrifice to God. Only when Abraham exceeds all expectation of anything in return from God (what could God give to compensate for such a deed?), does God remove the command and, in so doing, give Abraham everything.

Such generosity, a giving that exceeds every expectation of a balance sheet, every hope for a return, is what Derrida admires most in Christianity. When we face the other, Derrida is saying, we are called to give beyond any economy of expected return, even beyond the hope that we will feel good about ourselves. Since we are mortal and finite beings, we do not have the luxury of giving to one without denying some other. Thus the ethical subject will always find herself in an impossible position of seeking to express God's infinite goodness by a gift, all the while knowing that her gift will come up short:

> I have never been and never will be up to the level of this infinite goodness nor up to the immensity of the gift, the frameless immensity that must in general define . . . a gift as such. This guilt is originary, like original sin. Before any fault is determined, I am guilty inasmuch as I am responsible. . . . Guilt is inherent in responsibility because responsibility is always unequal to itself: one is never responsible enough.[17]

If we are to do good, if we are to be ethical subjects, Derrida is arguing, not only must we not expect a return from the other, we must also not anticipate some assurance that our gift proves our goodness. Insofar as we are mortal, our gifts will always fall short and our self-satisfaction will never be forthcoming. Only God, who is infinite goodness, can judge the relative worth of our meager, though necessary, attempts.

Toward an Anabaptist Response

Our desire to theorize a confident witness in a pluralistic world is motivated by all the right impulses: the impulse to tell the truth and the impulse to do so ethically—that is, defenselessly. As I argued at the beginning of this essay, I do not think we live in a pluralistic world in which all differences are valued the same. Still I believe the twin impulses to tell the truth and to do so defenselessly. That is because, though I am no relativist, I do recognize that we live in a world of differences that are not what they used to be. Whereas in the modern context differences were viewed as fixed by the laws of nature, these days they are hierarchized according to relatively transitory rules.

Because our world is ordered by hierarchies that cause tremendous suffering, we must speak the liberating truth of the gospel. However, because we now recognize that our differences are not natural but, instead, synthetic, we must think the manner of our telling anew. We must remake a witness for a world of differences in which there are no natural anchors for selfhood. Thus the question, put simply, is how do we witness to the other without defensively protecting the self.

The most relevant feature of the Anabaptist tradition for this witness in my view is its concrete rather than abstract character. As Robert Friedman argued, Anabaptist theology cannot in principle be formulated into a system, because of its "existential" refusal to separate faith from life.[18] Or, as John Howard Yoder has put it so well, "That Jesus Christ is Lord is a statement not about my inner piety or my intellect or ideas but about the cosmos."[19]

If our witness is to be, as Yoder and Friedmann have suggested, concrete in character and cosmic in scope, then we must offer our witness without reservation and with both body and spirit. We must give up those forms of Christianity which, as Michael Sattler wrote, seek "to obey God with soul and not also with the body."[20] However, as we have learned from Derrida, such full-bodied and spirited efforts to tell God's truth must, to be ethical practices, at every instance choose whether such witness will take the form of a confident claim or a critical question.

The Aporetic Witness

For our witness to be confident yet ethical, it must be aporetic. That is, it must be structured by an aporia, or two options that are as necessary as they are mutually exclusive. These two options will not be subject in the final instance either to a hierarchy or a synthesis. We will not be able to settle on always privileging one over the other. Nor will we be able to create out of the two of them some third option that resolves the tension between them. They will be irreducibly opposed.

Therefore, every time we come to a moment of witness we will have to choose all over again. That will always be our burden. But that will also be the condition of possibility for our doing witness as ethical subjects since the undecidability of the aporetic witness will put us in a position to choose.

Of course, in choosing, we will also always come up short since, in truth, whatever we do will be only part of the full task. As Gayatri Chakravorty Spivak has recently said:

> A dilemma is just a task of thinking, whereas an aporia is a practical fact. An aporia is a situation where one choice cancels out another, but a choice must be made. You can't exist in an aporia.[21]

Insofar as aporia represents a moment that demands an impossible choice, it is, so to speak, where the action and, thus, ethics is.

So what will be our options? One option of the aporetic witness will require that we tell the truth as we know it and that we do so as persuasively as we can. We will make compelling arguments with strong evidence and solid reasoning. We will also make appeals that seek to motivate our hearer's desire toward Jesus' teachings.

Of course, we will seek to make of ourselves an example for our case. Thus our truth telling will not be limited to our words—it will consist in every mode of our daily living as well. We will tell the truth of all things to the other so that we might be instruments for that person's transformation. We will evangelize. That is, we will witness in the sense of testifying to the truth we have come to know.

How shall we come to know such truth? We will come to know it through careful readings of biblical texts, as well as texts of our Anabaptist heritage in the context of our community of believers. We will discover it in the life and teachings of Jesus as we come to these through our historical tradition. Thus we will read as a community the texts of the New Testament and especially the Sermon on the Mount alongside the *Martyrs Mirror*, our confessions of faith, and a wealth of historical and theological interpretations of that rich heritage.

We know that we cannot learn the truth either alone or from a neutral position. We must do it together, so that we can discuss competing interpretations, hear the differences, and seek to choose the truth. We must do it from within the perspectives and biases of our tradition because that is who we are. We neither can nor should seek to escape our history. Rather, we should bring our history, and thereby ourselves, into a lively engagement with biblical texts and especially Jesus as our model to discern the truth.

The other option of the aporetic witness will require that we not give witness to the truth as we know it, but rather that we seek to witness precisely the truth we do not know. Since we are not omniscient, since we do not know all, we are assured that we do not own the truth. Our tradition, no matter how rich, cannot contain God's truth.

If we ever were to come to know all truth, Genesis tells us, we would be mortals no more. We would be gods. And that is simply not for us to be. Whenever we proclaim the truth as we know it, then, we are surely also telling nontruth. The whole truth is simply not ours to tell. God's full truth always eludes us precisely because it is, as God is, other than us. So just as we are telling the truth as best we know it, we can be sure that somewhere in some trace we are leaving behind is something of God's truth that we have missed. We will miss a point or smooth over a paradox or even out a tension and, just as we do so, some truth of God will escape our notice.

As witnesses, then, we must put ourselves on the track of those truths that elude us. We must be relentlessly on the lookout for what we have missed or ignored or hidden.

When we choose this option, we will be undoing the rules, pushing through the boundaries, shaking up the logics by which we have perhaps ordered our community or by which others have organized our world. As we seek out the truth that has not yet been, we will take on a terrible burden. Chances are we will cause confusion, loss for ourselves and for others. That will be our doing, and we will have to take responsibility for it. To be sure, if our pursuit involves upsetting the status quo for those who enjoy disproportionate power, we will be held accountable. But we will have to choose this option now and again because, if we don't, we will have forfeited our relationship to God as the wholly other.

As should be clear, we cannot reiterate the truths of our tradition and community while at the same time pursuing the traces of those truths which would undo our truths. There can be no synthesis or balance between these two options. We will have to choose one or the other, and we cannot know for sure and in advance which is the better choice. Perhaps we have some truths right, or right enough, that they ought not to be contested as much as reaffirmed. Perhaps these truths or others of which we are absolutely convinced are downright wrong.

I am, for instance, totally convinced that pacifism is true. I am certain that God wants us to eschew violence. Therefore I think we should reiterate that truth as often and as compellingly as possible to anyone we can persuade to listen. But I also wonder what we may be missing in that witness. As we have construed pacifism in opposition to militarism, what have we put out of our view? Have we imagined peace witness too narrowly? Have we failed to live it in as challenging a manner as we could?

If we pursued such inquiry, what would become not only of our pacifism but also of us? Who would we be? Who will we be if we do not engage in such inquiry? These questions could not be more difficult, because they are all about choosing one or the other of the options of an aporetic witness that will surely have consequences for whether we speak the truth or falsehood, as well as implications for who we will be as Christians.

The Aporetic Witness as Gift

"Go ye therefore, and teach all nations, baptizing them in the name of the Father, and of the Son, and of the Holy Ghost: Teaching them to observe all things whatsoever I have commanded you: and, lo, I am with you always, even unto the end of the world" (Matthew 28:19-20, KJV).

As we give ourselves over to the great commission, I wonder whether we aren't a bit like Abraham on hearing God's command that he sacrifice Isaac. What is more precious to us than the truths of Christianity as they have come to us, whether through tradition or its traces? Jesus commands us to teach all nations; that is, to give these truths as gifts to others, so that they might transform those others as well. But what will come of these gifts and of us as we give them? Which gifts will we give? Will they help or harm? If they do harm, will we bear that responsibility? How will they be received? Will they be accepted or altered? Will we be praised or martyred?

If Derrida is right about what it means to make a gift to another, then we cannot answer these questions except to say that if our gift is to be a gift, if it is to be given in the spirit of God's infinite goodness, then we will have to give it expecting nothing in particular in return. Nothing, perhaps, except a sense of not having given enough.

We may not give in anticipation of gratitude or of self-righteousness. When we give in that way we make no gift at all since we are really only making a trade of God's gifts for our satisfaction. In truth, we cannot say what the reception of our gift of witness will be. The other may receive it as precious, may transform it into something else, may take it as a threat. Since the other is, as we have said, truly other, that person is beyond our expectation, just as the future is beyond our prediction. If we are to give this most precious gift, and we must, for Jesus tells us that it is not ours to keep, then we will have to give it as Abraham gave Isaac—in fear and trembling and faith.

Notes

1. For an example of a prominent communitarian response, see George A. Lindbeck, *The Nature of Doctrine: Religion and Theology in a Postliberal Age* (Philadelphia: Westminster Press, 1984).

2. For his discussion of "unsurpassability," see Lindbeck, 48. Recently Nancey Murphy has taken up Lindbeck's notion of "unsurpassability" as a criterion for truth claims within a postmodern theology that she hopes may bridge the divide between evangelical liberals and conservatives. See Nancey Murphy, "Philosophical Resources for Postmodern Theology," *Christian Scholar's Review* 26, no. 2 (winter 1996), 200. For an excellent review and critique of Lindbeck's theology from an Anabaptist perspective, see J. Denny Weaver, "Review of *The Nature of Doctrine: Religion and Theology in a Postliberal Age*, by George A. Lindbeck," review, *Conrad Grebel Review* 3, no. 2 (spring 1985), 221-224.

3. For an example of a prominent triumphalist response, see Diogenes Allen, "The End of the Modern World," *Christian Scholar's Review* 22, no. 4 (1993), 339-47.

4. For examples of the constructionist response, see the following: Joe Holland, "The Postmodern Paradigm and Contemporary Catholicism," in *Varieties of Postmodern Theology*, ed. David Ray Griffin, William A. Beardslee, and Joe Holland, SUNY Series in Constructive Postmodern Thought (New York: State University of New York Press, 1989), 9-27; Scott Holland, "How Do Stories Save Us?: Two Contemporary Theological Responses," *Conrad Grebel Review* 12, no. 2 (spring 1994), 131-153.

5. Scott Holland, 153.

6. David Ray Griffin, for example, posits the constructionist project as positive and productive against Derrida's deconstructionist efforts which Griffin considers extremist and destructive. See David Ray Griffin, "Introduction to SUNY Series in Constructive Postmodern Thought," in *Varieties of Postmodern Theology*, ed. David Ray Griffin, William A. Beardslee, and Joe Holland, SUNY Series in Constructive Postmodern Thought (New York: State University of New York Press, 1989), xi-xiv.

7. If structuralism sounds similar to the communitarian response, that is because the communitarian response is based in a structuralist view of language that has been translated into a theory of the way religious discourses work.

8. John D. Caputo, "A Commentary: Deconstruction in a Nutshell," in *Deconstruction in a Nutshell: A Conversation with Jacques Derrida*, ed. John D. Caputo (New York: Fordham University Press, 1997), 101.

9. Ibid., 104.

10. For the remainder of the paper, I will refer to Derrida's reading of Kierkegaard's interpretation of the story of Abraham and Isaac as Derrida's reading of

Abraham and Isaac, because the former phrasing is cumbersome. The intertextuality of Derrida's reading of the story of Abraham and Isaac through Kierkegaard's reading is important. So I am asking the reader to bear that in mind when I refer to it as Derrida's reading.

11. I believe Derrida understands himself to be on the track of one of the traces of history, namely, Christianity as it might have been had Plato's philosophy not influenced our understanding as much as it did. Thus he writes,

> Something has not yet arrived, neither at Christianity nor by means of Christianity. What has not yet arrived at or happened to Christianity is Christianity. Christianity has not yet come to Christianity. What has not yet come about is the fulfillment, within history and in political history, and first and foremost in European politics, of the new responsibility announced by the *mysterium tremendum*. There has not yet been an authentically Christian politics because there remains this residue of the Platonic polis. Christian politics must break more definitively and more radically with Greco-Roman Platonic politics in order to finally fulfill the *mysterium tremendum*.

Jacques Derrida, *The Gift of Death*, trans. David Wills (Chicago: University of Chicago Press, 1995), 29.

12. Ibid., 93.

13. Ibid., 5.

14. Ibid., 54.

15. Ibid., 44.

16. Ibid., 56.

17. Ibid., 51.

18. Robert Friedmann, *The Theology of Anabaptism: An Interpretation* (Scottdale, Pa.: Herald Press, 1973), 27-34.

19. John Howard Yoder, *For the Nations: Essays Public and Evangelical* (Grand Rapids, Mich.: Wm. B. Eerdmans Publishing Co., 1997), 24.

20. Michael Sattler, "On the Satisfaction of Christ," in *The Legacy of Michael Sattler*, ed. and trans. John Howard Yoder (Scottdale, Pa.: Herald Press, 1973), 117.

21. Gayatri Chakravorty Spivak and David Plotke, "A Dialogue on Democracy," in *Radical Democracy: Identity, Citizenship, and the State*, ed. David Trend (New York: Routledge, 1996), 211.

CHAPTER EIGHT

The Church in the Pluralistic African Experience

Tite Tienou

"Pluralism in Africa? I didn't know there was any!" Presentations on pluralism in the African experience regularly elicit this kind of response in North America and in Europe. Images of a tribal Africa, where traditional religion is the factor of social integration, seem to have left an indelible mark on the minds of Westerners. That is why some find the association of Africa with pluralism incongruous.

Yet for African Christians, pluralism is one of the major issues the church faces. Tokunboh Adeyemo places religious pluralism at the top of the list of "competing forces or realities to face."[1] Kwame Bediako remarks that, "for the modern African theologians, religious pluralism is their *experience.*"[2]

Adeyemo and Bediako are not alone in their assessment of the religious scene in Africa. The African experience is indeed pluralistic.[3] This pluralism must, however, be understood on its own terms and in the context of African realities. Understanding the specificity of pluralism in Africa is necessary if the Church in that continent is to address its situation meaningfully and continue in the bold proclamation of Jesus as Lord.

African Pluralistic Experience in Religion

The nature of religious pluralism in Africa is best understood if contrasted with common understandings of pluralism in Western democracies. It is almost an axiom in the West that pluralism implies the privatization of religion, the rejection of truth claims, and the flourishing of relativism. In Africa, however, it can be argued that pluralism is understood as the absorption of many religions into a previously existing religion. The previously existing religion is, of course, the traditional ethnic religion.

Ali Mazrui is one of the well-known advocates of this view of religious pluralism in Africa. He has argued that "African traditional religion can be combined with either Christianity or Islam."[4] For Mazrui, Nigeria and particularly Yoruba society illustrate the African genius of insisting "on the supremacy of the indigenous" religion while accepting other religions.[5]

It can be debated whether the African religious synthesis, described as a "triple heritage" by Mazrui, is pluralism or syncretism. Mazrui and others seem to base their opinion on African societies' ability to adopt and adapt alien religious ideas. So a look at the nature of religious borrowing in Africa may be helpful.

Over the years, African religions have survived the onslaught of competing, and sometimes more "powerful," religions. This resilience of traditional African cultures and religions has surprised many people and has been the object of studies. For Achille Mbembe, indocility is what explains the resurgence or revenge of African traditional religions in postcolonial African states.[6]

One cannot dispute the fact that Africans have resisted the advances of Islam and Christianity. The "Africanization" of both religions should also be acknowledged. Yet limiting analysis of the situation to the encounter between African indigenous religions and "conquering" outside religions may not tell the whole story. It may be more fruitful to look first at intra-African religious borrowing.

Religious buying and selling between African societies has occurred and may continue to occur. Sometimes this is explained in terms of "clan memory"—that is, in the form of stories about the origin of specific clan deities. For example, the present ethnic identity of the Tienou clan of Worowé is Bobo. The Tienous, however, claim to come from the Bwa ethnic group originally. This claim of ethnic origin is authenticated in the clan's memory by the existence of clan deities whose "language" is Boomu, the language of the Bwa. Even today, these deities must be addressed in Boomu. But they are incorporated into Bobo religion, though they are recognized as foreign both in terms of origin and liturgical language.

Clan memory is not the only way by which Africans have acquired other ethnic groups' deities and adapted them to their own religious systems. There are indications of conscious importation of deities from more or less distant people.

Some southern Bobo, or Bobo people living in the vicinity of Bobo-Dioulasso (Burkina Faso), have Kono and Komo, deities that belong to the Bambara and Minyanka of Mali. Likewise, the Baoulé of Côte d'Ivoire have incorporated *Do*, the most important deity of Bobo society, into their own religion. In both these examples, the borrowed deities retain their names, but their functions are transformed and absorbed into the religious fabric of the ethnic group doing the borrowing.

Such examples of intra-African religious borrowing are not meant to prove a pattern or establish a rule. They simply show that African traditional religions as we now know them may be the result of previous adaptations. Consequently, explanations of the "supremacy of indigenous" religions must not be limited to how Islam or Christianity tend to be absorbed by African religions.

Whether it occurs through the absorption of elements from Islam or Christianity, or by the acquisition of divinities from other African peoples, this adaptability of ethnic or traditional religions points to Africans' propensity toward religious tolerance. But it is a tolerance in which the indigenous is reinforced, enlarged, revitalized, and readied to face the future.

This kind of tolerance, not unlike similar ideas found in Hinduism, is at the heart of the African experience of religious pluralism. It is a pluralism built on the conviction that God belongs to all peoples, though he may be called by many names, and that the ways to approach God may vary.[7] In fact, many Africans believe that the lesser divinities are mediators given by God himself.

In many ways, then, the African experience of religious pluralism is a situation in which it may be possible for every clan to adjust the religion of the wider ethnic group for its needs. This creates a religious environment inimical to conversion and exclusivism. In such an environment, conversion that demands the repudiation of the old religious ways is especially difficult to accept and live by. This sheds light on the often-noted superficiality of African Christianity, despite the numerical growth reported by Christian groups. It vindicates Kwame Bediako in his contention that the religious pluralism of the second and third century and that of contemporary Africa make "Christian identity . . . *the issue*. Religious pluralism therefore does not lie outside of theological existence itself."[8]

The church in Africa still needs to articulate how Christian identity is possible even with religious pluralism. This is an important item of unfinished business on her theological agenda. Yet I fear that, at present, the church does not fully realize the urgency of dealing with the issue of Christian identity. She is distracted by the political and economic scene.

Politics and economics, in much of contemporary Africa, tend to reinforce religious pluralism or accentuate religious mercantilism.[9] Therefore, it may be useful to look at how politics and economics affect the African pluralistic experience.

Religious Pluralism as a Political Doctrine

We have seen that the African experience of religious pluralism is one in which outside religions are incorporated into the existing religion, so that the new strengthens the old. The question is not, What religion do you adhere to? Rather, it is, Are you religious? Greater value is attached to letting people practice religion than to asking them to declare exclusive allegiance to a particular religion.

In Côte d'Ivoire, religious tolerance and the pursuit of peace were essential elements of nation building for President Félix Houphouët-Boigny, who led the country from 1960 to 1993. His successor, Henri Konan Bédié, has maintained the same outlook. President Houphouët-Boigny's attitude towards religion was a mixture of African pluralism and certain eighteenth-century American views of religious pluralism, such as those espoused by Thomas Jefferson and John Witherspoon.

For Houphouët-Boigny, one does not choose a religion. Instead, one is born into a religion or has the religion of one's environment. This reflects the assumption that a person must keep the religion he or she inherited. In Houphouët-Boigny's view, all religions are equal. The following saying is attributed to him:

> Fate made me Catholic. I was born in a town influenced by missionaries; I therefore found myself totally Catholic. Had I been born in a Muslim town, I would have been Muslim. But I would have never been without God.[10]

For Houphouët-Boigny, religious equality was not theoretical. He put his ideas into practice by a generous and vigorous support of all religions in his country. He helped build churches, cathedrals, and mosques. The Basilica in Yamoussoukro, named Our Lady of Peace, is the most grandiose sign of his generosity.

Houphouët-Boigny's views continue to be promoted in Côte d'Ivoire today. President Konan Bédié, himself a Catholic like his predecessor, makes annual financial contributions for pilgrimages to Mecca. Moreover, during his presidency, a major and strategically located mosque commenced construction in the Plateau, the financial and business district of Abidjan. The belief that religious tolerance is the foundation of civic peace links the politics of the two presidents. Many efforts go into convincing the population that all believers are equals, regardless of their religion.

Religious tolerance, equality of all religions, civic peace: these words have an American ring to them. We know that in the United States there is "the common belief in religious tolerance as a civic virtue to be observed by all the churches."[11] Thomas Jefferson and John Witherspoon are important eighteenth-century advocates of this American view of religious pluralism. For Jefferson, "doctrinal diversity could be tolerated because it is incidental."[12] We noted how unimportant religious dogma was to Houphouët-Boigny. In that sense he had a Jeffersonian view.

David Little notes that in Witherspoon's understanding "religious pluralism has civil utility. . . . Therefore, the state has a direct interest in maintaining religious pluralism, but only insofar as the arrangement actually promotes and extends true piety and virtue."[13] One can see how Houphouët-Boigny might have agreed with Witherspoon.

Houphouët-Boigny's African, Jeffersonian, and Witherspoonian vision of religious pluralism has now been institutionalized in Côte d'Ivoire. In September 1997, representatives of religious bodies founded a "Forum of Religious Confessions" (*Forum des Confessions Religieuses*). Among the many reasons for the creation of this body we find this: only tolerance and love of neighbor can safeguard civic peace.[14]

Article Two of the constitution provides a list of the organization's goals. It is interesting to note the following: "de cosolider et perpétuer la coexistence pacifique et l'espirt de fraternité qui a toujours existé entre confessions religieuses en Côte d'Ivoire;"[15] that is, "to consolidate and perpetuate peaceful coexistence and the spirit of brotherhood that has always existed between religious confessions in Côte d'Ivoire."

In the case of Côte d'Ivoire, then, politics reinforce religious pluralism. The state protects all religious bodies. This encourages religious entrepreneurship and mercantilism. People point to the multiplicity of religious entities and the crowded places of worship as signs of religious vitality. For the Christian faith, however, the current proliferation of denominations in Africa may prove to be something else. There may be power struggles involved. Statistical growth may also be achieved for purposes of gaining political prestige or benefiting from the state's favors. Moreover, people may have multiple religious affiliations. Consequently, religious identity remains an open question.

Religious Pluralism and Economics

For some politicians and economists, the current proliferation of religious sects must be understood as a response to the contemporary economic and political crisis in Africa. One recalls how Jean-François Bayart and his school analyzed the postcolonial African state in terms of scarcity and survival: the state is guided by urgency of eating.[16]

In this analysis, religion is perceived as a strategy for survival. Such is the background for Achille Mbembe's claim that "religious identity no longer exists in Africa."[17]

Mbembe's thesis rests on the presupposition that the purpose of religion is to help the individual face the immediate practical problems of life. For the African, life is precarious; survival is problematic.[18] The African has come to realize that playing the political or religious game can be a means of satisfying one of his basic needs, the need to eat. Indeed, belonging to a party or professing allegiance to a religious body may bring relief in times of famine. Thus, the way to ensure one's survival is to have multiple political or religious identities. People may even sell their "souls" to the highest bidder![19]

The situation may not be as bad as Mbembe describes it. Not all Africans are pragmatic materialists. There is, nevertheless, reason for concern. Multiple religious affiliations are, indeed, widely practiced. Religious workers also use material incentives to encourage adherents. In Africa, as elsewhere, economics do shape religious behavior and sometimes determine religious choices. The economic crisis in Africa creates religious confusion and provides a fertile ground for the blossoming of religious pluralism.

Conclusion

Christians in Africa have always known that they lived in contexts of religious pluralism. After all, in most situations Christians are a minority. Even in places where Christians today comprise the majority of the population, many in the church can still recall the time when they were a minority. In such a context, African Christians have lived their faith as "strangers and pilgrims." Many have been joyful and bold witnesses of the grace of God in Christ. The contemporary church in Africa owes an eternal debt of gratitude to them.

Emerging forms of pluralism present new challenges to the church in Africa. In some ways the church is just discovering the implications for Christian life and witness. She is faced with many questions, and her leaders seem able to provide few answers. Will the church in Africa

continue in the tradition of bold witness of her ancestors? Will she ca-
pitulate to the manipulations of politicians who use religion for their
own purposes? Will she buy the privatized, lukewarm religion of Western democracies? Time will tell, but appropriate steps can be taken now.

Notes

1. Tokunboh Adeyemo, "The Church in Africa Today," in *Church and Society
. . . Can They Work in Harmony?* ed. Gilbert Okoronkwo (Nairobi, Kenya: Association of Evangelicals of Africa and Madagascar, 1990), 19. Adeyemo emphasized that his list is partial. Nevertheless, the order and what he chose to include are significant: religious pluralism, cultural authenticity, Roman Catholicism, theological liberalism, cults, and pragmatic humanism.

2. Kwame Bediako, *Christianity in Africa: The Renewal of a Non-Western Religion*
(Maryknoll, N.Y.: Orbis Books, 1995), 257. Italics in the original.

3. The theme for the 1998 Annual Meeting of the African Studies Association
(held Oct. 29-Nov. 1) was "Africa's Encounter with the Twentieth Century." African Religions is one of the subthemes for discussion. "Africa is a continent of
many religions" is the first sentence introducing Section D: African Religions,
ASA News 21, no. 1 (January/March 1998): 13.

4. Ali A. Mazrui, "A Trinity of Cultures in Nigerian Politics: The Religious Impact," *Africa Events* 2, no. 10 (October 1986), 13. See also his *The Africans* (Boston:
Little, Brown and Company, 1986), particularly chapter 7 entitled "Africa at
Prayer: New Gods." Kwame Nkrumah, *Consciencism* (New York: Modern Reader,
1964), makes a similar argument.

5. Mazrui, 14.

6. Achille Mbembe, *Afriquest indocile* (Paris: Editions Karthala, 1988), 13.

7. It is instructive that Hinduism is often characterized as a "federation of
faiths." The same designation, *mutatis mutandis*, applies to African religions. I have
benefited from Ken Gnanakan's study of pluralism in the Hindu context; see his
The Pluralist Predicament (Bangalore: Theological Book Trust, 1992), particularly
chapter 4. In *Tierce Eglise, ma Mère* (Bobo Dioulasso: Imprimerie de la Savane,
1977), 180, Anselme Titianma Sanon notes that for the Bobo Do, the most important secondary deity is God for them but not for all peoples; other deities "actualize" God for other people. The African experience in religion is therefore quite
different from that of African Americans, for whom pluralism is a rather recent
phenomenon (see C. Eric Lincoln and Lawrence H. Mamiya, *The Black Church in
the African American Experience* [Durham, N.C.: Duke University Press, 1990], 8,
390-391).

8. Kwame Bediako, 257. Italics in original. See also *Theology and Identity* (Oxford, England: Regnum Books, 1992). On conversion and Christian identity, see
Andrew F. Walls, "Old Athens and New Jerusalem: Some Signposts for Christian
Scholarship in the Early History of Mission Studies," *International Bulletin of Missionary Research* 21, no. 4 (October 1997): 146-153.

9. It is important to remember that very few generalizations are possible when
dealing with the African continent. This is especially true in matters related to re-

ligious ideology. Pluralism and religious mercantilism will not occur any time soon in Muslim states such as Mauritania, Morocco, Algeria, Tunisia, Libya, Egypt, Sudan, Somalia, or Djibouti. In addition, the countries within the area sometimes referred to as the belt of Christian–Muslim tension will continue to struggle with the question of religious freedom. Nevertheless, the idea that politics and economics reinforce religious pluralism should not be dismissed without examination.

10. President Houphouët-Boigny did not leave a body of writings. This statement on his religious affiliation comes from Arthur Comte, *Côte d'Ivoire ou les racines de la sagesse* (Paris: Grands Livres/Les Editions JA, n.d.).

11. David Tracy, "The Question of Pluralism: The Context of the United States," *Mid-Stream* 12, nos. 3, 4 (July-October 1983): 273.

12. David Little, "American Civil Religion and the Rise of Pluralism," *Union Seminary Quarterly Review* 38, nos. 3, 4 (1984): 406.

13. Ibid., 407.

14. *Statuts du Forum des Confessions Religieuses,* 2.

15. Ibid., 3.

16. See Jean-Francois Bayart, *L'Etat en Afrique: la politique du ventre* (Paris Fayard, 1989).

17. Mbembe, 69.

18. Mbembe (l'impératif majeure restant celui de la survie).

19. Ibid., 69. Mbembe's exact wording is worth noting: "A lalimite, il n'existeplus d'identité religieuse en Afrique. Il existe des agents qui scrutent les offres qui leur sont faites et les utilisent dès lors qu'elles réspondent àleurs interêts pratiques et immédiats."

CHAPTER NINE

The Church in Pluralistic North America: Decentering Conviction

Wilbert R. Shenk

Introduction

What if the world woke up one day and there were no Jews left? Would America be worse off? A strange question, perhaps, but an important one. American Judaism is in crisis, and the root cause of it is that most American Jews cannot answer that question. We can't explain why an America without us would be worse off, because we have spent the past century trying to become exactly like the culture that surrounds us.[1]

This melancholy observation can be applied to a wide range of religious groups in the modern world. It underscores the pervasive insecurity of religion in contemporary culture. A fundamental premise of modernity has been that religion is unnecessary at best and detrimental at worst to human well-being. Modernity offers the only adequate alternative: a world rid of the superstition and subjectivism that comprise religion.

Throughout the modern period, religious adherents have sensed intuitively that they were on trial, always needing to justify themselves vis-à-vis the modern view. It must be recalled that modernity has two faces: it has been both adversary and seducer. The astonishing achievements of modern science and technology have proved irresistible. In-

156

deed, important features of the modern project can gladly be affirmed. Yet in the end, modernity was the authority to which religion had to answer; it would brook no rivals.

Although modernity itself is now in crisis and beset by criticism from postmodernists, it remains true that the modern view has undermined and transformed religious life and belief during the past three centuries.[2] Indeed, no religious group has been exempted.

From Periphery to Center to Periphery

One way of understanding a culture is to describe it in terms of what defines its center and what its periphery. The center of a culture is the locus of authority and control, out of which influences radiate to the whole culture, giving coherence and definition. The cultural system of values and institutions is largely shaped by what is at the center. The further one moves from the center, the less power one can command. And yet center and periphery exist in a dialectical relationship. The center is dependent on the tribute it draws from the periphery.

This framework is useful in interpreting the history of the church. Historically, the Christian movement emerged on the margins of Jewish and Roman societies. The New Testament depicts Jesus as one who hails from the cultural, political, and religious hinterland and is put to death by the religio-political center. Earliest Christian history confirms this identity. To be a Christian disciple in the first three centuries conveyed neither sociopolitical advantage nor status.

A momentous change occurred in the fourth century. This erstwhile marginal group moved rapidly from the periphery to the power center of the Roman Empire; by the late fourth century the once fugitive Christian movement was relatively secure, due to official favor.

This, of course, marks the rise of historical Christendom. The church of Christendom henceforth would be identified as an integral part of the establishment. It was at the center of Western culture. For many generations Western culture was regarded as Christian culture, and the terms "Western" and "Christian" were used interchangeably. Christianity rode in the cockpit as copilot of Christian civilization.

This transition from periphery to center was based on a metamorphosis of the church, a change in form and character that indelibly imprinted every aspect of the church's identity and life. Being at the center called the church to develop a new theology, ethics, worship, and mission. What had been important to the church on the periphery no longer made sense viewed from the center.

From its new sociopolitical location of privilege and influence, the church proceeded to redefine its understandings of the world and its place in it. What had made the church on the periphery a threat to the state—for example, the proclamation that Jesus Christ alone is Lord— was now replaced by the rhetoric and theological rationale that transformed the church into a compliant and complicit member of the establishment. The position of the church at the center of Western culture went largely unchallenged until the seventeenth century.

The rise of modernity and the Enlightenment in the seventeenth century irreversibly altered the old balance of power. Forces were now unleashed that led to the disestablishment and marginalization of the church. Over the next two centuries the church was progressively displaced from the center. With this change the privileged status the church had enjoyed since the fourth century was surrendered.

Whenever a long-standing relationship is forcibly changed, there follows a long period of grief acted out as resistance and denial. The church in the West has, in fact, been in a state of denial for several generations. Nor can we say it has been a healthy or therapeutic grief process.

One form of denial is that found among the mainline Protestant churches. Since the late nineteenth century these churches have adopted an accommodationist stance toward modernity.[3] They have sustained steady decline since the 1960s, apparently unable to develop a constructive offensive that would address their situation.[4]

Denial is also evident among so-called free churches. In 1949 the eminent British historian Herbert Butterfield, a devout adherent of the free church tradition, noted that Christianity in the West had crossed a historical watershed. "We are back for the first time in something like the earliest centuries of Christianity," he argued.[5]

Butterfield felt elated because this indicated that no one need any longer feel compelled to affiliate with the church out of fear of official, social, or economic sanctions. Ironically, the impulse to restore this lost estate has been especially strong among those groups on the religious and political right in the United States that support movements like the Moral Majority and Christian Coalition, which keep beating the drums for a lost Christian hegemony.

Are not both of these responses distortions of what Jesus had in mind for his body? Scholars have suggested that a normative description of the Christian movement is that of faithfully following the marginalized Messiah, Jesus of Nazareth. Henri Desroche argues that "messianism is a plan for a Kingdom conceived in the lands of Exile."[6]

Such a movement is hardly one that is preoccupied with achieving and maintaining a dominant position in society. Too many Christians in the West pine for a restored Christendom rather than asking whether the new historical situation could be a providential opportunity—a chance for recovering the genius of Christian faith by accepting marginality as gift.

Thus, as we have seen, the church in late modernity is effectively marginalized by the dominant culture but continues to deny that this fundamental change in status has occurred. In effect, the church has been disestablished.[7] Yet in theology and structure it continues to act as if little has changed.

The marginalization of the church takes two forms. The first of these, disestablishment, has an even more crucial element than the removal of the church from its once powerful position. In the words of Colin Gunton, "Modernity is the era which has displaced God as the focus for the unity and meaning of being."[8] That is to say, modernity has attempted the radical move of marginalizing both God and church.

The second variety of marginalization is to be found in what results from pluralism.[9] Modernity has been highly successful in eroding traditional structures but has utterly failed to create viable replacements. The cultural center has been progressively eroded; indeed, the very logic of modernity has rendered the notion of center and periphery obsolete. Consequently, we live in a decentered world of competing power options in all areas. To analyze this process and outcome more closely, we must take account of the characteristics of modernity.

The Dynamics of Modernity

Among the range of factors in modern culture that impinge on religion, sociologists have singled out three as fundamental to the modernization process: functional rationality, cultural pluralism, and structural pluralism.[10]

Functional Rationality

The hallmark of modernity is the emphasis laid on rationality.[11] Rene Descartes is credited with introducing this notion in the 1640s. He lived in one of the truly dark periods of world history. His world was mired down in the devastating Thirty Years' War, and socio-religious conflict was intense. Descartes was looking for a new foundation for the human enterprise. Against the irrationalism of his day, Descartes proposed a mathematically based epistemology that would lead humankind out of this chaos and to open-ended human progress, enabling people to escape from the dreadful irrational conflicts in the Europe of that day. This appealing new perspective quickly gained acceptance and redefined the worldview that controlled Western culture. As modernity flowered, rational controls were extended and applied in all areas of human life.

Modern rationality has been institutionalized symbolically and structurally. One of the foremost examples is the way the modes of technology and bureaucracy have become indispensable to the production process. Applying principles drawn from modern rationality and science, around the turn of the twentieth century Frederick W. Taylor proposed organizing the factory on the basis of the assembly line. This revolutionized production. The process could now be broken down into discrete functions, then routinized and mechanized to insure uniform quality at the least cost. This innovation made possible systems of mass production that have decisively shaped the modern economy.

Symbolically, functional rationality has been institutionalized in terms of rational and utilitarian values that have been the undergirding of the modern worldview. Traditional societies interpret the natural world in terms of mystery, while modernity has sought to "disenchant" the world. The modern view treated the physical world as a mere factor of production to be exploited for economic gain. Although these modern values are difficult to reconcile with core characteristics of religious faith, the pressure on religion to accommodate to functional rationality has been intense.

Cultural Pluralism

Impelled by industrialization and urbanization, modernity has fostered cultural pluralism by drawing together many subsocieties—ethnic, linguistic, and cultural groups. These retain important aspects of their distinct cultural traditions while living under the canopy of modernity.[12]

All people in modern society now confront a bewildering array of worldviews and disparate value systems unrelentingly purveyed by the mass media. Inevitably, this has resulted in a dilemma for all religions. Each faith tradition is defined by a unique set of nonnegotiable core values; without them their religious identity will be lost. But modernity has promoted the homogenization of religious values.

The clash between modernity and religious commitment is ongoing. Consider this example. Recently, an immigrant from India living in Ventura County, California, brought suit against Taco Bell because he had mistakenly been served a taco containing beef; he had taken a bite before discovering the error. This incident caused the man such distress that he had sought the help of a psychiatrist and local Hindu priests. Ultimately, he traveled to a Hindu temple in London for ritual cleansing. Now he was seeking damages from Taco Bell for violating his religious convictions. (This story is of interest not least because of the fascinating mixing together of traditional and modern views and practices.)

Whenever religious values have come into conflict with modernity, as they inevitably must, it is presumed that religion has no rightful role in the public sphere and that redress will be found by effecting accommodations in the private sphere.[13] All religious claims are relativized against the prior claim of the modern worldview to control the public realm. It is assumed that those who remain loyal to a faith tradition in modern society will have to devise their own way of coping with two irreconcilable value systems.

Responses to this cognitive dissonance range from confusion to acquiescence. In the West it has long been taken for granted that the solution is to confine religious commitment and practice to the private sphere and maintain a secular stance in the public sector. But this is increasingly under challenge from the growing communities of Hindus and Muslims, among others, who have migrated to the West in recent decades and refuse to accept secular dominance as inevitable.

Structural Pluralism

This leads directly to the third factor, namely, structural pluralism. A clear line has been drawn between public and private. In contrast to traditional societies where religion was the overarching authority and glue, the public sphere in modern society is the arena of the nation-state, the professions, and specialized bureaucracies, all organized on the basis of an impersonal, abstract, and alienating functional rationality. The private world is the scene of family, social relations, sexuality, personal identity, and life meaning. This latter world is marked by expressivity, particularity, and subjectivity. The modern regime has looked to religion primarily to offer solace in moments of personal crisis and guidance when the individual faces important transitions in life.

Modernity is based on what is termed "reflexive ordering and reordering."[14] An attitude of skepticism is normative. Every finding is at best temporary, and each discovery is short-term, for we know that ongoing scientific investigation will continue to produce new possibilities.

The modern economy is geared to this process of innovation, and innovation is what is rewarded. But this attitude and process are inherently destabilizing. Nothing lasts long and we speak easily of "planned obsolescence." The culture of modernity is inveterately antitradition. The private sphere is especially vulnerable at this point, for the family and religion have been held together by traditions that have survived over long periods. Modernity continually challenges all such structures.

Religion in North American Culture

The path to the secular taken by Western societies has varied.[15] The French variety of secularization has been characterized as doctrinaire and radical. Other societies have managed to modulate secularization's effects somewhat.

In the United States religion seemed to flourish alongside the spreading secularization that accompanied industrialization and urbanization, with the result that warfare between religion and the secular was minimal. But this apparent religious prosperity came at a price. Religion was allowed to play a role so long as it performed its part outside the public square and confined itself to the religious. Public life and civic functions were securely in the grip of the secular. Religion was expected to show its loyalty to the public sphere by being present at civic functions and responding to the needs of individuals.

The founding documents of the United States were suffused with Enlightenment values that have become the basis for forceful rhetoric about the wall of separation between church and state. Ostensibly, the church has been protected from encroachments by the state, but, in fact, it is the secular state that sets the boundaries for the church in relation to society. Before the law all religions are equal, even as all citizens, in theory, are to enjoy equal civil rights.

What was not foreseen two centuries ago when the West was still Christendom was the pluralization that would ensue. In addition to the pervasive cultural pluralism described above, religious pluralism now characterizes many countries in the West.[16] Just as the founders of the United States did not interpret the phrase "all men are created equal" in the comprehensive sense it has acquired in the twentieth century, so the constitutional guarantee of the right of every citizen to decide which religion, or no religion, to practice has had unforeseen implications. This legal and political recognition of all citizens, based on the concept of a secular state that tolerates all religious faiths and establishes none, has effectively relativized and neutralized the authority of religion in the United States.[17]

Heirs of the radical Reformation and free church tradition ought to recognize that this legal and political arrangement is the recipe their spiritual forebears struggled to see adopted by society in the sixteenth and seventeenth centuries. Against a religio-political system that vigorously suppressed religious dissent, they argued for a political order that recognized the rights of individual conscience. To achieve this ideal required that the church be independent of state control.

The promise of the United States and Canada was that freedom of religion would be respected and guaranteed by government. That is to say, this theory of the proper relation between state and religion assumed that a secular state would be religiously neutral and an ally of the free exercise of religious conviction. What was unforeseen was the emergence of a secular ideology as the public philosophy, plus the multiple pluralisms engendered by urbanization, industrialization, and the mass migrations of people using modern means of transportation.

The Evangelical Response to Modern Culture

How have North American evangelicals responded to modernity? The hallmarks of evangelicals have been their fidelity to the Bible, passion for missions and evangelism, and disciplined lifestyle. Evangelicals maintain that they have kept faith with the Reformation, whereas theological liberals have abandoned the historic doctrinal commitment. Evangelicals also tend to be conservative in their social and political views and in their patriotism.[18]

In the 1940s, challenged by leaders like Harold J. Ockenga and Carl F. H. Henry, a new generation of evangelicals began pursuing advanced education with a view toward effective engagement with modernity. The goal was to be able to counter the effects of secularization by meeting modernity on its own ground. In retrospect, James Davison Hunter argues, this move actually undermined evangelicalism. "What began as an enterprise to defend orthodoxy openly and with intellectual integrity may result in the weakening or even the demise of orthodoxy."[19]

This generation of leaders, which has been the teaching force in evangelical colleges and seminaries for nearly fifty years, has breached the boundaries between traditional evangelicalism and the modern world. As a result, evangelical identity is changing. Modern education has proved to be a powerful and elusive counterforce.

Hunter's empirical study of students in evangelical colleges and seminaries in the United States was carried out in the mid-1980s as the Evangelical Academy Project. The study provides useful data for taking stock of evangelical attitudes and reactions.[20] Hunter focused on the cognitive boundaries embraced by self-identified evangelical students in four main areas: theological affirmations; work, morality, and the self; family life and values; and political philosophy and attitudes. We will examine two of these.

Evangelicals have guarded their theological identity by taking a strong stand on the authority of Scripture. The stakes were raised late in the nineteenth century when the concept of inerrancy was introduced.[21] In 1895 A. T. Pierson urged a "Baconian" approach to the interpretation of Scripture, by which he meant a thorough gathering of empirical facts that could then be sorted out and arranged according to general laws. Shortly before this, William Hoyt employed a novel term when he argued that the Bible was "kept inerrant" in every detail. This move paved the way for the fundamentalist hermeneutic based on the notion of inerrancy that dominated conservative Protestantism until after World War II.

While evangelicals have continued to affirm a high view of Scripture, the way biblical inerrancy is understood and applied has been changing. Hunter found that while forty percent of his respondents affirmed that the Bible is the inerrant Word of God, the earlier emphasis on literalism had been replaced by a view that the Bible contains various genres of literature. Each should be interpreted according to principles appropriate to its genre rather than the strict literalism of earlier fundamentalism. As one student put it: "History is to be read as history, metaphor as metaphor, symbol as symbol, parable as parable, and so on. The context of the passage and literary style of the author must be taken into account."[22]

Increasingly, evangelicals have tried to come to terms with the philosophical and methodological issues raised by biblical interpretation. Gradually, the earlier formulation has been modified.

A basic premise of the Christian faith is that men and women can be saved only through faith in Jesus Christ. This is taught by the leading historical confessions of the Christian church. The Westminster Confession affirms that only those who come to Christ are saved:

> [M]uch less can men, not professing the Christian religion, be saved in any other way whatsoever, be they never so diligent to frame their lives according to the light of nature and the law of that religion they do profess; and to assert and maintain that they may is very pernicious, and to be detested.[23]

Historically, the Christian church has understood its mission to the world to be based on this very premise.

But the exclusivism of this Christian claim is deeply offensive to the modern mind. The multiplying pluralisms of the past hundred years have heightened the pressure on Christians to modify this key Christian conviction. As Hunter points out, "Intensive cultural pluralism, one of the hallmarks of the modern world order has, at least in the United States, institutionalized an ethic of toleration and civility."[24]

Evangelical students continue to affirm other traditional convictions: ninety-five percent believe in a place of eternal torment for those who do not place their faith in Jesus Christ, and two-thirds affirm that one gets to heaven only by faith in Jesus Christ. Yet important modifications to doctrines that fundamentalist Christians might have embraced half a century ago are evident. On the question of who will get to heaven, one-third of the students qualified their affirmation that the only hope of reaching heaven is through faith in Christ, to say "except for those who have not had the opportunity to hear of Jesus Christ."[25]

The following statement reflects student response to this doctrine: "I think it would be unfair for those who have not heard of Christ to be sent to hell. What is important in their case is that they have conformed to the law of God as they know it in their hearts."[26]

Evangelical student responses reveal a growing tentativeness about a range of Christian convictions. The students continue to express a readiness to embrace orthodox tenets for themselves but hesitate to affirm that these truths can be regarded as authoritative for all people everywhere. The impact of pluralism is readily evident.

An equally important window through which to view changing evangelical culture is the political. Conservative Protestants have traditionally been politically conservative. When one listens to the popular interpretation of the founding of the United States as told by many evangelicals,[27] there is an intertwining of politics and religion. It is asserted that America was founded on conservative Christian principles held in place by stalwart evangelical forebears.

Hunter's survey demonstrates that the majority of evangelical college and seminary students largely adhered to the conservative political agenda of their parents. The students also were essentially anti-elitist, as were their parents. However, there were important points of difference as well. The students were preoccupied with the moral decline of American culture to a degree their parents were not. Along with this, the "texture of their political orientation" was different. Although still conservative, they were relatively less conservative than their parents. Supporting this was a growing attitude of tolerance toward deviations from the social norm.

This increasing tolerance can be traced to the growing emphasis on civility in modern culture. Not only has religion been displaced as a source of authority in modern society, but this has become widely accepted as the only proper arrangement for the civil order. The basic premise of the modern democratic society is that divergent viewpoints must be tolerated. Hunter summarizes this understanding well:

> Despite any ideological diversity and any attendant hostilities, the civil society remains intact as long as all parties agree to abide by the procedural norms of tolerance of opposing views, respect for civil liberties, and nonviolent, legally prescribed political action and dissent.[28]

The key requirement is to be tolerant of others, for each individual has civil rights. This ethic of civility inculcates gentility and moderation as primary civic virtues. "It speaks of a code of social discourse whereby religious beliefs and political convictions are to be expressed discreetly and tactfully and in most cases, privately."[29] Civility in society is rewarded with social approval; incivility is censured for being disruptive. Civility signifies the standard by which social tranquility is maintained.

The effect of the ethic of civility on religion has been considerable. It has contributed further to the muzzling of religion as a source of influence in society, for religion implies deeply held conviction. Civility requires toleration and noninterference in other people's lives.

The fact that evangelicals have accepted this ethic of civility is reflected in the following statement by a student:

> I like [the Moral Majority's] platform but I don't think they should go about pressuring people the way they do. If they want to say that they are against abortion, for example, they should just make their opinions known. They don't have to go into towns and have massive demonstrations picketing clinics. They should just be strong in their beliefs. . . . They just should not pressure people all the time like Jerry Falwell does.[30]

Such evangelicals do not wish to be identified with the aggressive tactics of the fundamentalists because they regard such behavior uncivil. They have increasingly joined the cultural mainstream by adopting the values of civility that reinforce cultural and structural pluralism.

The Impact of Postmodernity

Any discussion of contemporary culture must take account of the fact that modern culture has continued to evolve and in the twentieth century has reached a new stage. Scholars do not agree. Some argue that we are now in radicalized modernity or hypermodernity. But there is a large literature in many fields devoted to postmodernity, a new cultural stage that emphasizes developments that break with or move beyond the modern.

Zygmunt Bauman has characterized modernity and postmodernity in terms of four features. Modernity is marked by universality, homogeneity, monotony, and clarity. By contrast, postmodernity is defined by institutionalized pluralism, variety, contingency, and ambivalence.

Underlying homogeneity, monotony, and clarity is the Enlightenment emphasis on rationality and its application to all areas of human endeavor, including the rationalization of work represented by assembly line production. Breaking free from the perceived constraints of the modern machine, "the postmodern condition is a site of constant mobility and change."[31]

Bauman goes on to argue that postmodernity "'unbinds' time; weakens the constraining impact of the past and effectively prevents colonization of the future."[32] This has resulted in a postmodern consciousness that has been described as "the homeless mind."[33] Kenneth Gergen, a postmodern psychologist, suggests that the fragmentation of the postmodern life-world into competing parts is leading to "multiphrenia."[34]

Postmodern consciousness is creating a new outlook on religious experience. While religion is regarded positively by postmodern people, notions of truth and absolute claims are offensive to postmodern sensibilities. Postmodern people have been characterized as "seekers,"[35] people on a quest, unabashedly searching for spiritual answers. But it is a quest that assumes cultural and religious pluralism to be normative.[36]

Conclusion

Recent studies of popular opinion demonstrate remarkable congruence between the behavior of self-identified evangelicals and the general population.[37] This can be explained in one of two ways. Either the citizenry as a whole is moving to embrace ethical standards that comport well with biblical norms, or evangelical Christians are becoming so blended with the wider population that there is no discernible difference. This, of course, is the issue raised by Daniel Gordis with reference to the American Jewish community. He argues that it is the religious community that has done the adapting.

It is evident that religious communities that historically defined themselves in contrast to prevailing cultural norms are learning increasingly to be at home with the values and norms of the wider society.[38]

The apostle Paul warned the first Christians against allowing their identity to be determined by "the patterns of this present world" (Rom. 12:2, NIV). A world-shaped identity and convictions will reflect the world's values, not those of God's new order. In other words, the world will decenter—render ineffectual—the church's witness to God's reign.

Modern worldly forces are both subtle and aggressive.[39] A church conformed to this culture will deservedly disappear without anyone knowing or caring.

A faith community can be established and maintained only by a self-consciously affirmed convictional base. The first Christians were formed into a new faith community because they were convinced, against all odds, that Jesus was the Messiah of God who was inaugurating God's own order in the world, here and now. In a world whose religious pluralism easily rivals our own, they were ready to stake all on this conviction.

It is a futile exercise merely to criticize or decry the fact of modernity and postmodernity. The church is never given a choice as to the cultures in which it is called to work out its life and witness. The biblical vision is of the church so centered on its Messiah leader and filled with conviction that it spontaneously and faithfully witnesses to the messianic order in every culture. To do so effectively it must discern the nature of the challenge posed by each particular culture to the reign of God.

Notes

1. Daniel Gordis, "Blending In, American Judaism Finds Itself Without Identity," *Los Angeles Times*, December 31, 1997, B7.

2. Cf. Peter L. Berger, "From the Crisis of Religion to the Crisis of Secularity," in *Religion and America*, ed. Mary Douglas and Stephen M. Tipton (Boston: Beacon Press, 1983), 14-24.

3. William R. Hutchison, *The Modernist Impulse In American Protestantism* (New York: Oxford University Press, 1976).

4. One of the most thorough studies of this phenomenon is Wade Clark Roof and William McKinney, *American Mainline Religion: Its Changing Shape and Future* (New Brunswick, N.J.: Rutgers University Press, 1987). Note especially chapter 7, "The Future of the Mainline."

5. Herbert Butterfield, *Christianity in History* (New York: Scribners, 1949/50), 135.

6. Henri Desroche, *The Sociology of Hope* (London: Routledge and Kegan Paul,

1979; French orig. 1973), 112.

7. Summarized well by Douglas John Hall, *Thinking the Faith* (Minneapolis: Fortress, 1989), 200-201, with reference to the impact on the theological task:

The extremity within which the disciple community in North America finds itself today is not only the end of an age, it is also the end of a long and deeply entrenched form of the church. The single most far-reaching ecclesiastical factor conditioning theological reflection in our time is the effective disestablishment of the Christian religion in the Western world by secular, political, and alternative religious forces.

See also Douglas John Hall, *The End of Christendom and the Future of Christianity* (Valley Forge, Pa.: Trinity Press International, 1997).

8. Colin Gunton, *The One, The Three and the Many* (Cambridge: Cambridge University Press, 1993), 28. Gunton goes on to say:

The functions attributed to God have not been abolished, but shifted--relocated, as they say today. . . . God was no longer needed to account for the coherence and meaning of the world, so that the seat of rationality and meaning became not the world, but human reason and will, which thus *displace* God or the world. When the unifying will of God becomes redundant, or is rejected for a variety of reasons, the focus of the unity of things becomes the rational mind.

9. A point made by Alan J. Roxburgh, *The Missionary Congregation, Leadership, and Liminality* (Harrisburg, Pa.: Trinity Press International, 1997), 10-12.

10. Summarized by James Davison Hunter, *American Evangelicalism: Conservative Religion and the Quandry of Modernity* (New Brunswick, N.J.: Rutgers University Press, 1983), 11-14.

11. One of the most useful accounts is Stephen Toulmin, *Cosmopolis: The Hidden Agenda of Modernity* (New York: The Free Press, 1990).

12. Los Angeles, for example, now has communities of people drawn from 140 nationalities, making it among the most multicultural cities in the world. Yet pluralism in its manifold variety is present in all urbanized cultures.

13. Stephen L. Carter, *The Culture of Disbelief* (New York: Basic Books, 1993), argues this thesis.

14. Anthony Giddens, *The Consequences of Modernity* (Stanford, Calif.: Stanford University Press, 1990), 36.

15. Helpfully described by Martin E. Marty, *The Modern Schism: Three Paths to the Secular* (New York: Harper and Row, 1969).

16. The second largest religious group in several Western European nations today is Islam, and many other religions are present and growing in strength.

17. Marty, 101-118.

18. I speak intentionally of *tendency*. See the warning posted by R. Stephen Warner, "Theoretical Barriers to the Understanding of Evangelical Christianity," *Sociological Analysis* 40, no. 1 (1979): 1-9, against reifying certain analytical constructs that then lead to false findings.

19. James Davison Hunter, *Evangelicalism: The Coming Generation* (Chicago: University of Chicago Press, 1987), 33.

20. Ibid., 3-15. No effort will be made to draw direct correlations with J. Howard Kauffman and Leland Harder, *Anabaptists Four Centuries Later* (Scottdale, Pa.: Herald Press, 1975). General trends and patterns reported by the latter study, carried out a decade earlier, tend to be fairly congruent with Hunter's.

21. George M. Marsden, *Fundamentalism and American Culture* (New York: Oxford University Press, 1980), 56-57.

22. Hunter, *Evangelicalism*, 24 (male respondent, third-year master of divinity candidate, Church of Christ).

23. John H. Leith, ed., *Creeds of the Churches* (Chicago: Aldine Publishing Co., 1963), 206.

24. Hunter, *Evangelicalism*, 34.

25. Ibid., 35.

26. Ibid., 37 (female, senior, sociology major, Independent Fundamentalist).

27. Various evangelical scholars have recently produced studies that tell a quite different story, but this has yet to be accepted by the popular mind.

28. Ibid., 152.

29. Ibid.

30. Ibid., 153 (male, sophomore, history major, nondenominational).

31. Zygmunt Bauman, *Intimations of Postmodernity* (New York: Routledge, 1992), 189.

32. Ibid., 190.

33. See Peter L. Berger, Brigitte Berger, and Hansfried Kellner, *The Homeless Mind: Modernization and Consciousness* (New York: Vintage Books, 1974).

34. Kenneth J. Gergen, *The Saturated Self: Dilemmas of Identity in Contemporary Life* (New York: Basic Books, 1991), 73.

35. Wade Clark Roof, *A Generation of Seekers* (San Francisco: HarperCollins, 1993). Roof studied "baby boomers," but his findings are being applied to Generation X and even younger people.

36. For a perceptive examination of Generation X spirituality by a GenXer, see Tom Beaudoin, *Virtual Faith* (San Francisco: Jossey-Bass, 1998).

37. See, for example, George Barna, "The Sad Truth About Christians and Marriage," *Barna Report*, Premier Issue (1996). Barna reports the rate of divorce to be slightly higher among evangelicals than in the general population.

38. An example of how these external cultural forces operate is illustrated by the film *Amistad*. The filmmaker has deftly edited the story to minimize the role of deeply held and constructive religious convictions by replacing and upstaging a historical figure, evangelical abolitionist Lewis Tappan, with the fictional Theodore Joadson. Cf. Peter T. Chattaway, "Amistad Gives African Americans Their Due, Abolitionists Fare Less Well," *Books and Culture* 4, no. 2 (March/April 1998): 20-21.

39. See Anthony Giddens, op. cit., for an investigation of the long-term effects of modernity.

CHAPTER TEN

The Gospel
and Religions

Calvin E. Shenk

Biblical Perspectives on the Gospel

The New Testament overflows with the good news (gospel). Jesus came proclaiming the good news of the kingdom, curing every disease and every sickness among the people (Matt. 4:23; 9:35). He announced that the kingdom of God had come near and that people should repent and believe the good news (Mark 1:14). Jesus declared that there was good news for the poor, release for captives, recovery of sight for the blind, and freedom for the oppressed (Luke 4:18).

The Gospels both model and urge proclamation of the gospel (Matt. 11:5; 26:13; Mark 13:10; 16:15; Luke 20:1). The book of Acts records announcement of the gospel to Jews as well as to Samaritans (8:25) and Gentiles (14:7; 16:10).

The good news is called the gospel of God (Rom. 1:1; 15:16; 2 Cor. 11:7; 1 Thess. 2:2, 8-9; 1 Tim. 1:11; 1 Peter 4:17), the gospel of his Son (Mark 1:1; Rom. 1:9), and the gospel of Christ (Mark 1:1; Rom. 15:19; 1 Cor. 9:12; 2 Cor. 2:12; 9:13; 10:14; Gal. 1:7; Phil. 1:27; 1 Thess. 3:2). The gospel is described as good news of God's grace (Acts 20:24), peace (Eph. 6:15), truth (Gal. 2:5, 14; Col. 1:5), salvation (Eph. 1:13), light (2 Cor. 4:4), hope (Col. 1:23), and mystery (Eph. 6:19).

Believers are reminded that the gospel is the power of God for salvation to everyone who has faith, to the Jew first and also to the Greek (Rom. 1:16). They are entrusted with the gospel (1 Thess. 2:4) and are to have boldness in making known the gospel (Eph. 6:19). Believers are warned about the consequences of disobedience to the gospel (2 Thess. 1:8; 1 Peter 4:17). They are to suffer for the gospel (2 Tim. 1:8).

171

The Gospel of Jesus Christ

The gospel includes essential themes relevant to other religions. The first of these themes is the good news of the kingdom of God.

Kingdom of God

The kingdom of God is the rule of God inaugurated by Jesus. In Jesus we have the proclamation and presence of the kingdom. As Lesslie Newbigin says, the kingdom has a name and a face.[1] There is no kingdom of God without the king—Jesus. Jesus' words and works were witness to the kingdom "at hand" (Matt. 4:23; 9:35; Mark 1:14-15; Luke 4:43). He actualized the kingdom in his life, death, and resurrection. The kingdom came near in Christ; it will come in fullness when Christ returns.

The church is part of the kingdom movement, a sign and foretaste of the kingdom. The church does not embody the fullness of the kingdom but points to it. Though the kingdom has begun to manifest itself in the church and through the church, the church only partly and imperfectly models the kingdom. If the characteristics of the kingdom are not visible in the church, its witness to Jesus the Christ is invalidated.

When Jesus told us to pray, "Thy Kingdom come, thy will be done in earth, as it is in heaven" (Matt. 6:10, KJV), he implied that Christians can make a difference in the world. Jesus' own modeling of the kingdom suggests that religious, ethical, and social concerns are concerns of kingdom citizens. Jesus invites us to join the kingdom through repentance, new birth, and discipleship. A kingdom view, based on the life of Jesus, enables us to have a broad understanding of witness. As Henry Knight reminds us, "A reductionism occurs when one aspect of God's reign supplants the rest, as has so often happened in recent American history, with evangelism and social action."[2]

While the kingdom and the church are not identical, they should not be separated. Where God reigns, a new redemptive community is formed. Lesslie Newbigin says, ". . . [T]he only hermeneutic of the gospel is a congregation of men and women who believe and live by it."[3] There must be incarnational embodiment of the gospel in the church before the church makes its confession to the religions. The community around Jesus represents the content of witness and functions as an instrument of witness. The particular community witnesses to a universal invitation.

Incarnation of Jesus Christ

Knowledge of God is not merely subjective. The gospel is about events that have happened in history. Salvation is provided by the coming of God in the concrete history of Jesus of Nazareth. At the heart of the gospel is the belief that God is incarnate in a human person—Jesus.

Many Hindus believe the Absolute is impersonal and unknowable or that the impersonal aspects of God transcend the personal aspects of God. But Christians declare that the Absolute is in the person of Christ. By becoming flesh, God showed solidarity with humankind and revealed what God is like. Jesus is Immanuel (God with us). Revelation has come in a person—not just in a text, as in Islam.

Hindus speak of *avatar*, the appearance of God on earth. The god Krishna is considered the most important avatar of the god Vishnu. Though avatar resembles aspects of incarnation, the two concepts are not equivalent. The similarities are superficial. There is no clear dividing line between human and divine in Hindu thought. Avatars are based on mythology and fall short of moral perfection. They are temporary manifestations, and their historicity is not crucial.

The gospel understands revelation to have a focal point in Jesus of Nazareth. Jesus is the center of God's self-disclosure. He is the definitive revelation of God in history. The relation of Jesus to God is not repeatable. It is unique. God's activity in Jesus Christ reveals God's character. In him we see God's self-giving love and grace. Norman Anderson notes, "If God could have *adequately* revealed himself in any other way, how can one possibly believe he would have gone to the almost unbelievable length of the incarnation?"[4]

Carl Braaten insists, "God is never more divine than when he becomes human and never more self-revealing in his true essence, love, than in the death and resurrection of Jesus."[5] Divine love is exhibited in Jesus' person, ministry, and teaching.

Geza Vermes, a Jew, argues that the lifestyle of Jesus differentiated him from his contemporaries and his prophetic predecessors. The prophets spoke on behalf of the poor, defended the widows and the fatherless, and spoke against the wicked, rich, and powerful who exploited others. Jesus went further. He took his stand among the pariahs of the world, those despised by the respectable. Sinners were his table companions and tax collectors and prostitutes his friends.[6]

But Jesus was more than a teacher of divine truth. Jesus' teaching is dependent on his person. Gandhi had high regard for the life and teachings of Jesus but rejected his full claims. Yet one cannot fully understand the teaching without commitment to the teacher. The lifestyle of Jesus, the teaching of Jesus, and the person of Jesus must be held together. Christian faith rests on the person of the founder, not just principles. The gospel calls for personal response to Christ's person.

Though Jesus' teaching and lifestyle are attractive to persons from other religions, there remains resistance in religious communities to the idea that God was incarnate in Christ. A Jewish friend candidly admitted to me, "Incarnation is a scandal to my religion." And most Muslims cannot imagine a transcendent God becoming flesh.

One of my Jewish teachers noted that "Jews say the greatest gift of God is Torah, whereas Christians say the greatest gift of God is God's Son." Cannot we Christians affirm Jesus as the Torah of God (John 1)?

Incarnation is central to the gospel. It is not a myth, as John Hick states.[7] One cannot remove the scandal of the gospel and still have the gospel. Incarnation is a particular event with universal significance.

Suffering and Death of Jesus Christ

The cross is the key to understanding the gospel. In the cross the love of God is seen most clearly.

The message of the cross is that Christ was crucified for us (1 Cor. 1:23; 2:2; Gal. 6:14). The cross challenges human self-sufficiency, shattering arrogance. There is a redemptive character to Jesus' death. Humans cannot save themselves. Conversion is necessary—a change of direction, a transfer of allegiance. Religions emphasize the need for divine self-revelation but not the need for redemption. Christ brought revelation as well as redemption.

The proclamation of Christ crucified was a stumbling block to Jews and foolishness to Gentiles, but to Jews and Gentiles who believed, it was the power of God (1 Cor. 1:23-24). The cross was scandalous and absurd because it was a reversal of the world's order. Yet it is the God of pathos, the one who suffered wounds, who can heal our wounds.

The cross is scandalous because religious people prefer to work out their own salvation. They hope to achieve salvation because of their moral qualities, by doing their duty, by the degree of their illumination, by the merit of their sacrifices, or the depth of their religious commitment.[8]

Yet there are indications that humans feel needy. Hindus are attracted to the god Krishna who manifests aspects of grace. Some Buddhists rely on the assistance of Bodhisattvas or Amida Buddha's gracious assistance.

The cross of Christ is a stumbling block for many religious people because they cannot imagine a God who suffers. Christians believe in a vulnerable God who suffers for and with us. This idea is alien to Hinduism because Ultimate Reality is impersonal. To suggest that the burden of karma could be borne by another seems absurd.

One Buddhist said, "Buddha was superior to Jesus because even though Jesus lived a noble life, he was defeated through death in his battle for righteousness."[9] Muslims insist that a prophet like Jesus would not be abandoned by God to suffer on the cross.

Muslims do not understand Allah as one who suffers or who is involved in human suffering. Islam advocates the use of power rather than resignation in the face of suffering. Mohammed, deciding to fight on behalf of truth, marched toward Mecca. Jesus bowed his head in suffering, resisting the temptation to power.

The cross motivates Christians to take on voluntary suffering, modeling the Suffering Servant. Suffering can mold character. As Agith Fernando notes, suffering can be "positive endurance rather than quiet acceptance."[10] The cross is the model for Christian discipleship, as we declare that we "want to know Christ . . . and the sharing of his sufferings by becoming like him in his death" (Phil. 3:10).

Christians believe the universal lordship of Jesus Christ is related to his life, teaching, suffering, death, and resurrection. According to Phil. 2 he became Lord through self-sacrifice and self-giving, a "kenotic lordship."[11]

The Resurrection of Jesus Christ

Though for many religious people Jesus is remembered as a martyr, for Christians Jesus is remembered as the resurrected one. The supreme act of revelation and redemption is the resurrection of Jesus Christ. His resurrection is an endorsement of his Sonship, incarnation, suffering, and death. The final test of the validity of Jesus' claims was the resurrection. Resurrection confirmed Jesus as Savior and Lord (Matt 28:18; Acts 2:24ff; 4:10; 5:30ff; 17:31; Rom. 1:24). Resurrection provided the foundation for faith. The key message of the early church (Acts 1:22; 4:33; 17:18, 31) was that the promises of the Hebrew Scriptures had been certified in the resurrection.

The gospel of Jesus' death and resurrection for the whole world ultimately separates Christianity from the religions of the world. Clark Pinnock points out, "No one can deny that after the Resurrection the person and work of Christ is described strongly in terms of uniqueness and finality."[12]

Resurrection provides assurance of salvation (Rom. 4:25). Hindus and Buddhists, by contrast, have no assurance of when release from bad karma will come. Islam does not claim assurance of salvation.

Resurrection also promises new life (Rom. 6:45). Believers are empowered (Phil. 3:10) to become a new creation (2 Cor. 5:17). The Christian's deliverance from sin and death is an aspect of resurrection (Eph. 1:19-20). Because Christ was raised from the dead by the glory of the Father, believers are enabled to walk in newness of life (Rom. 6:4).

All religions teach one to be good. But dedicated followers experience frustration because they cannot live up to the ideals. The gospel, however, promises victory over sin and transformation of life.

Christ's resurrection is also the firstfruits guaranteeing our resurrection (1 Cor. 15:20ff). It became obvious to me in studying Jewish Talmud that Judaism is much more vague about "the world to come" than Christian faith is, partly because there is lack of clarity about resurrection. The hope of resurrection is absent in Hinduism and Buddhism, given their belief in reincarnation. For Hindus and Buddhists the possibility of liberation from the cycle of birth and death is uncertain and vague.

Resurrection not only affects the past and the present but has an impact on the future. The incarnation, death, and resurrection of Christ have dealt a blow against sin and evil, thus providing a basis for future hope. The gospel of hope is a sign of God's reign in the present and a pledge of that which is to come.

Resurrection is a hopeful word in the context of other religions. An African Muslim who was converted to Christ was asked why he became a Christian. He replied:

> Well, it's like this. Suppose you were going down a road, and suddenly the road forked in two directions, and you didn't know which way to go; and there at the fork of the road were two men—one dead and one alive—which one would you ask which way to go?[13]

Provisions of the Gospel

The attractiveness of the gospel is seen in the provisions that it promises.

The Gospel of Salvation

The gospel declares that faith in Jesus Christ is the basis for salvation (Acts 16:30-31). Salvation is available through a particular history, but it is offered universally. Stephen Neill said, "In Jesus Christ the turning of God towards the human race, and the turning of the human race towards God, have perfectly met."[14]

In the New Testament, salvation is not earned; it is a gift. God extends grace and mercy through Christ. But this gracious offer is often not heard, not understood, or spurned. Some people do not feel a need for salvation. Others want to achieve it rather than to receive it. Still others argue that there are multiple ways of salvation.

Religions vary in their understanding of salvation. Some religions focus only on this life. Some focus only on eternal life beyond this life. Others understand salvation in terms of this world and the next world.

Paul Clasper, writing from Burma, noted that there one lives amid a variety of the most time-honored religions of humankind. There are many roads that one can follow. But all these different roads have one thing in common. They are marked by the sign, "Save yourself by yourself."[15]

Therevada Buddhism and Zen Buddhism insist that humans can work out their own salvation. Hindus also take responsibility for their own salvation as liberation from space and time. Salvation for Hindus is not from moral guilt but from the human condition. Some Hindus believe that humans are sparks of the divine and not in need of salvation.

While it is true that Bhakti (devotional) Hinduism and Amida Buddhism seem to have elements of grace, such grace often differs from Christian understandings. Bhakti is not aware of sin's burden and does not emphasize forgiveness. Bhakti focuses on union with God and the religious experience of becoming a saint. Amida Buddhism bases its hope for salvation on merit transference from the grace of Amida Buddha.

The gospel reveals the depths of sin and the impossibility of self-justification apart from what God has done in Christ. Acceptance of the gospel demands self-criticism, confession, and repentance. The key to receiving salvation is to give up believing in oneself. We must lose ourselves if we are to find true life. Human effort cannot manipulate divine power or generate new life. We are called to abandon ourselves to God, not to use religions for self-justification.

The Christian gospel offers salvation experienced as grace, redemption, forgiveness, and reconciliation (Eph. 1:7; 2 Cor. 5:19). Though many would like to save themselves, the cross cuts at the heart of human pride. The gospel says humans are helpless but God did not abandon us in that state. Jesus has done what we cannot do for ourselves.

Salvation includes forgiveness of sins. Forgiveness is a creative act opening possibilities for reconciliation. By receiving forgiveness and giving forgiveness, we learn the joy of reconciling love, which makes possible restored relationships with God and with fellow humans. Reconciliation is two-dimensional: we receive it and we minister it to others.

The new covenant in Christ is a covenant of forgiveness (Matt. 26:26-28). Our reception of grace is conditioned by our willingness to extend forgiveness. Our ability to forgive is a sign of having received inward spiritual grace.

The community of Christ is a reconciled and reconciling fellowship. The social implications of reconciliation are crucial in a world torn by ethnic and social strife. The cross is a great equalizer breaking down distinctions between people. Social distinctions such as Jew and Gentile, slave and free, male and female lose their significance in the church.

Salvation results in service to God in active discipleship. We are not simply devotees (as in Hinduism); we are disciples who learn from and follow Christ. We make life's decisions out of love for God and concern for others. We can never fully attain Christian discipleship, but that is its value. The signposts to discipleship always point beyond us. Our self-surrender is never complete. The critics of Jesus had a set of rules which they hoped to keep, but Jesus taught that detailed standards of conduct can be burdensome and that the essence of ethical demands cannot be fulfilled by merely keeping laws.

Yet there is an equal danger. Misunderstanding of the gospel of grace can result in careless living. Hindus frequently say that forgiveness offered by Christ on the cross leads people to live irresponsibly. Forgiveness seems so cheap. A Hindu once told me that he does not believe in "a charge account for sin." He assumed that Christians ask forgiveness and then sin again hoping to "charge it" to Christ." Gandhi thought the Christian idea of grace opened the door to moral license. He cited examples of people who became morally lax after converting to Christianity.[16]

Genuine discipleship refuses to cheapen grace. Newness of life and ethical sensitivity are both part of the gospel.

The Gospel of Truth

The truth of the gospel is affirmed in Galatians 2:5, 14 and Colossians 1:5. Other religions might contain signs of the gospel, e.g., the sacrifice of an innocent lamb in the quest for reconciliation and forgiveness. Some religions even believe in a transcendent creator. However, Christian faith witnesses to something profoundly distinctive. God's true essence is known through the incarnation, crucifixion, and resurrection of Jesus Christ.

The truth of the gospel is expressed in doctrine, in experience, and in action. Formulations do not fully constitute the truth. But neither is lived faith by itself a full expression of truth. Our words and actions together must witness to something beyond our understanding, experience, and practice.

Hendrik Vroom addresses an important question: "Which is the absolute truth—the exegetical truth, the dogmatic truth, or the personal truth?"[17] Vroom says that these should not be set against each other. Rather, we confess in multiple ways that the gospel of Christ is the most profound truth about God, about people, and about the world. This does not mean that Christians or the church possess all the truth. We point people to Christ. Confessing the truth should honor Christ, not engage in boasting about one's own tradition.[18]

Vroom insists that the issue is not whether I am right or you are right, but whether it is true that God is revealed in Jesus in a unique way and whether it is true that God forgives sins of those who repent and seek justice. The question is not whether we are the best believers but whether the Crucified One and Resurrected One is the fullest revelation of God.[19] The conviction that, in Jesus, truth is disclosed more than discovered must energize our witness to religions.

The Gospel of Peace

A Jewish professor from Hebrew University said in class, "Our sages taught us how to deal with enemies, but only Jesus taught us to love enemies." Another professor from that university said, "Christianity surpasses Judaism in its command to love all people." Christians welcome these affirmations, even if our practice is often deficient.

Christians have the opportunity to announce the gospel of peace (Eph. 6:15). But this must be done in peaceful ways. Followers of other religions must not be enemies. The long shadow of Crusades, colonialism, media stereotyping, national enemies, insults, and verbal bashing too often keep the gospel of peace from being understood. Reconciliation with God must produce reconciled relationships and inspire ministries of reconciliation. Even if religions assault Christian faith, we are to love the enemy.

Peace theology can strengthen our witness to other religions. Much judgmentalism and conflict have emerged in interreligious contacts. Our stance must be characterized by servanthood, reconciliation, and defenseless communication. Witness must not be coercive. We must respect the dignity and freedom of others, even if they reject our message. We need to divest ourselves of unfair or illegitimate use of the power of Western culture and nationalism. The power of the gospel is not communicated with power but with weakness.

The lordship of Christ should not make us arrogant. We must guard against religious and cultural self-righteousness. But the opposite of arrogance, vulnerability, does not mean that we soften the message.

There is danger in either intolerance or indifference. We commend the gospel of peace.

The Gospel Engages the Religions

Two dangers Christians face are that (1) we can become over-familiar with the gospel and lose our conviction for its attractiveness, or (2) we may fail to realize the difficulties or resistance that people from other religions have with the gospel.

Christians must regain confidence in the good news. It must be believed, obeyed, and shared. The gospel is not *against* people but *for* people. If the crucified Jesus is alive his story must be told. The gospel is the power of God for salvation, now and in the future. It declares the universality of the kingdom of God for the whole world.

Our witness is most honest when we are candid about our core convictions. Witness is the test of our faith that the gospel is true. It is an expression of faith and thanksgiving.[20] We believe the message of Jesus Christ touches human need. Though it repels it also attracts. For some it is a stumbling block, but for others it is attractive because it responds to the longing of their souls.

Yet we must do more than assert the gospel's claims. We must seriously engage religions at the points of their strengths and their weaknesses. We must address the questions raised by other religions. These questions provide redemptive analogies, points of contact, bridges, or stepping-stones. Those who believe the gospel cannot withdraw from responsible engagement in religious and cultural life. Engagement calls for understanding of religion and its relationship to culture. It also calls for contextualization of the gospel in the world's cultures. The New Testament illustrates how faith in Christ's lordship can take shape in a variety of cultures. We will need to open our eyes to the variety of christologies, as the gospel penetrates cultures.

We announce the gospel, but how it is heard is crucial. Sometimes we confuse the gospel with our culture. Knight addresses this problem when he says, "Cultural accommodation occurs when we become too at home in our particular culture, and begin to transform the gospel in light of our cultural values instead of the reverse."[21]

We live with the temptation to Western superiority. Other religions often point to the moral decay of the West. The gospel must break out of the cultural molds in which we have tried to contain it. By the church's unfaithfulness it becomes a prisoner of its own scandal. Yet as Vroom suggests, "Jesus can't be reproached for the misuse of Christianity and the distortion of his message."[22]

Other religions must be approached with caution and graciousness. Criticism must be balanced with understanding. Sensitivity, respect, and humility in relationships are the conditions that enable others to recognize Christ as Lord. By openness and vulnerability we witness to divine vulnerability. Incarnational love is essential for communication.

We do not promote "our religion" in competition with other religions; we appeal to Jesus, not our religion. We should not pretend that we have a monopoly on God's grace. We point to the one who is utterly gracious. We share the gospel as those who have received the gift of salvation but who are also pilgrims who are learning more and more of God's abundant grace.

Witness is not argument but genuine caring. It is not imposed on another from a sense of compulsion. Arrogance and triumphalism or anxiety and timidity must give way to confident witness.

Assessing Other Religions

We should look for and welcome all signs of God's grace in lives of those who do not know Jesus Christ as Lord. Barth called these signs "parables of the kingdom." Because God is providentially present in the religious histories of all people there are signs of truth in other religions. The New Testament recognizes such awareness of truth at Lystra, Athens, and Rome. To suggest that Christ is the unique salvation of God does not imply that the witness of God is absent in other religions. Religions echo God's activity. This calls for engaging witness, not denial of anything that is true.

We need to meet religions at the level of their experience and knowledge. If there is a universal enlightenment of all people, all people know something of God. God is wrestling with religions. God is behind the quest for God. As Augustine said, "Thou hast made us for thyself and our hearts are restless until they find their rest in thee."

We need to probe what God is doing beyond the walls of the church. Why do Christians want to ignore beauty, truth, and goodness in persons of other religions? Must we make them look bad to strengthen the gospel?

At the same time, there are negative aspects of religions. As Vroom says, "Not everything is good, let alone equally good."[23] The positive in religions is often mixed with the negative, and truth is mixed with error. Religions can be false and evil. They can manifest ignorance, blindness, and rebellion. Religious worldviews are often in conflict with the gospel. They fail precisely in the kinds of salvation they offer.

Religions do not all make the same claims. They are not variations on the same theme. There are differing concepts of God and differing concepts of salvation. There is no generic salvation with different religious labels. Religious pluralism which assumes a common religious experience is seriously flawed.

Religions are best understood not as alternate revelations, but as people's varied responses to God. It is unwise to make judgments about religions in general. Specific encounter is necessary, for without contact with people we don't know how God is working with them. In conversation we understand our agreements and differences. We not only share our personal experiences but probe our understandings of God's purposes in the world. We may agree or disagree on many issues. As we work together and converse together, we discover where our paths converge and where they separate. Here is where conversation about real issues can take place.

As Christians we accept that in other religions which is compatible with Christ and reject that which is contrary to Christ's lordship. Values in other religions can prepare the way for the gospel. We know what God is doing in other religions in the light of Christ. The light of Christ shining on other religions enables us to see meaning there.

Yet while we take seriously what humans have believed and experienced about God before hearing the gospel, the word of the cross is the central norm by which we interpret other religions. In the presence of the cross and the grace of Christ, we are all sinners in need of salvation.

Justification by faith cuts at the root of human pride and self-justification. Faith opens us to the work of God for salvation and achieves that which human effort cannot. Braaten insists, "Sin negates every human capacity to do something on the basis of which to make things right with God."[24] Religions are often the place where humans intensify their rebellion and seek to hide from the judgment of God. Religions find it difficult to let God be God. Indeed, religions are often used as a shield against God.

Witness to Other Religions

Recognizing value in other religions does not diminish the cruciality of Christian witness, which must concentrate on the heart of the gospel, not on the often-flawed historical cultural expression of Christianity. Our witness must hold in tension the presence of God in the religious histories of people and the lordship of Christ. Christ is the light of the world, but not all have been exposed to or are open to the light. As Stanley Grenz points out: "The gospel is the only gift we have to offer our world. More importantly, however, our obedience in announcing the gospel in word and action is the only gift we can offer to God."[25]

Witness must focus the distinctiveness of the particular story of Jesus. The story and events of Christ's life must come before theological statements. Jesus is Lord, and his life and teachings are normative.

We can only engage other religions when we are sure of our norms and convictions. We confess that the particularity of incarnation has universal significance, that the truth revealed in Jesus Christ is for everyone. The confession of Jesus as Lord is more than personal devotion or a private cult; it has universal validity. Charles Van Engen refers to the Christian confession as faith particularist, ecclesiologically inclusivist, and culturally pluralist.[26]

It is misleading to say Christ is my Lord and Savior but not the only Savior. Christians witness to Jesus as God's unique way of providing salvation for the world. The essential difference between the gospel and religion is Christ. Christianity without the gospel at the center is simply generic religion. The church does not claim its own authority but claims the unique authority of Jesus.

Our task in Christian witness is to answer the question, "Who is Jesus?" On the Damascus road Saul asked, "Who are you, Lord?" (Acts 9:5). In answering this question we announce the gospel by letting Jesus' life, suffering, death, and resurrection define the gospel. We must guard against recruiting Jesus for our own causes. Braaten warns, "Like plastic surgeons making over the face of the patient in their own image, Jesus becomes a prisoner of our own fads and fashions."[27]

We often discover that people in other religions want to talk about Jesus. He is more interesting than theological abstractions. Jesus is back on the Jewish agenda. He is often considered a rabbi, miracle worker, or prophet. Muslims have teachings about Jesus as prophet, messenger of God, and servant of God. Jesus has made an important impact on Hinduism. He is considered a yogi, a guru, an avatar, or one of the Hindu pantheon. Gandhi was inspired by the message of Jesus, especially the Sermon on the Mount. Buddhists interpret Jesus in light of their understanding of Buddha and his teachings. Both Jesus and Buddha are seen as wandering preachers with a message of salvation. Both told stories and proverbs and gathered disciples. Both criticized religious tradition.

But who is Jesus? People want to speak of Jesus, but it is *who* Jesus is and *what* Jesus offers that are often rejected. The controversy which he causes has little to do with his moral teaching. The controversy is about *who* he is. Christian witness must engage this question. Almost all the proclamations in the book of Acts are in response to questions asked by those outside the church. The gospel needed to be explained. Religions in our pluralistic environment also raise questions we must respond to. The church must address itself to real questions people are asking.

But truth is not always accepted by assertion of formulas. It must be recognized. Witness should generate recognition of the truth. Kwame Bediako suggests, "Once the point is granted that Christian affirmations about the unique Christ are not assertions, but rather invitations to recognition, it becomes essential to engage the major question: 'What then is it that in Christ confronts us, which calls for recognition?'"[28]

The task of witness is to interact with other religions to bring about an encounter with Christ. The uniqueness of Christ is not a proposition that can be proven true or false by argument from Scripture or tradition. The uniqueness of Christ needs to be demonstrated and recognized in the encounter with other religions.

Sometimes we discover truth already hidden in religion, as insights that partly embody God's intentions for us. We can explore new theological idioms without surrendering Christian content. Spiritual disciplines in other religions may be preparation for Christian spirituality. Ideas of sacrifice in some religions can help explain Christ's sacrifice. Merit transference in Amida Buddhism can point to grace in Christ.

The gospel calls us to focus on the whole humanity and the whole person. Ramachandra said, "The gospel constituted a new category of human being and a new way of being human."[29] The gospel of the kingdom should be announced in word and deed. Debate and conflict about word and deed weakens witness. To set word and deed, preaching and action against each other is absurd. Pronouncements need responsible actions. Words and deeds need to reinforce and interpret each other. The words explain the deeds, and the deeds validate the words.

We need to recover the whole gospel instead of dividing it into parcels. Message and lifestyle can both be subversive as the gospel upsets socioreligious systems. Early believers developed a new social grouping where gender, ethnicity, and economic status were reconciled. Justice and peace in these relationships were not secondary or marginal.

Peace with God and working for peace and justice in the social order are equally important. Though not the same, they both witness to the kingdom. Eternal peace and peace on earth, eternal salvation and social liberation, righteousness of God and justice for the social order are all part of the gospel. Both dimensions are valid and strengthen witness. It is the gospel which holds each dimension together.

Christian witness requires communities of faith that live the gospel. Kenneth Cragg asserts that the "Christ event" must be followed by the "church event." While there can never be a totally Christian community, the church must represent the kingdom. Jesus did not write a book but formed a community.

The engagement between Christian faith and other religions must be mediated by the Holy Spirit. The same Spirit who works in the church is at work in the world. Assurance of resurrection and the continuing presence of the Spirit are part of the theology of Acts. We never know precisely how the truth of the gospel is recognized by people. We only know that it is the sometimes mysterious work of the Spirit as it makes Christ present in the world.

Today there are many questions raised about the gospel. Some equivocate about the gospel and speak of "the myth of Christian uniqueness." Others believe in the truth of the gospel but are reluctant to witness to other religions. But when we surrender the missionary identity of the church and fail to witness to other religions, we are in danger of apostasy and of losing the gospel. We are granted the privilege of announcing the gospel. Let us do it with joy.

Notes

1. Lesslie Newbigin, *The Gospel in a Pluralist Society* (Grand Rapids, Mich.: William B. Eerdmans Publishing Co., 1989), 134.

2. Henry H. Knight III, *A Future for Truth, Evangelical Theology in a Postmodern World* (Nashville, Tenn.: Abingdon Press, 1997), 165.

3. Newbigin, 227.

4. Norman Anderson, *Christianity and the World's Religions: The Challenge of Pluralism* (Downer's Grove: InterVarsity Press, 1984), 139-140.

5. Carl E. Braaten, *No Other Gospel! Christianity among the World's Religions* (Minneapolis: Fortress Press, 1992), 112.

6. Geza Vermes, *Jesus the Jew, A Historian's Reading of the Gospels* (Philadelphia: Fortress Press, 1986), 224.

7. John Hick, ed., *The Myth of God Incarnate* (Philadelphia: Westminster Press, 1977).

8. Anderson, 100.

9. Agith Fernando, *The Supremacy of Christ* (Wheaton, Ill.: Crossway Books, 1995), 149.

10. Ibid., 216.

11. See the chapter by Tom Finger in this volume.

12. Clark H. Pinnock, *A Wideness in God's Mercy, The Finality of Jesus Christ in a World of Religions* (Grand Rapids, Mich.: Zondervan Publishing House, 1992), 60.

13. John T. Semands, *Tell It Well: Communicating the Gospel Across Cultures* (Kansas City: Beacon Hill, 1981), 69.

14. Stephen Neill, *The Supremacy of Jesus* (Downer's Grove, Ill.: InterVarsity Press, 1984), 156.

15. Paul Clasper, *New Life in Christ* (New York: Association Press, 1961), 8-9.

16. Fernando, 180.

17. Hendrik Vroom, *Christian Belief in Dialogue with Buddhism, Hinduism and Islam,* trans. Lucy Jansen (Grand Rapids, Mich.: Eerdmans Publishing Co., 1996), 136.

18. Ibid., 136-137.

19. Ibid., 137-140.

20. Newbigin, 127.

21. Knight, 165.

22. Vroom, 143.

23. Ibid.

24. Braaten, 76.

25. Stanley J. Grenz, "Toward an Evangelical Theology of Religions," *Journal of Ecumenical Studies* 31, nos. 1-2 (1994): 65.

26. Charles Van Engen, *Mission in the Way, Issues in Mission Theology* (Grand Rapids: Baker Books, 1996), 183.

27. Braaten, 88.

28. Kwame Bediako, "The Unique Christ in the Plurality of Religions," in *The Unique Christ in a Pluralistic World,* ed. Bruce J. Nicholls (Grand Rapids: Baker Book House, 1994), 50.

29. Vinoth Ramachandra, *The Recovery of Mission, Beyond the Pluralist Paradigm* (Grand Rapids: Eerdmans, 1996), 226.

CHAPTER ELEVEN

Confident Witness for Cultural Transformation

Linford Stutzman

Around the world, Christianity has transformed cultures. It continues to do so today, even in North America. This chapter is not about hoping that Christianity can make a contribution in pluralism, make peace with pluralism, or win individuals to Christianity in the midst of pluralism. This chapter is about the gospel competing powerfully in pluralism against the cacophony of strident voices proclaiming that which is not good news, voices that promote ideas and worldviews that contradict the vision of the kingdom of God and its righteousness. This chapter is about followers of Jesus—the church—competing for and winning influence in pluralism to transform culture.

Confidence

We Christians in the West must recover the confidence of Jesus and his followers throughout history who have changed the world through their witness. We must recover the vision of the kingdom of God as transforming culture, as filling the whole earth. The kingdom of God, as described by Jesus, is like mustard seed or leaven. It begins to grow, small and unnoticed, and in the process transforms all cultures for the benefit of all humanity. This vision motivated the early Church, the Anabaptists, and others to succeed and to suffer.

Authentic Christian confidence is neither arrogant nor silent. Such confidence was a feature of Jesus' life. As a twelve-year-old boy, Jesus conversed with the learned and explained to his mother why he was doing so. Confidence is evident in Jesus' prophetic acts of cleansing the temple, in private dialogues with seekers of all kinds, in confronting demons, in enduring suffering, and in making promises from the cross. Jesus' confidence consistently elicited powerful responses, either enthusiastic admiration or hatred. His confidence played a central role in his life and ministry that cannot be overlooked.

Consider the impact of the confident claims of Jesus about himself, God, and the kingdom in his context of Jewish religious pluralism and the climate of moral ambiguity and uncertainty this pluralism produced. "I and the Father are one" (John 10:30, NIV). "I am the way, the truth and the life" (John 14:6, TEV). "I am the light of the world" (John 8:12, 9:5). Jesus' unshakable self-understanding shook those who heard these statements, some out of their despair and confusion, others out of their self-assurance and hypocrisy.

The great commission, among other things, can be seen as the basis of Christian confidence in witness that enables Jesus' followers to have powerful effects in the cultures of the world, in all times and places. It is an affirmation of the kind of power derived from confidence that is capable of transforming culture.

Authentic confidence, then, is the confidence that is derived from Jesus' own example of confidence of identity, purpose, and the ultimate success of the kingdom of God in the world. Confidence centers on several related truths that Jesus communicated: first, that Jesus reveals the Creator, God Almighty, ruler of heaven and earth; second, that Jesus is making the kingdom, or reign of God, present in the world now; and third, that this kingdom is not contingent on human or any other kind of resistance. It will ultimately succeed. For those who live on the basis of these unqualified central truths, confidence is reinforced by observation and experience.

The confessions and actions of the early church echoed the confidence of Jesus with similar effects, prompting both hope and retaliation among those who recognized that their witness was indeed "turning the world upside down" (Acts 17:6). Martyrdom was both the result and the demonstration of the confidence accompanying the invasion of the Christian witnesses to the very heart, as well as the peripheries, of the Roman empire.

This pattern of authentic confidence is characteristic of the varieties of Christian movements that produced significant historical shifts. Such confidence is visible in the Anabaptist movement of the sixteenth century. The ability this movement had in gaining strength, momentum, visibility, and social impact has been well documented. The confidence of the leaders, empowering the followers in the movement, has not been as clearly recognized as other factors in explaining the explosive growth of early Anabaptism.

This confidence was sometimes misdirected, resulting in the apocalyptic and moral recklessness of an early Hans Hut or a revolutionary Thomas Müntzer. Yet we must acknowledge the more enduring confidence of the Anabaptists based firmly in the example of Jesus, a confidence displayed by leaders and martyrs, women and men, and even by children. This confidence had a power that shook European society to its very foundation and eventually contributed to the religious freedom of the new world.[1]

In North America, freedom and equality, including religious freedom and dissent, were understood to be self-evident truths—"inalienable rights" that were confidently incorporated into the ethos of the newly independent colonies. This provided a foundation on which the politics and culture of the United States were to be built. Confidence in the truth of these insights has contributed to the growth of a confident and powerful culture that continues to exert positive and negative power throughout the world. For better or worse, this culture is magnetically attractive to youth everywhere.

Missionaries from the United States often display confidence that is derived both from the confidence of the kingdom and the secular confidence of the culture from which they come. My research among evangelical missionaries in Albania from 1994 to 1998[2] demonstrates that confident people exercise power in society, whether this confidence derives from faith in Jesus, from a culture confident that its founding principles are sacred truths, or from a combination of the two.

Confidence is power. Like all power it can be destructive when it is practiced and understood in ways not authentically Christian. History, including church history, is filled with examples. The influence necessary for cultural transformation is partly achieved by the power of confidence. Confidence, especially in cultures undergoing rapid change, in pluralistic and morally ambiguous societies, can be an extremely attractive power.

On the other hand, if Christians lose confidence in their witness in culture, other confident powers fill the vacuum in ways that can also be destructive. Witness without confidence is, like salt without saltiness, good for nothing.

Pluralism is the context in which confidence is challenged. Pluralism, and the related phenomenon of the relativization of truth, erodes the ability of everyone to make universal truth claims. When the church loses its confidence in the message it proclaims, the power of the gospel to transform culture is neutralized. To witness in pluralism, we need to recover the confidence of Jesus and, in so doing, the power of the good news of the kingdom of God—its relevance, its attractiveness, its threats, and its impact.

Witness

With the loss of confidence, Christian apologetics has become an exercise in apologizing for Jesus' radical and powerful message. The church in the context of pluralism must recover the skill and the spirit of the early Christian apologists. Apologetics, if understood and practiced in the manner of Jesus, is a potentially powerful and appropriate tool in pluralism. Debate that sharpens differences rather than dialogue that attempts to synthesize them, the truth of Jesus as a claim in competition with counterclaims rather than in coexistence with them, apologetics rather than apologies, all need to be considered as appropriate for Christian witness in pluralism if Jesus, the early church, and the Anabaptists are taken as seriously as models.

Authentic apologetics is based on Jesus' role as apologist of the kingdom of God. The apologetics of Jesus includes confident affirmation, persuasive confession, powerful demonstration, and relevant argumentation about the presence of the kingdom of God in the context of public life, values, popular opinions, social institutions, and contemporary issues that shape culture. Authentic apologetics is a way of relating, ministering, living, and speaking that results in local change.

Authentic Christian apologetics, following the model of Jesus, is potentially a powerful force in pluralism. Such apologetics evaluates and interprets local human experience in terms of the universal kingdom of God. Authentic apologetics is a confession and application of the truth that Jesus is Lord of all. This affirmation cannot be qualified or diminished for any reason, or it is not authentically Christian.

Authentic apologetics is action that is intentional and public by local congregations in their context, that demonstrates the reality of this confession. This action includes the idea of "performing the kingdom": that is, demonstrating the relevance, appeal, validity, and power of the kingdom deliberately, creatively, and faithfully.

Authentic apologetics is primarily the task of local congregations engaged in their own neighborhoods. It involves social identification as a prophetic actor, rather than a power broker. The local congregation as authentic apologist has the role of a prophet rather than a pundit, a populist rather than an elitist. From this position of identification with those marginalized from institutional power, the local congregation makes the case in its public actions and words that the kingdom of God is, among other things, a way of viewing reality that liberates, explains, offers hope, empowers, and corresponds to the experience of life of those who hunger and thirst for righteousness.[3]

Jesus and the early Christians were apologists in this way. The confidence of Jesus built a community of confidence that embodied the message of the kingdom and changed history. The priesthood of believers as practiced by the early Anabaptists enabled each of the movement's participants to function as an apologist of the kingdom.[4] The Anabaptist community gave purpose, identity, and meaning to the individuals that joined it and promoted publicly the same understandings to all with whom they related. In this way, the kingdom of God as an alternative way of viewing reality became believable and powerfully persuasive.

The same phenomenon is visible in the public apologetics of modern martyr/prophets such as Dorothy Day, Dietrich Bonhoeffer, and Dr. Martin Luther King Jr. These people not only embodied the message of the kingdom of God in a variety of ways relevant to their own situation, but led history-changing social movements toward alternative goals of the kingdom that challenged the status quo of their own culture in powerful ways.

The authenticity of apologetics can be evaluated, in part, by the attitude, or spirit, in which it is engaged. Because the Christian church seems to be so susceptible to the temptation of either triumphalism (abusing its power to achieve positions of control in society) or timidity (neglecting to exercise any power that would jeopardize peaceful coexistence with society), two central characteristics of Jesus' apologetics must be continually affirmed.

The first attitude, which is necessary to resist the temptation of timidity, is a desire to win. While embracing pluralism as the context in which the power of persuasion will be exercised, the authentic apologist does so with the intention of winning. Throughout the gospels and the New Testament record, it is clear that competition is inevitable. There are winners and losers in pluralism. Authentic apologists compete to win.[5]

The second attitude, which is necessary to resist the misuse of power in the spirit of triumphalism, is an acceptance of suffering. The readiness to suffer without retaliation in the midst of resistance and reaction directed against the apologist is a powerful mark of authenticity in Jesus' life and death and in Christian martyrs through the ages. In pluralism, acute suffering often takes the forms of strident and public charges of being intolerant, unloving, judgmental, or arrogant—blasphemy in the context of pluralism. These accusations are equivalent to the false charges of blasphemy made against Jesus to discredit him and his message of the kingdom. The suffering caused by such accusations range from humiliation to violence, and the temptation to either alter the message to minimize these charges or to coercively silence the voices of those who make them is enormous. Jesus did neither. Instead, he suffered on the cross, exposing the true nature of evil behind the religiously correct facade of his accusers.

Cultural Transformation

Western culture is continuously undergoing transformation. Powerful hegemonic voices in pluralism compete against each other with conflicting versions of truth and goodness. The church is but one competing voice among many. The church—or for sake of practical application and theological concreteness, the local congregation—is the community of confident witness for cultural transformation. Using a classical sectarian understanding of church, the local congregation is a prophetic community of strangers and pilgrims in human society, continuing the social movement begun by Jesus towards the coming kingdom. The local congregation is an embodiment of the vision of the kingdom of God and as such is in tension and competition with all other groups of people that have alternative visions and competing agendas. The local congregation is thus an intrusive, powerful presence of the kingdom in society with the potential to transform it.

Does such a presence correspond to the model of Jesus in his society, the early church in the first several centuries, and the Anabaptists in the sixteenth century? I believe it does. One of the difficulties in reconciling sectarian intrusiveness with cultural transformation is that of definition. Either the meaning of cultural transformation is left ambiguous, which ensures that there is no way of ascertaining success or failure, or cultural transformation is so specifically defined, so linked to a particular cultural issue, that it is impossible to reach without coercion. Moreover, because many Christians are on opposite sides of specific issues, such a narrow definition divides the church.

What, then, is cultural transformation? From the parables of the kingdom of God as leaven and as mustard seed, and from Jesus' presentation and demonstration, several negative assertions can be made about the nature of cultural transformation that occurs as the kingdom is voluntarily accepted by people everywhere.

Authentic cultural transformation is never coercive domination. While the church possesses certain "hegemonic assets" that it may powerfully exercise in proclaiming and demonstrating the kingdom of God, these must never be used coercively. Coercion, whether violent or political, is always unauthentic power, for it is antithetical to the model of Jesus and his followers. Cultural transformation is not authentic when the church seeks to silence or eliminate the competition and their agendas through legislation, intimidation, or manipulation.

Although intrinsically connected to cultural transformation, making disciples does not define the extent of the cultural transformation that occurs as the kingdom of God grows in and through the life of the local congregation. Neither is cultural transformation defined completely by making the world a better place through socially relevant and necessary programs of development and reform, although this too is an intrinsic part of it. Finally, cultural transformation is not simply achieving and balancing success between the "spiritual" and the "social" agendas just mentioned.

In positive terms, cultural transformation can be defined as the creation of the conditions in human society for making ongoing progress towards truth, goodness, justice, freedom, or "righteousness of the kingdom of God" which benefits everyone. The vision of the kingdom of God, the prophetic imagination by which the church lives, which it demonstrates and publicly promotes for the good of everyone, provides direction for cultural transformation.

At this point the discussion of cultural transformation often takes polarizing political directions. What is the agenda of the faithful church? Christians divide and align according to the way they answer this question. It is necessary to affirm the primary objective of cultural transformation.

The primary objective of cultural transformation is a transformation of worldview, or the "heart," of human society in general, and of as many individuals in it as possible. The church seeks to achieve powerful social influence to reach that objective. Two concepts need to be defined according to the criteria of authenticity referred to thus far—cultural hegemony[6] and worldview transformation.

Cultural Hegemony

Cultural hegemony includes the ability to convince significant numbers of individuals of a particular view of reality, so that this view gains general acceptance in society, along with the responsibility this view of reality implies. Hegemony is the ability to influence, to exert power of all kinds in a society to achieve this. It can be, but is not necessarily, coercive. Rather, a variety of "hegemonic assets," or tools, are available, whether or not the visionary group is in control of institutional power. Influence exerted by groups with a vision of reality and the future contributes to shifts in the way the world is viewed, resulting in concrete social, political, and cultural change.

While hegemony is not a biblical term, it is a concept demonstrated in Scripture by the prophets in the Old Testament and by Jesus and the early church in the New Testament. All of these demonstrated the power, or hegemony, of a vision of the kingdom of God in culture that successfully countered other, self-interested ideas and visions of the ruling political, religious, and social powers of the day.

Cultural hegemony increases as the ideals of visionaries are powerfully embodied and communicated to those people in society whose life experience correlates with the message of the visionary individual or community. As this successfully attracts public attention and participants, historical hegemonic movements begin to achieve momentum towards a kind of critical mass, capable of social influence far greater than their size might suggest. Cultural hegemony begins to be achieved when accommodation of the visionary group begins to influence cultural perceptions of reality, creating the conditions for eventual shifts in public policy by those in official positions of power.

Cultural hegemony can be seen as successful when the state must accommodate not just the beliefs of the social group exercising power, but of public perceptions that have been influenced by that group. It is not necessary to control or dominate the institutions of power to achieve cultural hegemony. Indeed, cultural hegemony that is achieved through a change of perception of reality is more effective and durable than that achieved through manipulation, control, and coercion through institutions of power.[7]

With this understanding of cultural hegemony, it can be seen that the early church quickly became competitive with the hegemony of the ruling powers. The church did so by transforming the worldview not only of adherents of Christianity but of society on a large scale, to the point that the church could not be ignored. In the persecution that inevitably occurred, the progress towards hegemony continued, for the vision—the way the Christians explained reality and demonstrated the power of truth in their own willingness to die for it—was powerfully attractive and threatening in the empire.

The Transformation of Worldview

What could conceivably be an appropriate goal for Christians seeking cultural hegemony in a postmodern, pluralistic context? What vision of transformation does the church have for our culture? What would our culture look like if the church achieved cultural hegemony?

The transformation of culture begins and ends with the historic confession of the church, "Jesus is Lord." I submit that this confession, if consistently applied, embodied, communicated, and expected, is as revolutionary in pluralism at the close of the twentieth century as it was in the first century in the Roman empire. It is a worldview issue. It is more than that, of course, but it must never be seen as being less than that. The worldview of individuals, and the worldview of culture, when transformed by this reality, provides the foundation for the transformation of life itself.

The confident confession of the truth "Jesus is Lord" by the local congregation and by Christians everywhere in the world, is hegemonic—in direct conflict with all other claims of authority, morality, truth, and power on local and global levels. In the church, we have treated this confession fairly consistently as a *theological* statement, rather than a political and social truth. When limited in this way, the confession is relatively ineffective, both in the church and in the culture in which the church exists. The confession needs to be made visible, relevant, revolutionary, and believable, both in and outside of the church.

The reality of the kingdom is made present in the world beginning with this confession. Broadly understood, this means the same thing in Saudi Arabia, India, New York City, or small-town Virginia. When the reality of the kingdom of God through the witness of the church is broadly recognized in culture, when there is a general "glorifying the Father in heaven" by observing and experiencing the church's good works, this can be seen as constituting worldview transformation and the achievement of cultural hegemony by Jesus' witnesses of the kingdom of God.

Everywhere, the awareness that there is a transcendent, creator God, revealed in Jesus as loving, righteous, merciful, and just, will in the long run have culturally transformative effects. As this worldview increases, so does the potential for transformation. This way of viewing reality offers a powerful and attractive contradiction of other worldviews, if it is embodied and demonstrated in the life of the church.

In a further way, cultural transformation occurs through the recognition by growing numbers that this worldview gives them both meaning and purpose in life, a personal and social responsibility. Many, if not most, of those who assume the view of the reality and superiority of the kingdom of God, as demonstrated and promoted by a faithful church, may never acknowledge the lordship of Jesus in their own lives. Yet the effects of this worldview in culture are good for all, for conditions are created in which increasing numbers of people can legitimately accept the personal salvation in Christ. Conditions also increase for gradual or dramatic improvement for all of society, as the hunger and thirst for righteousness is secularized and incorporated into social policy. Conditions are created for spontaneous "people movements of the Spirit" that have a revolutionary quality about them.[8]

Appropriate Cultural Hegemony

We may now examine the hegemonic assets possessed by the church in the context of Western pluralism and address the question of appropriateness. Not all the power we possess is compatible with the kingdom. Jesus' temptations demonstrate that in making the kingdom of God a reality in the world, the ends do not justify the means. This section will examine the use of natural, human, and cultural power in the struggle for hegemony on the basis of Jesus' model. My conclusions are based on my research among evangelical missionaries in the country of Albania. In this research project, I sought to determine the kinds of power Western missionaries were exercising in their presence and work, and the appropriateness and effectiveness of the powerful hegemonic tools at their disposal.[9]

The faithful church struggling to achieve and exercise authentic cultural hegemony rejects the hegemonic tools of the state and its institutions of coercion to control culture. At the same time, it rejects and undermines the efforts of others seeking cultural hegemony. The authentic church, in the world as Jesus was, recognizes that the kingdom of God cannot be established by any human system. The fullness of the kingdom will be realized in the reign of Jesus alone.

A tempting option for the church is the kind of struggle and exercise of cultural hegemony demonstrated by Marxist revolutionaries. Marxism can be viewed as a secularized version of the kingdom of God, an extremely powerful movement of the twentieth century among populations who hungered and thirsted for righteousness. Marxism provided vast segments of the global population with a clear goal, the confidence of its eventual realization, and a worldview that explained life, raised hope among the masses, and motivated people to work together.

The Marxist worldview had religious dimensions. In the struggle for cultural hegemony, Marxism functioned as a religion and seemed to transform culture. The necessity of resorting to violence to establish this new hegemony, and eventually to repression and coercion to maintain it, was due in part to the fact that many were threatened by Marxist ideals. Many others were not persuaded of its validity, and increasingly those who once were convinced began to recognize Marxism's inadequacy to achieve what it promised.

Despite initial success of revolutions, or revolutionary changes at the ballot box, Marxism as an adequate ideology at the worldview level continues to be discredited. If a revolutionary theory is not eventually historically verifiable, it will not continue to have the power to transform cultures on a worldview level but must be enforced coercively. This ensures that sooner or later it will fail to maintain cultural hegemony.

This is as true for Christianity as for Marxism. The demonstration of the validity of the truth of the kingdom of God, the embodiment of the good news of the kingdom, is the power of the gospel, both as salvation to all those who believe and as positive influence to all those who live in a culture being transformed on a worldview level. The use of coercion indicates a failure of the power of the gospel as Jesus modeled and taught it.

To repeat a point made earlier, coercion is antithetical to the message of the kingdom. This is true whether the coercion is direct, through the use or threat of violence, or indirect, through manipulation of the cultural apparatus of influence.

The power of the kingdom is related to the truth of its ideals. When embodied and realized, it has the power to be sustained despite temporary setbacks, repression, and violence. The power of the kingdom that is authentic in all times and places, then, remains essentially that which Jesus exercised in his life and teaching in Palestine: never exercising coercive control in society, never inflicting punishment on others but rather absorbing it, transforming suffering into affirmation of truth of claims, never arriving, always on the way toward final salvation of all peoples in the future kingdom of God.

Pluralism is not the enemy, for in the conditions of pluralism the church can be faithful and effective. When pluralism is idealized as an alternative to the kingdom of God, when Christian witness is neutralized in it, then the presuppositions on which this view is built are appropriate to discredit. Yet the God revealed in Jesus does not violate the freedoms of others to establish the kingdom.

Following the model of Jesus, Christianity has at its disposal in the establishment of cultural hegemony the tools of persuasion, confrontation, reasoning, application, interpretation, education, use of symbols, and denunciation. Engaging in public discussion, interpreting history, and explaining events in light of the kingdom: all are authentic means of power in a free society. These activities are not only guaranteed for all in the context of pluralism but are demonstrated and recommended by Jesus himself to his followers.

The prophetic role is socially powerful in the ways just listed. The popularity of the prophet among the common people, who begin to act in accordance with the new truths in the manner that the prophet embodies them, begins to gather momentum as a movement. Although the prophet and the people who follow are acting locally, they understand their actions in terms of a global and ultimate vision. This remains the primary function of the local congregation in terms of cultural hegemony and is applicable anywhere in the world, especially in conditions of pluralism.

Let us examine several possibilities for the local congregation to exercise hegemony. One option can be referred to as "prophetic performance." Performance, referring to communication and entertainment in pluralism, is a powerful medium of influence on a worldview level, for the performer symbolizes the ideals which are being communicated and are connecting in some way with those of the audience. We talk of performers achieving "god-like status" whose fans "worship" them, not only by buying their records but by emulating their styles, speech, and actions.

Performers in pluralism give meaning, identity, and purpose to those who hunger and thirst for these. The answers performers give range across the spectrum of good and evil, from ignorant to intelligent. While performance is always an act, some performers are less hypocritical than others. While some perform messages of revolution, they are staunch defenders of the status quo in their private lives. Others perform messages of integrity and wholeness, while their own lives are in shambles.

Christians who are authentic performers, like Jesus and the Old Testament prophets, possess incredible power. Billy Graham, Mother Teresa, and Tony Campolo are examples of authentic performers who influence not only Christians but world leaders. They do so without compromising their message of the kingdom.

The power of Christians in the local congregation to be prophetic performers for kingdom is in the complete correspondence between performance and life. The message and the medium are one. Prophetic performance makes worldview clear and thus both attractive or threatening depending on the position of the recipients in relation to the message. The clarity of the prophetic performer persuades, convinces, and shocks, as is demonstrated in Jesus cleansing the temple, calling Zacchaeus down from the tree to go to his house for a meal, healing on the Sabbath, preaching from a boat, feeding the five thousand, or conversing with a Samaritan woman of questionable reputation.

The performances of the kingdom occur in authentic, attractive ways, entertaining the crowds and upsetting the hypocritical performers of the traditional and official religious leaders. As in Jesus' day, the excitement, the rumors, and the story telling spread the news. Interest builds, prejudices collapse, and general attitudes begin to change.

Several current options are vastly underused by local congregations in our culture. One is the media. While some costly attempts have been made with inconclusive results, it is not direct control of the media that is a reasonable objective. Rather, an appropriate goal is gaining coverage and exposure, through the media, of newsworthy demonstrations of the kingdom of God by the local church. Cultural hegemony does not occur by the congregation getting its own cable program, but when the congregation begins doing things that make the news, whether dramatically doing some unusually creative good or publicly resisting evil.

Local congregations need to learn to translate the good news of the kingdom into the language of contemporary culture in ways that attract attention and make an impact through the power of truth demonstrated as good. The church can no longer make assertions that it cannot defend in the arena of public debate. The church must learn to be prophetically correct rather than politically correct in making convincing historical, sociological, and demonstrable cases that unity in Christ is more desirable than tolerance of diversity, that forgiveness and healing are superior to alleviating guilt through popular consensus. The church must strive to make the vision of the kingdom connect to life as experienced, especially by the marginalized, using old symbols in new ways, exposing hypocrisy, and challenging conventional wisdom, to the delight of the common people and the consternation of the official intellectuals.[10]

Another hegemonic asset that is emerging and needs to be deliberately appropriated is the ability to form networks. In pluralism, unity and solidarity in diversity provide a demonstration not only of power but of the credibility of the agenda that a diverse group has in common.[11] The structure of hegemony in the future will not be centralization, or even organizational unity. Structure is important, but mobilization for movement, for flexibility, and for increased responsibility must occur. This must replace centralization and bureaucratization, which offer the sensation of power but make that power increasingly irrelevant in the culture by using so much energy to maintain the structure itself.

The principle of kingdom structures originates with Jesus himself, who declared that his kingdom was not of this world. It is not even in control of itself but is empowered by the Spirit. The Spirit continually leads the church into dangerous encounters with the opposition, mobilizes it for invasion, equips it for confrontation with evil, and in the process allows the church to be scattered, to suffer public scrutiny and humiliation, as well as irresistible success. The institutional structures of our churches deserve to flourish only if they are relevant and authentic in the work of the kingdom in the world. They need to adapt to the realities of pluralism with the sole purpose of making the kingdom real, attractive, and powerful.

Jesus told his followers, "By this everyone will know that you are my disciples, if you have love for one another" (John 13:35). In pluralism, the power of cooperation demonstrates an application of this assertion of Jesus. It is worth noting that Jesus did not say that this would necessarily result in people becoming Christians, although that certainly is included, but that people would become convinced on a large scale about the validity of the worldview. This is the goal of cultural hegemony that provides the conditions for cultural transformation.

I want to end with an additional reason I believe that the good news of the kingdom is inherently at home in pluralism, why it is good news for postmodern culture. This has to do with the fact that authentic power of the kingdom not only rejects coercion as an option for itself but rejects and opposes the use of coercion for worldview change or maintenance by any group. This idea, which underlies the U.S. Bill of Rights and modern understandings of free speech, religious freedom, and the separation of church and state, can be seen as originating with Jesus. It was asserted at great cost by the Anabaptists. The good news of the kingdom of God, if authentically exercised in power, is good for all, even those who reject, oppose, and compete against it.

The struggle for cultural hegemony for cultural transformation should not be confused with the familiar culture war on the level of issues such as abortion and homosexuality. These issues divide liberal and conservative Christians from each other while uniting them in opposing camps with non-Christian social groups. Rather, the struggle for hegemony is a culture war on the worldview level. The historical and unifying confession of the church that "Jesus is Lord" must remain the basis of united struggle for hegemony.

Conclusion

Local congregations around the world, especially in the context of pluralism, are seeing their influence on a worldview level decline. In the context of pluralism, alternatives to the good news of the kingdom of God are successfully competing with the gospel and seem to be achieving cultural hegemony. In this context, local congregations lose confidence and their witness becomes weakened. Self-preservation or congregational growth increasingly shapes their agenda in their society.

The power of the kingdom of God to transform culture is realized through the faithfulness of the local church in being authentic in its struggle for cultural hegemony—that is, the power of the kingdom of God, exercised in the world in the way of Jesus, visible in the early church and many subsequent movements of suffering and victory until the present. May we pray, participate, and witness with confidence to the truth of Jesus' prayer: "Thy Kingdom come, thy will be done in earth, as it is in heaven" (Matt. 6:10, KJV).

Notes

1. In his book *Brothers in Christ*, trans. Joseph Nordenhang (Scottdale, Pa.: Herald Press, 1961), Fritz Blank relates incidents that demonstrate the confidence that motivated women and even children to confront the religious and secular authorities on the basis of their understanding of Scripture. Blank writes: "In June, 1525 a peculiar procession wends its way toward Zurich--men, women, and children. . . . They are . . . from the farms of Zollikon. They proceed through the lanes and squares of Zurich. . . . They call the inhabitants of Zurich to repentance . . ." (p. 60).

2. This research formed the empirical basis of my dissertation, "Antonio Gramsci's Theory of Cultural Hegemony Applied to Evangelical Missions in Albania" (Ph.D. diss., The Catholic University of America, 1997). See pages 133-134, in which confidence as a hegemonic asset is discussed.

3. This chapter's analysis of visionary leadership owes to the writings of Marxist theorist Antonio Gramsci. For Gramsci's argument, see *Selections from the Prison Notebooks of Antonio Gramsci*, ed. G. Hoare and G. N. Smith (New York: International Publishers, 1971), 5-14. For a discussion and analysis of Gramsci's central concept of cultural hegemony, see T. J. Jackson Lears' article, "The Concept of Cultural Hegemony: Problems and Possibilities," *The American Historical Review* 90 (June 1985): 567.

4. John Howard Yoder wrote, in "The Hermeneutics of the Anabaptists,"*Men-*

nonite Quarterly Review 41, no. 4 (October 1967): 301, "The first implication of this conception of the congregation listening to the Word of God is that the common man becomes a full member of the church . . . thus placing theological authority in the hands of the congregation. . . . "

5. Walter Wink points out that in the metaphorical language used to describe spiritual weapons, Paul is assuming an offensive engagement with the powers, not merely defensive action. Paul, Wink notes, "depicts the church taking the fight to the enemy, and *he expects the church to win.*" In *Naming the Powers: The Language of Power in the New Testament* (Philadelphia: Fortress Press, 1984), 88. Emphasis in the original.

6. The term "cultural hegemony" is admittedly problematic, for it seems to connote domination, coercion, intimidation, triumphalism, and other un-Christlike exercises of power. However, if we take a primary definition of hegemony as the achievement of powerful social influence, and if we carefully reference this to the model of Jesus and New Testament concepts of the kingdom of God, this term allows the social influence of Jesus' followers to be compared and contrasted to that of other social groups that are seeking to influence society.

7. See Michel Foucault's description of the superiority of "strong power" (the power to attract) over "weak power" (the power to coerce). Strong power is more effective than weak power, in that the ideas and arguments presented by those exercising it are clearly "natural" and right. See *Discipline and Punish: The Birth of the Prison* (New York: Vintage, 1979), 27.

8. The Wesleyan revivals, the American Awakening, and the preaching of Dr. Martin Luther King Jr., are examples of religious events that had significant social impact. For a more thorough discussion of the concept of the Anabaptist movement as comprising a "people movement of the Spirit," see chapter 4 of my book *With Jesus in the World* (Scottdale, Pa.: Herald Press, 1992), 72-86.

9. This research was conducted from 1994 to 1998 among evangelical missionaries, Albanian Christians, and others among both the expatriate and Albanian populations. My dissertation, cited above, was based on this case study of hegemony.

10. Gramsci describes this as the work of "organic intellectuals," who connect new, superior truth with the common sense of those people struggling to cope with life that is difficult and in which traditional answers are unsatisfactory, irrelevant, and oppressive. See Gramsci, *Selections*, 330.

11. My research in Albania among evangelical missionaries demonstrates the power of networking. See pages 140-142 of my dissertation, op. cit.

CHAPTER TWELVE

Confessing Truth in a Pluralistic World

Thomas Finger

The Current Cultural Climate

During the last twenty years or so, a swiftly spreading tide of relativism has been sweeping over the Western world. In its most extreme forms, it is espoused by academic elites who seem to take special delight in challenging as many traditional beliefs, and in promoting as unconventional an array of behaviors, as possible. Yet these efforts cannot be dismissed simply as intellectual fads. For their proponents are articulating, even if sometimes in sensational fashion, an orientation towards life that influences increasing numbers of people around the globe. Many church members have been significantly affected by it.

A basic claim of this outlook is that it is impossible to make statements about reality[1] that are universally true—true for all people everywhere. For whatever any individual or group of people perceives to be true about reality is so conditioned by particular experiences, interests, and limitations that it can be valid only for those who share their specific vantage point. Nowhere is this claim more emphatically stressed, and even celebrated, than by many individuals and circles that call themselves "postmodern."

Postmodernism is usually contrasted sharply with "modernism," which attained clear expression in the Enlightenment. Modernism involved the effort to erect all knowledge on foundations that were universally true, so that nature and society might be transformed on the basis of knowledge that would be as certain as possible. One such universal foundational truth was the proposition that "all men are created equal, with inalienable rights to life, liberty, and the pursuit of happi-

203

ness." Postmodern critics, however, often critique such features of this affirmation as the following.

First, in many forms, the list of such rights included property. Thus, postmodernists complain, this general list sanctioned the tendency for individuals to accumulate as much property and wealth as possible, unhindered by limitations that safeguarded the larger community. Second, these rights were limited literally to "men" and, in fact, only to adult, propertied ones. Women were excluded. In the United States, a slave counted as only three-fifths of a person, while native Americans were ignored. Third, because the Western world considered itself to be the most advanced in affirming universal truths, westerners could regard their civilization as superior to other cultures. This sanctioned the colonization and exploitation of other peoples in the name of progress. Cultures which seemingly did not recognize such truths could justifiably be forced to submit to the Western vanguard.

Many postmodernists reject affirmations of universal truth and champion the expression of very diverse kinds of truth claims to avoid these kinds of oppression and imperialism. They encourage the expression of beliefs of groups that have historically been oppressed by white Western males. Only if the pretensions of any culture to universal truth are undermined, they insist, will real equality, reciprocity, and mutual enrichment be possible among races, nations, cultures, and genders.

Anabaptists need to be careful about how they evaluate the relativistic claims of postmodernism. On one hand, Anabaptists have tended to regard their beliefs about Jesus as universally true. Seen from this angle, postmodernism appears as an opponent. Yet on the other hand, universal truths have apparently been vehicles for imperialism and inequality. Jesus, Anabaptists, and others who have experienced oppression have strongly opposed such misuse of "truth."

In any case, the issue of universal truth claims cannot be dismissed as simply an academic matter. Whether, or in what sense, we regard our beliefs as universally true has much to do with how we express our faith to persons of different cultures, and with our social, cultural, and economic dealings with them.

Truth Claims in Contemporary Theology

Many theologians today are stressing the particularity of Christian truth claims. Anabaptists might well regard current discussions of this issue with an ambivalence similar to that aroused by the postmodern challenge. On one hand, this emphasis might seem to counter their traditional universalist understandings. Indeed, some theologians are doing this to reduce the ultimacy of the gospel; to claim that it is merely a culturally conditioned expression, perhaps of basic truths which all religions share, or perhaps of beliefs quite different from those of other religions.[2] On the other hand, many who emphasize the cultural shaping of all truth claims are concerned to emphasize the uniqueness of the gospel. This is being done by various theologians who regard themselves as "post-liberal" or "narrative theologians." Perhaps the best known among these who are close to Anabaptism are the Methodists Stanley Hauerwas and James McClendon, and Nancey Murphy, currently of the Church of the Brethren.

This second group is concerned that many theologians, in their desire to be culturally relevant, may not really be emphasizing a distinct Christian orientation to life but viewpoints which are widely accepted in modern culture. For instance, some liberal theologians base their accounts of personal development on theories stressing the kind of self-actualization and autonomy idealized in our individualistic society.[3] On the other hand, conservative Christians often base their understandings of Christian social behavior on the assumptions of market capitalism. In both cases, Hauerwas and others complain, what Western people mistakenly regard as universally true is providing the foundation for theology, while what is unique to the gospel is being minimized. In order both to expose the cultural relativism of such views and to emphasize the gospel's particularity, such theologians challenge the notion of universal foundational truths. Whatever one thinks of this strategy, its motives should resonate with Anabaptists, who have stressed that following Christ results in a critique of the prevailing culture.

Antifoundationalist theologians like Hauerwas, McClendon, and Murphy seek to emphasize not universal beliefs or ethical principles on which all can purportedly agree, but those derived from Jesus' distinctive way and teaching. In discussing the Christian life, they stress development of character, which involves practicing what ethicists call the virtues. However, character and specific virtues can be nurtured only in communities that emphasize particular behaviors and are guided by certain historic understandings. These understandings will be rooted in the narratives, or stories, of how such communities originated and have survived. Accordingly, the beliefs and practices of such communities, including Christian ones, will be rooted largely in tradition and authority, not in rational judgments as to what is universally true.

This means that in conversations among adherents of world religions, participants ought not to first search for common truths on which they can all agree as foundations for dialogue. Instead, each person or faith community should simply tell their own story, unperturbed by how odd it may sound to others. Antifoundationalist theologians are not worried about letting significant differences among religions remain. At the same time, they assume that in such conversations, certain similarities will also emerge.

Antifoundationalist theologians, then, oppose the practice of grounding theology in philosophical or purely rational concepts or arguments alleged to be valid for all people. Nonetheless, many of them employ philosophy in a more paradoxical manner. To support their own procedure, they often rehearse antifoundationalist arguments from philosophers themselves. In this strange fashion, their antiphilosophical theologies seem to be supported by a certain kind of philosophical foundation. Moreover, the arguments they rehearse are taken by some philosophers as evidence for relativism—for the invalidity of all claims to universal truth.

Since I am dealing with the intellectual issues surrounding universal truth claims, it will be helpful to consider briefly two such arguments often enlisted by antifoundationalist philosophers and theologians.[4] The first aims to refute the modernist belief that one can speak with certainty, and thus universality, if one's statements are grounded in undisputed empirical facts and consist only of implications carefully drawn from these facts. This belief assumes that it is possible to identify certain bare, hard-core facts that are distinct from any kind of interpretation.

Antifoundationalists argue, however, that it is impossible to discover or speak of any fact without perceiving or describing it through some kind of interpretive scheme. For instance, it might seem that scientific observation is surely in touch with bare, uninterpreted facts. Yet consider the kinds of sensory data that scientists commonly observe, such as blips on radar screens or globules on microscopic plates. One must know extensive interpretive theory to even recognize what one is seeing. And if theories concerning the significance of those blips or globs change, so will the most basic apprehension of what one observes.

Still, it might be thought that if one could describe one's sense perceptions in their rawest form, one could point to some facts on which all possible observers would have to agree. Suppose I describe a given perception simply by saying, "Here is a red circle." Would not all other observers affirm that they saw the same thing, and could not some universally agreed-on truths be based on data like this?

Antifoundationalists would object that the distinctions I make between, say, red and orange, and between a circle and an ellipse, depend on an interpretive scheme learned from my culture. Other cultures divide up colors and shapes in different ways. Consequently, their members would describe this basic experience differently than I. Thus, antifoundationalists conclude, "We cannot build knowledge on a foundation of uninterpreted sense-data, because we cannot know particular sense-data in isolation from the conceptual schemes we use to organize them."[5] In this way they reject the possibility of finding in sensory experience some undisputed foundation for universal truths.

A second common argument challenging universal truth claims concerns "incommensurability." This issue arises in science, an area many people suppose enjoys the firmest claim to universal truth. Philosophers have recognized that in various historical periods, science operates according to different "paradigms," or overarching views, of how the universe operates and what composes it. Major transitions in science take place through dramatic "paradigm shifts."[6]

Under the Newtonian paradigm, for instance, it was assumed that matter is ultimately composed of minute particles whose exact position and momentum can be plotted, at least in theory, by means of precise spatiotemporal coordinates. This paradigm, however, was replaced by the Einsteinian, in which it was recognized that the very nature of matter's smallest entities makes it impossible to tell whether they are waves or particles and to designate particular locations for each of them.[7]

This paradigm shift raised great problems. For according to the Newtonian paradigm, scientific truth could be established when the location and momentum of individual particles and forces, or aggregates of them, were identified and measured. But what happens when the smallest entities can neither be unequivocally identified as particles nor assigned to particular places? How should science speak of them, and what criteria will now determine whether these statements are true or false? The major point is that such questions were answered only as work suggested by the new paradigm proceeded and as the particular characteristics of its phenomena became better understood. Only in light of a new way of seeing things can it be decided what kinds of explanation are best suited to a new paradigm. In other words, criteria for determining truth and falsity in science depend significantly on which paradigm is being followed.

This means that Newtonian criteria for good scientific explanation, which are shaped significantly by the Newtonian way of seeing things, cannot be directly translated into—are not "commensurable" with—Einsteinian criteria for good science. Each paradigm, in other words, has its own criteria.

In a general sense, of course, one can specify criteria which any good scientific paradigm will exhibit: accuracy, comprehensiveness, simplicity, predictive fruitfulness, and the like. Yet these are extremely general. It is not possible to specify exactly what accuracy, say, might mean when the smallest entities are no longer particles until considerable work guided by an appropriate paradigm has been done.

What are the implications of this incommensurability among paradigms for the issue of universal truth claims? Simply that even in science far-reaching changes in foundational concepts and in truth criteria occur. Scientific notions of truth are at least somewhat conditioned by the state of scientific knowledge at the time and by other intellectual and cultural factors that enter into the fashioning of paradigms. Science at any one stage does not seem able to definitively establish any unshakable universal truth. (Strangely, however, this does not stop science from seeking, nor from progressing to some extent toward, greater truth.)

Antifoundationalist theologians often endorse philosophical arguments of this sort. Yet while such arguments at least question the entire possibility of universal truth, these theologians usually want their Christian theological claims to be understood, as they traditionally have been, as universally true.[8] I can appreciate their desire to stress the distinctiveness of Christian faith and to avoid grounding theology in current cultural values masquerading as universal ones. Yet in accepting antifoundationalist arguments so readily, do they not raise unanswered questions as to why anyone should regard their own theological affirmations as universally true? In a culture increasingly pervaded by postmodernism, do they not risk being understood as reducing the gospel itself to one more culturally relative preference? In short, if they oppose modernity mainly in this way, do they not risk losing the global significance of the very thing with which they wish to challenge it—the saving lordship of Jesus Christ?

Since I believe these dangers are real, I want to engage the postmodern sentiment against universal truths more fully than these theologians usually do. I want to suggest a way in which antifoundationalism can be generally affirmed, but its possible anti-universal implications rejected.

Postmodernism and Universal Truth

Both postmodernists and antifoundationalist theologians challenge the notion of universal truth. This seems to clash with Anabaptism's traditional understanding of the gospel. Let us remember, however, that they do so largely to resist the culturally oppressive way in which alleged universal truths can function and to open up conversations which include marginalized voices. This seems congruent with Anabaptism's intention.

I believe postmodernism can be challenged not only on the basis of Christian theological presuppositions but by examining the internal consistency of its own claims. Essentially, it can be argued that postmodernism's general rejection of universal truth is inconsistent, for the notion of universality is in fact presupposed in some of the basic arguments postmodernists make against it and underlies some of their most important reasons for making these arguments. In other words, postmodernists' acceptance of some notion of universal truth is a condition of the very possibility of their arguing against it. If postmodernists were not tacitly presupposing what they claim to deny, they could not make such arguments in the first place.

I find the common postmodern rejection of universal truth inconsistent in three main ways. First is the often recognized but seldom emphasized fact that any statement that seeks to categorically deny universal truth or affirm complete relativism contradicts itself. To say that it is impossible to make statements about reality that are universally true is to affirm a universal truth: that, among all statements that could ever be uttered about reality, all those that claim universality are false. This statement attempts to do what it says cannot be done—to utter a universal truth. One might say that while it *intends* to be entirely, or universally, true, its particular content which denies that universality contradicts this basic intention.

Postmodernists can also say, as I paraphrase them, that whatever any individual or group of people perceives to be true about reality is so conditioned by particular experiences, interests, and limitations that it can be valid only for those who share their specific vantage-point. This statement also intends to state something universally true: that all human perceptions are shaped by factors which keep them from being universally true. Yet the statement itself expresses the perception of some human individual or group about reality. Once again we observe a contradiction between the statement's basic intention (to affirm something universally) and its particular content (which denies that this is possible).

Something strange is occurring in such utterances. Postmodernists seek to insist that knowledge is inescapably limited to the knower's particular context, yet they can do so only by attempting to stretch beyond that context and affirm something about all knowledge in all contexts whatsoever. If our knowledge really is wholly limited to our own context, whence comes our ability to rise above it and even *intend* to compare it with all others? Perhaps we are not only embedded in our cultural contexts but also in some way beyond them, and maybe in a certain sense beyond all of them.[9]

Second, remember that postmodernists reject claims to universality largely to undermine the oppressive effects that such claims can have when wielded by dominant groups and to open up conversations among all kinds of voices. Perhaps no ideal is more lauded by postmodernism than the vision of authentic, uncoerced conversation, and eventually cooperation, among all social, cultural, racial, and gender groups.[10] Much of postmodernism's considerable rhetorical force emerges in protests that modernism has denied this or that group its freedom or its voice.

This ideal of open conversation, however, along with corresponding critiques of its absence, implies that certain universal values and rights are assumed to belong to all persons. It tacitly presupposes that every person's voice and experience is valuable and that every person has the right to be respected and to be heard in free, uncoerced dialogue. The assumption that equal rights and dignity belong universally to each person is a necessary, even if unrecognized, condition of the possibility of such conversations and also of criticisms of the oppressive function of universal truths.

I would even suggest that perhaps the criticized modernist notion of the equal rights of all persons to life, liberty, and the pursuit of happiness may express some of these underlying values. To be sure, use of this principle in the past has been accompanied by the exclusion of certain groups and by Western domination. Yet over time, the inner, universal meaning of this principle itself may have criticized such arbitrary limitations, until today this notion of equality actually underlies much of postmodernism's critique of modernism. To the extent that this is so, postmodernism represents the culmination, rather than a rejection, of modernism.

Although profound notions of universal equality underlie the postmodern emphasis on conversation, I acknowledge that their exact meaning and significance can emerge only as such interchanges occur. For instance, it is often not evident what speaking privileges should be exercised by formerly marginalized voices. Should they be allowed to speak far more often than traditionally dominant voices? A little more often? Less often? In addition, it is difficult to know how to include voices which resist some notions of equality. For instance, are men allowed to speak who, on principle, deny equal time to women?

Only as such dialogues proceed will the nature of the equality that they presuppose become clearer. Nevertheless, if some universal rights and values are not embraced beforehand—even if mostly as goals to be actualized, as obscure yet powerful hopes for what someday might attain partial realization—such conversations can never begin.

Third, notice another feature of authentic conversation. My views might be very different from yours on many subjects. Yet if we truly wish to communicate, we both must be willing to let our views be revised or critiqued. I have to acknowledge that as you express your beliefs, you might present arguments based on truth criteria which I could accept and which would obligate me to change my views. And you must acknowledge that I could mention truth criteria which would cause you to change yours. In fact, if our discussion is to produce greater agreement, we must be searching, even if only half-consciously, for some standards of truth on which we can concur and in light of which we can draw compatible conclusions.

Now let this dialogue widen to conversation among many diverse partners—to the kind valued by postmodernists. If communication is to occur here, these heterogeneous persons must also search for broad truth criteria in terms of which they too might come to agree. All participants must be committed to revising their views in light of such criteria, with conversation likely to continue only if such can be found.

Let us suppose that this conversation keeps expanding to include more and more kinds of people. As long as the participants are seeking better understanding, they will keep searching for broader truth criteria acceptable to all and commit themselves to altering their perspectives in accordance with them. Ultimately, sincere partners will be willing to accept truths and truth criteria acceptable to all, if such can be found.

To be sure, such participants will likely find that they differ on many things, but conversation will probably not continue unless they are also discovering some deeper agreements. My basic point is that in order for conversations recommended by postmodernists to succeed, participants must presuppose that broader and broader criteria for agreement at least might exist, must be searching for them, and must be coming to some wider agreements on the basis of them. In other words, for such conversations to continue, participants must be moving, to some extent, towards universally agreed-on truths. Some movement towards universal truth, then, is a condition of the possibility of postmodern kinds of conversations taking place.[11]

I have outlined two ways in which postmodernists themselves presuppose, even if unknowingly, the reality of universal truth: in their very attempts to deny universality and in the ethical values which underlie the conversations that they recommend. I have sketched a third activity in which postmodernists presuppose at least the possibility of universal truth: the search for agreements and truth criteria that keep such conversations alive. In none of these cases, however, have I affirmed that universal truth consists in clear foundational statements on which agreements can be built. Instead, I have claimed that universality is something towards which postmodern thought, despite itself, aims—a goal that it, perhaps unknowingly, seeks. When postmodernists deny universal truths, they nevertheless intend to affirm something universal. When postmodernists invite all voices into conversation, they intend to discover and actualize more fully what universal equality among them entails. They also intend to discover how widely, and possibly even universally, agreement among them can extend.

Using theological language, one can affirm that universal truth, which functions chiefly as a goal, is eschatological in character. It is a reality which humans "already" apprehend dimly and on the basis of which they actually function. Yet complete awareness of universal truth is something we can only hope for and strive towards, for it has "not yet" fully appeared. Theologically, I would affirm that some significant agreement about truth will indeed be shared some day by all nations, races, tongues, and tribes of the earth.

I have sought to show that even that outlook which most sharply challenges universal truth—the postmodern—must nevertheless presuppose its reality as a condition of possibility which underlies all thought. I would recommend that antifoundationalist theologians support the plausibility of universal truth claims as clearly as they critique the notion of universal foundations. For, by not doing so, they often create the impression that their own theological assertions, which they intend as universal, are also vulnerable to the postmodern critique.

Confessing Universal Christian Truth

First, perhaps I should give a clear answer to a basic question, even though I have already dealt with it in principle. Simply put, the question is this: does the Christian message make universal truth claims? Are the central New Testament beliefs valid only for people in those cultures in which they were formulated and in cultures that have been rooted in them?

Postmodernists, after all, insist that all human concepts are shaped by the particular contexts in which they originate. Are such concepts therefore unable to reach beyond these contexts? Is the notion of truth which applies to all people an impossible one? Are we then mistaken if we assume that gospel affirmations that sound as if they are applicable to everyone should be interpreted as such?

So far, I have argued that human thought involves the intention to make universal statements. Among such universals are statements that people intend to be true of reality as a whole: for example, "everything that exists has a spiritual dimension." Of course, it is extremely difficult to formulate plausible affirmations of this second kind. Nonetheless, humans can surely attempt this; they can distinguish between statements which intend to be true of only part of reality and those which intend to be true of reality as a whole. Consequently, despite the origins of all concepts in particular cultural contexts, we can intend some of them to apply to reality as a whole.

If this is so, humans can also distinguish between the notion of a power which rules only part of reality and that of a power which rules reality as a whole. Although it may be difficult to say much about *what* the latter is like, humans can grasp the basic intent of statements that assert that such a power exists and affirm at least something about it. Thus, the notion of a universal power about which some universal claims may be made, claims which apply to everybody, is an intelligible one.[12]

Now the Old Testament surely claims that the Yahweh whom it proclaims is such a power. Think of the many declarations like this one from Isaiah: "I am the first and I am the last; besides me there is no god" (44:6). And this one:

Turn to me and be saved, all the ends of the earth!
For I am God, and there is no other.
By myself I have sworn,
from my mouth has gone forth in righteousness
a word that shall not return:
"To me every knee shall bow, every tongue shall swear!" (45:22-23)

In the New Testament, the most basic affirmation from the early *kerygma* is "Jesus Christ is Lord." Now "Lord" (*kurios*) is the Greek Old Testament's primary name for Yahweh. Thus when New Testament Christians apply this name to Jesus, they clearly mean that he is to be accorded the same cosmic ultimacy which is given to Yahweh. Notice especially the following text (Phil. 2:9-11), in which the declaration which I just read from Isaiah finds fulfillment:

> Therefore God also highly exalted him [Jesus]
> and gave him the name that is above every name,
> so that at the name of Jesus
> every knee should bend,
> in heaven and on earth and under the earth,
> and every tongue confess
> that Jesus Christ is Lord, to the glory of God the Father!

In texts like these, the New Testament writers clearly intend to affirm that Jesus is the ultimate power in the cosmos, even if it is difficult to understand much of what that means.

I think it is evident that, despite the shaping of all biblical and theological concepts by limited cultural contexts, the basic Christian gospel intends to make some universal claims. But if this is so, how can Anabaptists avoid expressing this universality in ways that are oppressive? How can they avoid associating Jesus' lordship with the imposition of social constraints or practices that are really culturally relative?

A good solution begins with noticing more exactly what kind of universal is being affirmed by "Jesus Christ is Lord." This declaration identifies a certain person (Jesus) who exercised a particular messianic function (Christ) as being the cosmic "Lord." What were this person's human life and the messiahship like? The Philippians text from which I just quoted tells us (2:7-8):

> [He] emptied himself (*heauton ekenosen*),
> taking the form of a slave,
> being born in human likeness.
> And being found in human form,
> he humbled himself
> and became obedient to the point of death—
> even death on a cross.

Jesus' lordship is what I would call "kenotic lordship," a kind that does not domineer over its subjects but which gives itself totally and utterly for their sakes. Furthermore, it gives itself for all its subjects. Consequently, it can never favor one social, cultural, racial, or gender group over another. As we know from Jesus' life and death, this lordship identifies with the downtrodden and opposes injustice and oppression. Consequently, allegiance to this person's lordship can never be validly associated with allegiance to unjust or oppressive forces; indeed, when rightly grasped, it frees people from adherence or servitude to them.

Accordingly, those who proclaim this kind of lordship can never knowingly be messengers of any power which brings people into any kind of bondage. Such messengers must seek to be heralds of a universal truth which liberates people from the appalling spectrum of dominations that have been dressed up as truths. And Anabaptists, given their emphasis on Jesus' kenotic lordship and their own history of oppression, may be well suited to emphasize this dimension of mission.

Implications for Mission

Let me close by suggesting four ways in which this kind of truth may be confessed in our pluralistic world, particularly in mission. First, confession must include not only verbal affirmation but also actions. The important Philippians text begins with the entreaty, "Let the same mind be in you that was in Christ Jesus. . ." (2:5). If we do not seek to live as Jesus did, we are not authentically confessing the truth that this text affirms. We must communicate it with our lives as well as our words.

I would stress this point much more were it not that this sometimes seems to be the only kind of point that Mennonites make. When confronted with a truth claim, Mennonites often respond by saying, "It is meaningless to affirm it if you don't live it," and then go on to speak entirely about living it. In this way, it seems to me, they often avoid dealing with the cognitive dimension of such claims and with the uncertainties and conflicts with other claims that dealing with this dimension often involves. It is largely to redress this kind of omission that I have focused chiefly on the cognitive element in confessing truth.

Second, confessing this kind of universal truth does not suppress cultural pluralism but enables it to flourish, for it is precisely confession of this kenotic universal that critiques and unmasks all false claims to universality. If Jesus Christ alone is Lord, then no merely cultural value can exercise lordship over people's lives. Cultural values are emptied of their false claims to absolute allegiance and deprived of their power to incite peoples to hate, despise, and slay each other. Cultural values are freed to be what they truly are: rich, contrasting ways of organizing and expressing reality that can bring exhilarating variety—rather than hardened oppositions—into many people's experience. Those who confess the truth of Jesus' lordship should promote the expression of authentic cultural diversity wherever they live.

Third, confessing the truth of Jesus means that verbal expression of it must always involve, or at least be open to, genuine conversation. For this kenotic truth does not seek to domineer over its hearers but to elicit their genuine response and to win their hearts. To be sure, this truth will sometimes be communicated in a somewhat monologic form, as in an evangelistic appeal or a sermon. When this is the case, speakers need not pretend that they have no important, particular beliefs, nor attempt to express these without conviction and passion. Nevertheless, all rhetorical techniques which pressure or frighten hearers must be abandoned. All persuasion must address itself to the hearers' capacity for authentic decision. And all such presentations must be accompanied, if at all possible, by opportunities for continuing, friendly, respectful conversation.

Fourth, what I have just said implies that no absolute line can be drawn between evangelism and dialogue. Confessing Jesus' truth involves affirming some deep convictions. Though I may sometimes take the initiative to present these in some kind of connected presentation—what is often called "evangelism"—such a presentation, as I have just said, must be open to further conversation. There is nothing inconsistent about acknowledging, in such a conversation, that I am also ignorant or unsure about many things. In particular, I may be ignorant about many features of my conversation partners' culture and also of their religion. In such a situation, I can have a genuine interest in learning about such things from them by entering into what is often called dialogue.

Moreover, I can acknowledge that I do not know everything even about my own faith. I will fully affirm that Jesus Christ is Lord, but I may not know a great deal about what this means, particularly in the context of another culture. If universal truth is not only something that I already possess in part, but also something that is not yet fully known to me and toward which I strive, dialogue with sincere partners can help me better understand my own faith as well as theirs. Perhaps unsuspected similarities between our faiths will emerge. Perhaps some differences which initially appeared enormous will prove to be less.

At the same time, authentic dialogue usually sorts out deeper differences from less important ones and throws the former into sharper relief. I may well become more convinced of the importance of certain distinctive Christian convictions that I hold. And as I seek to articulate these in dialogue, nothing prevents me from expressing them in as coherent and convincing a fashion as I can. Moreover, so far as I can see, nothing prevents me from wishing and praying—so long as I present my convictions without pressure or coercion—that my dialogue partners might embrace them too.

In short, if the universal truth about Jesus is eschatological, I can safely acknowledge that I do "not yet" know it all and can strive toward fuller apprehension of it in partnership with others who may hold different views. At the same time, I can be confident that those features of that knowledge that are essential for my salvation have "already" been revealed, and I can affirm them, rest in them, and rejoice in them.

Conclusion

Today Christians are challenged as to whether any universal truth claims at all can be made. Postmodernists in particular ask whether any such claims that we attempt to make are not really cultural preferences dressed up as universals and therefore oppressive of other peoples. Even on a philosophical level, and even on postmodernism's assumptions, humans cannot avoid presupposing universal truths and intending or striving towards them as goals of knowledge. On a theological level authentic confession of Jesus' universal kenotic lordship will free people from all false and oppressive pretensions to universality.

Notes

1. With the words "about reality," I mean to exclude consideration of statements that philosophers often call "analytic"—statements in which the predicate simply defines what is meant by the subject. To say, for instance, that a meter is 100 centimeters long is merely to define what "meter" means and not to give any information about reality. If such a definition were universally agreed upon, this would only be because all people decided to accept this arbitrary convention.

2. The first kind of emphasis is often made in support of an inclusivist understanding of religions, while the second often promotes a pluralistic understanding.

3. According to George Lindbeck, this approach can make religion marketable in our society, as a "commodity needed for transcendent self-expression and self-realization"; *The Nature of Doctrine* (Philadelphia: Westminster, 1984), 22.

4. The clearest approach of this sort is perhaps William Placher, *Unapologetic Theology* (Louisville, Ky.: Westminster/Knox, 1989).

5. Placher, *Unapologetic Theology*, 29. Placher stresses the work of W. V. O. Quine and Wilfred Sellars, esp. *Science, Perception and Reality* (New York: Humanities Press, 1963).

6. The major work on this theme is Thomas Kuhn, *The Structure of Scientific Revolutions*, 2nd ed. (Chicago: University of Chicago Press, 1970). In relation to the following discussion, see Richard Bernstein, *Beyond Objectivism and Relativism* (Philadelphia: University of Pennsylvania, 1983), 61-93; and Placher, 47-51.

7. Almost all scientists and philosophers of science would stress that these limitations are not due simply to our knowledge, but result from the actual character of these entities.

8. Placher, *Unapologetic Theology*, 135. Stanley Hauerwas affirms that "Christian ethics . . . claims truthfulness and therefore a certain universality. . . ." Its affirmations "are true and objective" in that they give us skills "to see and act in the world, not as we want it to be, but as it is. . . ." *The Peaceable Kingdom* (Notre Dame, Ind.: University of Notre Dame Press, 1983), 35. Nancey Murphy finds "relativism . . . the besetting problem for the postmodern epistemological era," as she puts it in *Beyond Liberalism and Fundamentalism* (Valley Forge, Pa.: Trinity Press Interna-

tional, 1996), 89, and she seeks to oppose it (106-108).

9. I indicate towards the end of this section that the sense in which humans are beyond the limits of all particular cultural contexts (though not disconnected from them) is eschatological. Eschatologically, we "already" apprehend to some extent truths which embrace all cultures, and we strive towards their fuller apprehension, which has "not yet" occurred. Philosophically, thought points beyond the limits of all cultures in intention; theologically, it does so in hope.

10. See Placher, *Unapologetic Theology*, 105-122, and Bernstein, *Beyond Objectivism*, 226ff, and frequently throughout his volume; cf. Gordon Kaufman, *In Face of Mystery* (Cambridge, Mass.: Harvard University Press, 1993), 64-69.

11. This kind of argument can be found in Juergen Habermas. See Bernstein, *Beyond Objectivism*, 182-197, and Stephen White, *The Recent Work of Juergen Habermas* (New York: Cambridge University Press, 1988), 22-24, 48-65. I am not arguing that participants must fully agree that universal truths exist, but only that it is meaningful, and even necessary, to attempt to move towards wider and wider kinds of agreement, and ultimately to arrive at universal agreement if such can be found. Participants may not agree that universal truth is an existing reality, but they must seek it as at least a possible goal.

12. Indeed, how can anyone assert that some kind of knowledge is "only particular" unless it also makes sense to speak of knowledge which is not particular, but refers to the whole? The intelligibility of at least some speech about the whole, or the universal, even if one is seeking to deny its existence, is a condition of the intelligibility of speech about the parts.

CHAPTER THIRTEEN

Practicing
Truth as a Global
Christian Community

Sara Wenger Shenk

The Need for Roots

As an educator, I approach this topic asking how we come to know what is true. How do we establish frames of reference to help make sense of what we learn? How do children develop a sense of their unique identity and where they belong in the huge array of possibilities? How do they develop internal confidence in a good and trustworthy God?

You may wonder what these questions have to do with the mission of the church and how it relates to pluralism. A story told by William Willimon illustrates the connection.

The congregation Willimon served in Greenville, South Carolina, stood next to a synagogue. Over coffee with the rabbi one day, Willimon talked about his surprise that his church was experiencing an influx of single young adults of college age and just beyond.

The rabbi replied, "Hardly a week goes by that we don't have a twenty-something person show up at the synagogue saying, 'I want to be a Jew again. My parents were only nominally Jewish, but I want to be Jewish for real.'"

"Is this some new conservative trend?" Willimon asked.

The rabbi answered, "We've got a generation who have been so inadequately parented that they are desperate for roots and identity. I think they're looking for parents."

Many parents, faced with the realities of pluralism, have adopted an attitude that says, "I want my child to grow up open-minded, so I'm going to wait until he or she is old enough to choose for himself or herself." Many educators question the wisdom of such an approach. How can children make informed choices unless they have a sense of perspective and criteria for how to value and evaluate? Those who are going to learn well from other religions need a deep rooting in a particular religion, in the rituals, symbols, and stories of a tradition that they have come to own in their community.

The Embodiment of Truth in Communities

I like to play with images. Imagine yourself at home right now. What do you like about that home? What did you like about your childhood home?

The quality of life at home varies. Sometimes there is more at home that you don't like than that you like, or it becomes too uncomfortable and the time arrives to move and establish a new home. If you have to move out, would you seek to establish another home? Why?

In imagining, you've no doubt experienced a whole kaleidoscope of emotions, thoughts, bodily sensations, pictures, and memories. All of us, I would guess, have fairly deep, elemental feelings about home. The quality of life at home is woven into the fundamental fabric of our early formation. And while for those of us who are adults, home isn't so profoundly formative, it still provides us with an essential point of reference, of rest and regrouping.

I want to invite us home. Because if we seek to address how to give a confident witness in our pluralistic world, we will miss the point unless we look carefully at the quality of life in our particular formative communities. It is the quality of our life together that provides the most powerful witness to others experiencing the metaphysical homelessness endemic in this age.

Robert Coles tells a story about one of his Harvard University students. Marian reached a breaking point one day and decided to withdraw from the university. She came to his office to unload.

She spoke at length about her classmates, who apparently had forgotten the meaning of "please" and "thank you" despite their high SAT scores, and who did not hesitate to be rude, even crude, to each other. She spoke of being not so subtly propositioned by a young man she knew to be very bright, a successful pre-med student and an accomplished journalist.

"That guy gets all A's," she said. "I've taken two moral reasoning courses with him, and I'm sure he's gotten A's in both of them—and look at how he behaves with me, and I'm sure with others. . . . I've taken all these philosophy courses, and we talk about what's true, what's important, what's good—well, how do you teach people to be good? What's the point of knowing good, if you don't keep trying to become a good person?"[1]

The invitation to come home is an invitation to come and see how truth is embodied, where goodness is cultivated, and where truth is practiced in particular communities of faith.

New Testament scholar Richard Hays insists that without the embodiment of the Word, none of our other deliberations matters. We can do an excellent job of exegeting Scripture, looking for coherent themes that unify diverse New Testament passages and interpreting what relevance those Scriptures, from a world much different from our own, have for us today. And yet the value of our exegesis, our hermeneutics, our theological and philosophical deliberations, will be tested by our capacity to produce persons and communities whose character is commensurate with Jesus Christ and thereby pleasing to God. The test that finally proves the value of our theological and philosophical labors is Jesus' comment, recorded in Matthew, "Thus you will know them by their fruits" (Matt. 7:20).[2]

The most powerful argument for the Scriptures, Hays argues, is a community of people who exemplify the love and power of the God that they have come to know through the New Testament. Furthermore, apart from the witness of such communities, formal arguments for the truth and authority of Scripture carry little weight.[3] I'm reminded of Paul's yearning to the Colossians, "I want their hearts to be encouraged and united in love, so that they may have all the riches of assured understanding and have the knowledge of God's mystery, that is Christ himself, in whom are hidden all the treasures of wisdom and knowledge" (Col. 2:2-3).

Before we focus on particular communities of faith and the practices that enhance communal discernment and embodiment of the truth, I want to set the larger frame of reference out of which I work.

Opportunities and Challenges of Postmodernity

Others have very ably described the philosophical machinations that depict our current so-called postmodern era. Others have described the cultural contortions, fragmentation, and dead-end streets that characterize the uncertainty of the times in which we live. I don't want to attempt a description of the contours of postmodernity. I simply want to allude to some of the opportunities that I think become available to us, given the current shifts and creative ferment.

It is really a historical fiction, though a useful one, to draw sharp boundaries between one historical era and another. There are always continuities as well as changes, and the changes don't come at the same time in all disciplines or geographic regions.[4]

Much of what is called postmodern, suggests Nancey Murphy, is actually nothing but a recognition of the failure to find indubitable foundations for universal knowledge. She finds this so-called postmodernism to be essentially modern in that it still assumes the modern ideal of knowledge—but with the bitter conclusion that this is not available. She suggests that perhaps a truly *post*modern approach would look more like a return to the values of the Renaissance: an appreciation for the timely, the local, the practical, and the particular.[5]

Murphy further suggests that perhaps the clearest break with modern thought is the replacement of foundationalism by holism. Whereas modern epistemology was dominated by the image of a building needing to be supported by an adequate foundation, postmodern epistemology is dominated by another image: that of knowledge as a web or net, suggesting a new strategy that recognizes a complex mutual conditioning between part and whole. This represents a significant enough departure from the predominant modes of modern thought to mark the beginning of a new, postmodern era.[6]

Helpful Conceptual Frameworks for Postmodernity

How, in this time of realigning and readjusting frameworks of interpretation and meaning, can we most helpfully conceptualize our task for practicing truth, embodying truth, and witnessing to the truth? One very helpful approach, I think, takes us back to a tradition-based community in dialectical relationship with the individual and his or her needs and visions: a faith community that knows itself to be a distinctive, minority group with unique practices and purposes in relation to the larger society.

In this approach, the community is viewed primarily as a linguistic community, shaped and governed by its language traditions and its social life-forms and practices, a web of relationships. This approach underscores the social nature of human life. It has a particular focus on life practices that express the importance of a deep, tacit participatory knowing, one that must be nourished by tradition, communal experience, and social responsibility. Above all, central importance is given to narrative and story as providing identity and meaning to the community and its members.[7]

Alasdair MacIntyre argues that knowledge and truth are rooted in culture and need a narrative context to become intelligible. An action requires a context to be intelligible. Behavior, he claims, can only be characterized adequately when we know its setting, the beliefs that informed it, and the long- and short-term intentions of that behavior. Behavior and communication only become intelligible by finding their place in a narrative informed by the past, living in the present, and moving toward the future.[8]

There is a teleological character to lived narratives, he notes, hearkening back to an Aristotelian notion of *telos*. We live our lives in light of certain ideas of a possible shared future. Our present is always informed by some image of some future and that image presents itself in the form of a telos—or of a variety of ends or goals.[9]

In attempting to make sense of that telos, the human being is essentially a story-telling animal, argues MacIntyre, a teller of stories that "aspire to truth." Deprive children of stories and "you leave them unscripted, anxious stutterers in their actions as in their words." The story of a life is always embedded in the story of the communities from which a person derives identity, he continues, suggesting that in this way the possession of a historical identity and a social identity coincide. What a person is, he notes, is in large part what the person inherits. Thus each person finds himself or herself part of a history and, whether acknowledged or not, one of the bearers of a tradition.[10]

MacIntyre argues convincingly that in order for our human communities to thrive, we must give vigilant attention to the tradition of the virtues, narratives, and practices that sustain our community life together. To put it bluntly, our salvation lies in our traditions, and it is the exercise of the relevant virtues that sustains and strengthens our traditions.

Murphy suggests that no philosopher has done more to show a helpful way beyond the current epistemological crisis than MacIntyre and the tradition-based rationality and morality that he outlines. She claims that MacIntyre provides an alternative to the demand for universal reason and to the cynicism and relativism that appear when such a search is found to be futile. It is our traditions that give us the resources for justifying our actions as well as our truth claims, he argues. Outside of all tradition one is morally and intellectually destitute. He also argues that it is possible for traditions to compete meaningfully with one another, and occasionally to argue, in the public forum, that one tradition is rationally superior to its rivals.[11]

MacInyre further suggests that all inquiry is tradition-constituted and tradition-dependent. Translation of concepts from one tradition to another is difficult and not always possible. Yet we can learn the language of another tradition and can even show that a rival tradition has key problems it cannot answer and that our tradition may have resources to solve those key problems.[12]

The work of George Lindbeck has also been helpful in recognizing the value of concrete religious traditions and reclaiming the value of particular and local traditions and practices. Lindbeck argues (along with many other postliberals), that followers of Christ have something to say to the world only to the extent that they can produce communities which embody a distinctive way of life. He claims that religious communities are likely to contribute more to the future of humanity if they preserve their own distinctiveness and integrity than if they yield to homogenizing tendencies.[13]

If we accept the assertions of MacIntyre, Lindbeck, and others that *particular* traditional communities of faith provide the most potent resource for withstanding the loss of Christ's presence in postmodernity, what must characterize a given church community so it functions dynamically to preserve its own tradition while becoming a community "for the world?"[14]

Multiple Ways of Knowing

Many scholars have begun to demonstrate the need for and possibility of ways of knowing that are deeper and more encompassing of the fullness of reality than purely discursive, quantitative, and instrumental ways of knowing.

More and more, thoughtful people are acknowledging that the roads to knowledge are many and cannot be defined by any single system of thought. In fact, knowledge is distorted when single paradigms are used to speak of it. Is there a quality of knowing that makes all the difference? What does it mean to say there is a practical, a spiritual, a bodily, or a communal way of knowing?[15]

Knowing and Ethical Practices

Ways of knowing are not morally neutral, as might have been supposed. They are morally directive, and there are ethical implications that grow out of our assumptions about how we come to know.[16] Ethics, it is argued, is not something that comes into play only after our ways of knowing have done their work. The foundations of morality are already built into our ways of knowing, and it is crucial that we examine the kinds of images we allow to guide our moral discernment and action. Because of the enormous impact epistemological assumptions have on our ethical behaviors, one can argue rather convincingly that the central task of all ethics may be the transformation of our ways of knowing.[17]

Feminist epistemologies, primarily, have critiqued detached and controlling modes of knowing, making us more aware of the possibility of participatory, involved, communal, and relational ways of knowing.[18] They draw our attention to knowledge that has bodily roots and majors in finding connections and integrating ways of thinking rather than separating knowledge into discreet, manipulable pieces. Truth is not thought of as a disembodied concept or proposition but is derived out of the concrete practices of daily life together, practices that include bodily manifestations of care, liberation, and justice.[19]

Knowing by Indwelling an Authoritative Tradition

Michael Polanyi's epistemology is helpful. Polanyi's most basic assertion is that we must reconsider human knowledge by starting from the fact that "we can know more than we can tell." Observing that our bodily processes participate in the perceptions we make, he notes that all thought has bodily roots, including our highest creative powers.[20]

Polanyi suggests that knowing involves commitment. We must tacitly indwell the particulars internal to our awareness to be able to do what we are consciously intending to do. We must also commit ourselves either to indwell the particulars of our own subliminal knowledge or the particulars of the tradition before we can push on to new understanding and action. A kind of knowing that involves indwelling the tradition of one's teacher or one's community is a more adequate understanding of how we come to truly know than is scientific rationalism that must have explicit verification before one may believe. We need authoritative, traditional frameworks to place limits on our self-determination, he asserts, and it is by functioning out of them that we come to truer understanding.[21]

The implication of Polanyi's epistemology as it relates to practicing truth will not be about scientific verifiability but about the character of life together as a church community, and a community's ability to make sense of life for its participants as well as make sense in the public forum. It is in the church community that one discovers firsthand whether God speaks through the gathered community and whether God acts to make a difference in people's lives.

Knowing and Intuitive Imagination

Intuitive imagination is by far the most important and most neglected of all the components of knowing. It is intuitive imagination that grasps reality in its concreteness, its relationalities, and its complexities. All understanding depends on intuitive imagination. Imagination, as Edward Farley uses the word, does not refer to "mere fancy," but to the capacity for experiencing and understanding the noumenal, immaterial realities that are the sources of inspiration and revelation. This needed transformation of knowing might best be thought of as the development of imagination in the fullest sense, involving the whole human being in the work of knowing, in "thought, feeling, will, and character."[22]

It requires an act of imagination to enter the strange and distant world of the Scripture, and yet it is such an approach that is required if Scripture is to have the power to shape our present world of understanding and behavior. It takes imagination to perceive the relationship between the tradition or the experiences of truth of previous generations and our current reality.

Practicing the Gospel

Epistemology, Rodney Clapp argues, must be placed firmly in the bed of ecclesiology. It is the community called "church" that teaches people the language and culture that enables them to know Jesus as Lord. It is the church, in the fullness of its life practices—not primarily its arguments—that draws others to consider the Christian faith.[23]

Doing, then, is a kind of knowing, and knowing is a kind of doing. Previous approaches to Scripture (arguments about its inerrancy) often had the effect of postponing obedience until we could establish as certain the truth of the Scriptures. What is needed is a new paradigm of biblical authority, one that is rooted in practicing the gospel rather than in establishing an inerrant text "in performing the Scriptures," where the proper interpretation of Scripture is not found primarily in a commentary or a theological text but in Christian discipleship.[24] This approach highlights ethical practices as critical for coming to know the truth of the gospel.

What do we mean when we talk about practices? Practices are shared activities through which persons come to know and through which perspectives on reality are formed. Practices are sites of learning that join ethical and epistemological dimensions.

Practices, when woven together, provide a coherent and sustained way of life. They are concrete, physical, and down-to-earth. They make

ethical resources available and become the place where humans cooper-
ate with God in caring for community. Practices are embodied thought.
They bear traditions which have taken shape over centuries as people
respond to God's presence. They bear standards of excellence and are
ancient and larger than we are. Practices are schools of virtue. We use
them to express faith, but in turn they form us.[25]

John Howard Yoder suggests what it means for a practice to qual-
ify as "evangelical." It must communicate good news, he says. Among
other things, it tells the world "what is the world's own calling and destiny, not by announcing either a utopian or a realistic goal to be imposed
on the whole society, but by pioneering a paradigmatic demonstration
of both the power and the practices that define the shape of restored
humanity."[26]

Arenas for the Communal Practice of Truth

Let me propose a variation on a popularized African proverb: if it
takes a village to raise a child, how should we shape the Anabaptist village to find and raise children for the kingdom of God? How should we
shape the Anabaptist village so it becomes an inviting home for those
who wander homeless through the haphazard and dead-end streets of
postmodernity? I want to look at three arenas involving these questions.

The Church

Hays observes that the unity we discover in the New Testament
isn't the unity of a dogmatic system. Rather, the unity is that this collection of documents retells, in various ways, a single fundamental story
summarized as follows:

> The God of Israel, the creator of the world, has acted (astoundingly) to
> rescue a lost and broken world through the death and resurrection of
> Jesus; the full scope of that rescue is not yet apparent, but God has
> created *a community of witnesses to this good news, the church*. While
> awaiting the grand conclusion of the story, the church, empowered by
> the Holy Spirit, is called to *reenact the loving obedience of Jesus Christ and
> thus to serve as a sign* of God's redemptive purposes for the world.[27]

Hays further suggests that the unity and sense of Scripture can be
grasped only through an act of metaphorical imagination that focuses
the diverse contents of the texts in terms of a particular "imaginative
characterization." He identifies three images in the New Testament that
he says concretely represent its narrative coherence, one of which is
community.[28]

The church, he asserts, is a countercultural community of discipleship, and it is this community that is the primary addressee of God's imperatives. The community in its corporate life is called to embody an alternative order that stands as a sign of God's redemptive purposes in the world. And the coherence of the New Testament's ethical mandate will come into focus only when we understand that mandate in ecclesial terms: when we seek God's will not by asking first, "What should *I* do," but "What should *we* do?"[29]

What practices ought to characterize what we do as we reenact the loving obedience of Jesus Christ and thus serve as a sign of God's redemptive purposes for the world? Some that come to mind as central and vital for the quality of life I hope will characterize our global Anabaptist communities include assembling together regularly for worship; corporate, prayerful discernment of the Scriptures for our community practice; baptism; the Lord's table; the towel and basin; service on behalf of the neighbor; table fellowship; singing together; simplicity of lifestyle; nonviolence in relationships as modeled by Jesus' cross; honoring each other's physical well-being with mutual care; welcoming the stranger into our community circle; and testifying about God's work in our lives.

Worship is the core of congregational life and provides the paradigm for its peculiar form of life. It is worship, most fundamentally, that provides the church's primary source of freedom from patterns of mutual self-destruction. The practices of worship—primarily, confession, repentance, prayer, and proclamation—when entered into in spirit and in truth, provide a powerful context for freedom of discernment about the quality and integrity of life together.[30]

Yoder highlights the formative power of worship:

> Worship is the communal cultivation of an alternative construction of society and of history. That alternative construction of history is celebrated by telling the stories of Abraham (and Sarah and Isaac and Ishmael), of Mary and Joseph and Jesus and Mary, of Cross and Resurrection and Peter and Paul, of Peter of Cheltchitz and his Brothers, of George Fox and his Friends.[31]

Worship, I would argue, is a core practice essential to shaping our life together as Anabaptist communities of faith. In worship, we draw imaginatively on our tradition's stories and find the courage to shape our lives in obedience to Jesus' invitation to choose life. Central practices of baptism, the Lord's supper, and the towel and basin provide the opportunity to be deeply formed in Christlikeness.

Another core practice in an Anabaptist community will be that of discernment. Murphy calls discernment as it is practiced in Radical-Reformation churches a "Christian epistemic practice"—a communal practice aimed at the pursuit of truth.

In general, this practice involves criteria for judging teaching, prophecy, and decisions as being or not being of the Spirit of Christ. Consistency with the Scripture has served as the primary criterion for decision making, but the practical test of consistency is the agreement of the church community. The means of reaching agreement is open discussion in the context of prayer.[32] Murphy suggests in particular the practices of nonviolence, simple living, and revolutionary subordination as necessary to produce people with the virtues needed for the practice of discernment (for her, the central and critical practice of community life) to succeed.

Also important to note as a core practice of an Anabaptist village is a principled commitment to nonviolence. By remaining steadfastly obedient to God even unto death and refusing to be co-opted into the systemic power game, Jesus unmasked the powers. Jesus' nonviolent love for enemies and his willingness to absorb hostility by forgiving the perpetrators of violence set the high standard for our practice of nonviolence.

Yoder assumes this nonviolent ethic is not primarily personalistic or individualist but includes a communal political intent. "What needs to be seen," he asserts, "is rather that the primary social structure through which the gospel works to change other structures is that of the Christian community." The church is called to contribute to the creation of structures more worthy of humankind, he writes. The church is called to make known to the powers, as no other proclaimer can do, the fulfillment of the mysterious purposes of God by means of Christ.[33]

In our communities, service practices will be a vital expression of who we are. Service involves a commitment to make Jesus' style of self-giving the model for every profession and vocation. And our practices of mutual care assist us in the honoring of each other's physical, bodily well-being, remembering that every body is a temple of God's Spirit and worthy of care. Our community service must be shaped by acts of generosity, where each member takes responsibility for the well-being of every other and where each learns to live simply so there will be more to share with others.

We serve each other's well-being by caring for our children with tenderness and affection. We serve each other when we practice committed marital relationships, in which loving partners model reverence toward and delight in one another. We serve each other when we honor singleness and celibacy and relate to one another as a people who cherish chastity. We serve each other by taking care in the way we clothe ourselves, being vigilant about the effects our decisions have on others, and making choices that express our primary identity as children of God. We honor each other's well-being by touching only in ways that seek to respect and not exploit another for one's own sexual gratification.

How can we renew our communal practices of table fellowship and hospitality to each other and to strangers? Over and over again we see Jesus associating with persons thought to be unfit, indecent, and unwelcome at the table. Where in our congregations and homes do we welcome the sort of persons that Jesus sought out to break bread with? Far more often, we look for churches and neighborhoods peopled with persons like ourselves: persons who have similar tastes, who like our kind of music, sermons, books, home furnishings, and style of worship, and who have educational degrees like ours. We will renew our communal life, even across racial, economic, and educational barriers, by paying attention to Jesus when we choose whom to sit with at table. It is urgent that we renew the practice of hospitality to the stranger and to those we know and love.

The practice of communal singing together is one of the few remaining places where words and music actually form human beings in a communal identity. When people meet to worship, singing together in public forms us in a shared identity—a communal identity that flows out of an ancient story and takes on new life, in words, tunes, and actions today. Where people sing of God, an embodied theology is formed and expressed, and bonds of loyalty and love are forged.[34]

The Family

The family, more than any other context of life, is foundational to a child's formation. Children learn what they live. They learn more from what adults *do* than what adults *say*. If one accepts, as many studies find, that the family has more influence on our character, values, motivations, and beliefs than either church or school, then one can readily argue, as do more and more social scientists, politicians, and church leaders, that renewing families is one of society's and the church's most urgent and crucial tasks. How are we to practice truth in a family culture?

A child is a witness, an ever attentive witness of grown-up morality. Children look for clues from the day they are born as to how they ought to behave. And they find them aplenty as we who are parents and teachers go about our lives, making choices, showing in action our rock-bottom assumptions, desires, and values, and thereby telling them much more than we may realize.[35]

Children crave moral strength. Our conscience doesn't descend on us from on high, argues Robert Coles. We learn a convincing sense of right and wrong from parents who are themselves convinced as to what ought to be said and done. Children can be quite angry at being denied the protection of a strong guiding conscience.

To master the instincts, children have to find a reason to do so, a source of moral energy that enables them to do so. Where, they wonder, are the grown-ups in their lives on whom they can really rely and whose values are trustworthy and believable because they have been given out of the shared experience of a life together?[36]

What truly distinguishes people, says Coles, is how they behave toward one another, no matter what crosses their bedeviled minds. Are we teaching children to be generous or selfish, to have an eye out for others, or to be wrapped up in themselves?

Henry James's nephew, the son of William James, once asked the great and thoughtful novelist what he ought to do with his life, how he ought to live it. The nephew received this advice: "Three things in human life are important. The first is to be kind. The second is to be kind. And the third is to be kind."[37]

Where do we find the moral energy to live with kindness and loving, equal regard at home? Stanley Hauerwas reminds us that marriage and family life are possible only if they are sustained by a community more significant than the marriage or the family itself. If we have not first learned what it means to be faithful to self and others in the church, then we have precious little chance of learning it through marriage and the family. It is through learning to be faithful in relation to God's faithfulness that I have the character capable for loving through thick and thin.[38]

Each church must join with other churches to create a new critical marriage and family culture that can, simultaneously, proclaim the New Testament ideals for covenantal marriage in which Christians make unconditional promises and mean them, and also handle shortcomings with grace and forgiveness.[39] Covenantal fidelity is bigger, deeper, older, and wiser than any individual who enters into it. We need married Christians to live lives of fidelity so we can learn to recognize the God of faithfulness, the God of Israel and Jesus Christ. We need single Christians to live lives of celibacy, uniquely witnessing to true Christian freedom.[40]

How can we practice truth in a family culture? We need to recognize again how critical home-based worship is for the transmission of faith and family traditions. Praying and reading Scripture, discussing faith and moral commitments, and talking about views of sexuality, marriage, and family are essential to a healthy family practice of truth.

Continuity between the gathered church and the church at home has been a constant theme throughout Christian history. Because the early church met in homes, sacred actions around rituals and common meals in the gathered church spilled into home life. Home became a little church.[41] In order for our children to thrive, we must integrate authentic, loving practices of faith into the rhythms of our daily lives. There is perhaps no more important agenda for building healthy communities.

The School

Mark Schwehn urges the recovery of certain spiritual virtues as essential to the process of learning, even in the secular academy. He undertakes a critique of the modern university, acknowledging a widespread blindness to the relationship between spirituality and learning in the secular university, in part due to notions of knowledge that grew out of "enlightened" secular rationalism.[42] So long as the activities of teaching and learning involve communal questioning in search of the truth, he argues, the exercise of virtues such as humility, faith, self-denial, and charity will be indispensable to higher education.[43]

Schwehn cites Parker Palmer, the well-known educational philosopher, who has argued that "we must recover from our spiritual tradition the models and methods of knowing as an act of love."[44] Schwehn insists that both knowledge and truth are communal terms and that knowledge is not the result of the isolated individual's efforts to mirror the world but rather a form of responsible relationship with others. Knowing "becomes a reunion of separated beings whose primary bond is not of logic but of love"; and truth is the name of this "community of relatedness."[45]

Another strategy Schwehn suggests involves strengthening those church-related or religiously affiliated institutions of learning that have maintained a clear sense of their own distinctive vocations.[46] Such alternative institutions can provide resources for a recovery of the spiritual virtues essential to a communal quest for knowledge and truth.

Conclusion

We are stewards of magnificent and varied traditions. As communities of faith throughout the world, we either intentionally or haphaz-

ardly select practices from those traditions to characterize our life together. Can we imaginatively and lovingly find vital links between our
traditional stories and our own lives? Can we, by the way we live, provide a home for the homeless, inviting all the children to come home?

Notes

1. Robert Coles, *The Moral Intelligence of Children* (New York: Random House,
1997), 180-181. Coles is a renowned professor of psychiatry, medical humanities,
and social ethics at Harvard Medical School. He has authored many books, including the Pulitzer Prize-winning, five-volume *Children of Crisis* and the best-
selling *The Spiritual Life of Children*.

2. Richard Hays, *The Moral Vision of the New Testament* (San Francisco: Harper-
Collins, 1996), 7, 212.

3. Ibid., 10.

4. Nancey Murphy, *Beyond Liberalism & Fundamentalism: How Modern and Postmodern Philosophy Set the Theological Agenda* (Valley Forge, Pa.: Trinity Press International, 1996), 4.

5. Ibid., 3. Stephen Toulmin suggests that we are not compelled to choose between sixteenth-century humanism and seventeenth-century exact science;
rather, we need to hang on to the positive achievements of both. We can neither
cling to modernity in its historic form nor reject it totally. The task is rather to reform and even reclaim our inherited modernity, by humanizing it. The "modern"
focus on the written, the universal, the general, and the timeless, he says, which
monopolized the work of most philosophers after 1630 is being broadened to include once again the oral, the particular, the local, and the timely. *Cosmopolis* (New
York: The Free Press, 1990), 180, 186.

6. Nancey Murphy discusses this image, developed by Willard V. O. Quine, in
Anglo-American Postmodernity (Boulder, Colo.: Westview Press, 1997), 26-27, 34-35.

7. Douglas Sloan, *Faith and Knowledge; Mainline Protestantism and American
Higher Education* (Louisville, Ky.: Westminster John Knox Press, 1994), 223, 233.
Here Sloan is referring to the work of Lindbeck, MacIntyre, and Hauerwas.

8. Alasdair MacIntyre, *After Virtue* (Notre Dame, Ind.: University of Notre
Dame Press, 1981), 208-210.

9. Ibid., 215-216.

10. Ibid., 216, 221.

11. Murphy, "A Theology of Education," a paper presented at a consultation
on Mennonite Higher Education, Winnipeg, Manitoba, June 13-15, 1997, 4, 10; also
referred to extensively in several of her books. MacIntyre describes tradition as a
historically extended, socially embodied argument about how best to interpret
and apply the formative text or texts of a tradition.

12. Rodney Clapp, "How Firm a Foundation: Can Evangelicals Be Nonfounda-
tionalists?" in *The Nature of Confession: Evangelicals & Postliberals in Conversation*,
ed. Timothy Phillips and Dennis Okholm (Downers Grove, Ill.: InterVarsity Press,
1996), 89-90.

13. George A. Lindbeck, *The Nature of Doctrine: Religion and Theology in a Post-*

liberal Age (Philadelphia: Westminster Press, 1984), 128.

14. It is important to acknowledge, if one chooses a communitarian approach to make truth claims, the danger of tribalism and the violence that arises among rival tribes when each is wedded to its respective version of the truth. Mark Schwehn argues that objectivism arose primarily as a way of avoiding violence. Any alternative to foundationalism or objectivism will seem to open the prospect of renewed violence among different communities that seem to have no rational foundation on which to adjudicate disagreements. The fear of tribalism and violence is likely the foremost difficulty that communitarian accounts of knowledge must face, argues Schwehn in *Exiles from Eden* (New York: Oxford University Press, 1993), 29-32.

15. One fascinating study that illustrates this point comes from Jerome Bruner, who argues that there are two irreducible modes of cognition, the "paradigmatic" (or logico-scientific) and the "narrative." Each mode comes spontaneously into existence in the functioning of human beings, but each provides a different way of ordering experience, constructing reality, filtering perceptions, and organizing memory. The paradigmatic mode leads to good theory, tight analysis, and empirical discovery. It can be subjected to verification and seeks to be context-free and universal. The narrative mode leads to good stories and gripping drama; truth is multifaceted and elusive, context sensitive and particular. Both modes seek to express truth, but each judges truth values differently. Efforts to reduce one to the other or ignore one at the expense of the other fail to capture the rich ways people "know." Jerome Bruner, "Narrative and Paradigmatic Modes of Thought," in *Learning and Teaching The Ways of Knowing*, ed. Elliot Eisner (Chicago: The University of Chicago Press, 1985).

16. Mark R. Schwehn, *Exiles From Eden: Religion and the Academic Vocation in America* (New York: Oxford University Press, 1993), 94.

17. Sloan, *Faith and Knowledge*, 233.

18. Ibid., 215.

19. Rebecca Chopp, *Saving Work: Feminist Practices of Theological Education* (Louisville, Ky.: Westminster/John Knox Press, 1995).

20. Michael Polanyi, *The Tacit Dimension* (Gloucester, Mass.: Peter Smith, 1983), 4, 15.

21. Ibid., 62. A pertinent question which will need some attention if one uses this concept: while frameworks make it possible to know, what may they make it impossible to know? It may not be possible to answer this question from within the framework itself, but only from another framework or context. Another question follows: whether in order to be able to function epistemologically within one framework, one may have to exclude certain knowledges by filtering or selecting what one sees and hears.

22. Sloan, *Faith and Knowledge*, 219, 234, 236. Edward Farley is Professor of Theology at The Divinity School, Vanderbilt University, and is author of *The Fragility of Knowledge: Theological Education in the Church and the University* (Philadelphia: Fortress Press, 1988) and *Theologia: The Fragmentation and Unity of Theological Education* (Philadelphia: Fortress Press, 1983).

23. Clapp, "How Firm a Foundation," 90.

24. John R. Wilson, "Toward a New Evangelical Paradigm of Biblical Authority," in Phillips & Okholm, 153-157.

25. Dorothy Bass, ed., *Practicing Our Faith: A Way of Life for a Searching People* (San Francisco: Jossey-Bass Publishers, 1997), 4-11. This discussion builds on MacIntyre's *After Virtue*.

26. Michael G. Cartwright, ed., *The Royal Priesthood: Essays Ecclesiological and Ecumenical—John Howard Yoder* (Grand Rapids, Mich.: Eerdmans, 1994), 373.

27. Hays, *The Moral Vision*, 193, with my highlighting.

28. Ibid., 194. The three images he identifies are community, cross, and new creation.

29. Ibid., 196-197.

30. Craig R. Dykstra, "The Formative Power of the Congregation," in *Theological Perspectives on Christian Formation*, ed. Astley, Francis, and Crowder (Grand Rapids, Mich.: Eerdmans), 260.

31. John Howard Yoder, *The Priestly Kingdom: Social Ethics as Gospel* (Notre Dame, Ind.: University of Notre Dame Press, 1984), 43.

32. Nancey Murphy, "A Theology of Education," 7, 8, and far more extensively in *Theology in the Age of Scientific Reasoning* (Ithaca, N.Y.: Cornell University Press, 1990), chapter 5.

33. John Howard Yoder, *The Politics of Jesus* (Grand Rapids, Mich.: Eerdmans, 1972), 157-161. Yoder refers extensively in his book to Hendrik Berkhof's book *Christ and the Powers* (Scottdale, Pa.: Herald Press, 1962).

34. Bass, *Practicing Our Faith*. The discussion of honoring bodies, hospitality, and singing is drawn, in part, from this book.

35. Coles, *The Moral Intelligence*, 5.

36. Ibid., 58, 59.

37. Ibid., 195.

38. Stanley Hauerwas, "The Family as a School for Character," *Religious Education* 80, no. 2 (spring 1985): 272-285.

39. Don S. Browning et al., eds., *From Culture Wars to Common Ground: Religion and the American Family Debate* (Louisville, Ky.: Westminster John Knox Press, 1997), 273.

40. Rodney Clapp, *Families at the Crossroads: Beyond Traditional and Modern Options* (Downers Grove, Ill.: InterVarsity, 1993), 91, 119, 127.

41. Browning et al., *From Culture Wars*, 308.

42. Schwehn, *Exiles From Eden*, 46.

43. Ibid., 48.

44. Cited in Schwehn, *Exiles from Eden*, 25.

45. Schwehn, *Exiles from Eden*, 40.

46. Ibid., 81.

CHAPTER FOURTEEN

What Difference Does Jesus Make?[1]

Chris Wright

The title of this chapter reminds us of the real focus of this book—namely the Lord Jesus Christ. For a Christian, confident witness has to be founded on personal allegiance to the one who said, "I am the truth." So for us the issue can never be reduced to a mere conflict of ideas or ideologies.

We are not struggling for the survival of a religion; nor, as the Anabaptist tradition reminds us, are we conspiring to regain cultural hegemony or social power. Rather, like every generation of believers since the New Testament, we are summoned to bear witness to Jesus and the difference he has made and makes now. Our task is to commend Christ, not just to win arguments. Indeed, our understanding of mission and of eschatology is that ultimately the argument belongs to the Lord himself and he will win it. We are the witnesses he calls.

The Difference Already Prepared for Jesus

The task laid on the disciples of Jesus to bear witness to him, however, has its own roots in the Scriptures that shaped Jesus himself. There we find Israel similarly summoned to be Yahweh's witnesses. Indeed the language of Luke 24:48 and Acts 1:8 is drawn from Isaiah 43:10-12, where Yahweh commissions Israel as witnesses to his own uniqueness among the gods in the context of Mesopotamian pluralism.

Thus the shape of Jesus' uniqueness was already carved by Israel's faith. What was different about him was built on what was already different about Israel and Yahweh. Indeed the opening verses of the New Testament direct us back as if to say, "If you want to understand Jesus, you must see him in light of *this* story of *this* people with *this* God."

Unfortunately, many discussions about the significance of Jesus Christ in the context of world religions virtually cut him off from these historical and scriptural roots and speak of him as "the founder of a new religion." Now, if this means merely that Christianity as a worldwide religion goes back historically to Jesus and then became separate from Judaism, in which it was born, the statement may be superficially true.

But certainly Jesus had no intention of launching another religion as such. Who Jesus was and what he had come to do were both already long prepared for through God's dealings with the people he belonged to and through their Scriptures. This can be examined from two angles: the uniqueness of Israel and the uniqueness of Yahweh. I shall concentrate on the former.

The Uniqueness of Israel

After the profound analysis of the roots of our human predicament in our rebellion and sin (Gen. 1–11), the Bible shows how God began providing a solution through the call of Abraham and the creation of Israel as God's people. God's covenant with Abraham makes clear that what Yahweh has in mind is blessing for all nations (Gen. 12:3, 18:18, etc.). The narrative shows that the effects of sin are universal: all nations are implicated in the story of human rebellion illustrated by the tower of Babel in Genesis 11. The narrative also shows us that God's redemptive intention is equally universal: all nations will be blessed through Abraham. But at the same time, the biblical story shows us that God chose to achieve that goal through a very particular historical means—initially, the nation of Israel.

The Bible is quite clear that God's action in and through Israel was unique. Now this does not mean that God was not involved and active in the histories of other nations. The Old Testament explicitly asserts that he was.[2] It does mean that only in Israel did God work in the terms of a covenant of redemption, initiated and sustained by his grace. As Elmer Martens has observed, Amos was very well aware of God's moral and historical sovereignty over the other nations.[3] (See Amos 1–2, 9:7.) But about Israel he asserts in God's name, "You only have I known of all the families of the earth" (Amos 3:2).

Deuteronomy says that Israel had experienced God's redemption (the exodus) and God's revelation (at Mt. Sinai) in a way that was unparalleled among any other nation in the whole span of time and space (Deut. 4:3-24). Isaiah went on to tell Israel that it was because of their unique historical experience of Yahweh that they were qualified to bear witness to Yahweh's uniqueness as the only living God (Isa. 43:8-13).

Even the holiness of Israel was a means of expressing their uniqueness. It meant being set apart by God for his special purpose through them in the midst of the nations (Exod. 19:56; Lev. 20:26; Num. 23:9; Deut. 7:6).

To emphasize this truth about Israel (their unique particularity) does not take away from the other truth—that God's purpose through them was ultimately universal in scope. Israel only existed at all because of God's desire to redeem people from every nation. But in his sovereign freedom, he chose to do so by this particular and historical means.

The tension between the universal goal and the particular means is found throughout the Bible and cannot be reduced to either pole alone. What it comes down to is that, while God has every nation in view in his redemptive purpose, in no other nation did he act as he did in Israel. That was their uniqueness, which can be seen to be exclusive. No other nation experienced what they did of God's revelation and redemption. God's purpose is also inclusive. Israel was created, called, and set in the midst of the nations for the sake of the nations.

Now when we look at Jesus and ask what difference he made and what he achieved, we have to remember that he completed what God had already begun to work out through Israel. Matthew makes this clear from his opening genealogy. Jesus as a historical, particular man has to be understood against the background of a historical, particular people. His uniqueness is linked to theirs.

But we can go further than simply noting how Jesus brings the unique story of Old Testament Israel to its climax and completion. We have to reckon with the vitally important fact that the New Testament presents him to us as the Messiah: Jesus, the Christ. And the Messiah *was* Israel. That is, he represented and personified Israel. The Messiah was the completion of all that Israel had been put in the world for—God's self-revelation and his work of human redemption.[4]

The Messiah fulfilled the mission of Israel, which was to bring blessing to the nations. For this reason too, Jesus shares in the uniqueness of Israel. In fact, he was the whole point and goal of it. What God had been doing through no other nation, God now completed through no other person than the Messiah, Jesus of Nazareth.

The paradox is that precisely through the narrowing down of his saving action to this unique, singular man, God opened the way to making his saving grace available universally to all nations, which was his purpose from the beginning when he made that promise to Abraham. God called Abraham to make a difference to the fallen world of nations; God sent Jesus to achieve that mission and to inaugurate its historical completion through the mission of the church.

It had been a mystery all through the Old Testament ages how God could bring about for Abraham what he had promised him—namely, blessing to all nations. Paul saw this clearly and expounds it in Ephesians 2–3 and Galatians 3 especially. What the Gentile nations did not have before, because it was at that time limited to Israel, is now available to them in the Messiah, Jesus.

It is significant how regularly Paul inverts the normal order and puts Christ before Jesus in these passages. This is not accidental; Paul is making a point. It is precisely because the Messiah has come in the person of Jesus of Nazareth that the Old Testament hope of redemption is fulfilled in him (cf. Luke 1:33, 54f., 68-79; 2:25-32, 38; 24:21ff.), and also that redemption can now be extended to include people from all nations who are "in the Messiah" through faith. It is worth quoting some of Paul's key texts:

> He redeemed us in order that the blessing given to Abraham might come to the Gentiles through Christ Jesus, so that by faith we might receive the promise of the Spirit. (Gal. 3:14, NIV)

> For in Christ Jesus you are all children of God through faith. As many of you as were baptized into Christ have clothed yourselves with Christ. There is no longer Jew or Greek, there is no longer slave or free, there is no longer male and female; for all of you are one in Christ Jesus. (Gal. 3:26-29, NRSV)

> Therefore, remember that formerly you who are Gentiles . . . were separate from Christ, excluded from citizenship in Israel and foreigners to covenants of the promise, without hope and without God in the world. But now in Christ Jesus you who once were far away have been brought near through the blood of Christ. (Eph. 2:11-13, NIV)

> The mystery [of Christ] was made known to me by revelation. . . . In former generations this mystery was not made known to humankind, as it has now been revealed to his holy apostles and prophets by the Spirit: that is, the Gentiles have become fellow heirs, members of the same body, and sharers in the promise in Christ Jesus through the gospel. (Eph. 3:3, 5-6, NRSV)

Unquestionably, then, there is a universal dimension to Paul's gospel because of its roots in the Abraham covenant and its promise to "all nations." But it is firmly based on an exclusive foundation—only through the Messiah Jesus, just as it had previously been only through Israel. The uniqueness of Jesus is thus bound to the uniqueness of Old Testament Israel because both are the expressions of the unique saving work of God in history. Jesus made the crucial difference for all the nations because that was exactly the purpose for which God had prepared the way in the calling and creation of Israel among the nations.

The Uniqueness of Yahweh

There can be no more powerful affirmation in the Old Testament than the claim that Yahweh alone is truly God. This indeed was the lesson that Israel was to expected to learn from its unique experience of his revelation and redemption. Thus after Deuteronomy 4:32-34 has affirmed the unparalleled experience of Israel, verses 35 and 39 go on to draw the consequences:

> You were shown these things so that you might know that the Lord is God; besides him there is no other. . . . Acknowledge and take to heart this day that the Lord is God in heaven above and on the earth below. There is no other. (Deut. 4:35, 39, NIV)

It is important to realize that in the Old Testament this monotheistic faith is not merely a matter of arithmetic but of character. That is, what Israel was to learn from its encounter with God in history was not merely that there was only one deity, not many. The point, rather, was who that God was. *Yahweh is God.* Therefore, deity is being defined in terms of the nature, character, and actions of Yahweh, and especially in terms of his justice, his faithfulness to his promises, and his great power to save and deliver his people.

This too is the ringing declaration of the great prophecies in Isaiah 40–55. Read especially Isaiah 40:12-31; 43:10-12; and 45:5, 22-24 and hear the strength of the claim that Yahweh is utterly beyond comparison. He is unique as God because he is in reality the only God, and therefore he is in sovereign control of history from beginning to end. The future belongs to Yahweh as much as the past.

Yahweh, then, makes all the difference because he is himself so utterly different from all rivals. This indeed is a major dimension of what it meant to speak of his holiness. The word has a strong connotation of distinctiveness. That too is how it is then transferred to Israel. They were to reflect among the nations the distinctiveness of Yahweh among the gods.

The strong concern for this in Leviticus is expressed most succinctly in the command (and challenge), "You shall be holy for I, the Lord your God, am holy" (Lev. 19:2). More colloquially expressed this could be translated, "You must be a different kind of people because I, Yahweh, am a different God." The rest of the chapter shows that this was far from merely ritual or religious distinctiveness but affected every aspect of ethical life—private, family, social, legal, economic, and political.

The Difference Jesus Made in His Context

As we look forward from the Old Testament to understand the difference that Jesus made in his own world, we need to recognize that a crucial ingredient in Old Testament Israel's hopes for the future was the conviction that at some point (often phrased in the prophets as "in that day" or "in those days") Yahweh himself would come and take action in the world, bringing both redemption and judgment. This had entered into Jewish expectation and apocalyptic writing at every level.[5] Isaiah 35, for example, announces "Your God will come" (v. 4, NIV), and then goes on to list the signs and blessing that will be proof of his coming: the blind will see, the deaf hear, the lame walk, and the dumb speak (v. 5f.).

Jesus himself pointed to these signs in his reply to the questioning disciples of John the Baptist. But if these things were now taking place, what did that mean about the identity of Jesus (Matt. 11:4-6)?

In other places in the Old Testament, the promise that Yahweh himself would "take over" is linked without explanation to the expected coming and rule of a messianic figure. This is clearest in Ezekiel 34. There God, in response to the failure of Israel's historical kings ("shepherds"), promises a restoration of full divine government ("I myself will be shepherd of my sheep," v. 16.), but at the same time promises the rule of a future "David" (v. 23f.). When Jesus claims to be the "good shepherd" (John 10:11, 14), or to be the one whom even David called Lord (Matt. 22:41-46), again the question arises: who has really come?

The Old Testament closes with the warning that Yahweh himself will come but that he will be preceded by "Elijah" (Mal. 2:1, 4:5). In the light of this text, Jesus could declare that this prophecy about "Elijah" was fulfilled in John the Baptist. But if "Elijah" was to precede the coming of God himself, and John the Baptist was "Elijah," who must Jesus be? The expected sequence was: "Elijah, then Yahweh." Everybody knew that they had heard John first and then Jesus had come.

So Jesus *who*? "If you are willing to accept it," said Jesus, when he made the statement about John being Elijah (Matt. 11:14). The difficulty of accepting what he was saying was probably not so much that he identified John with Elijah as what that would then mean for the identity of Jesus himself. For those who were willing to accept it, it meant beyond doubt that God had indeed come in the person of Jesus of Nazareth, to bring in the new age of his kingdom and salvation. Yahweh had come, and it made all the difference.

In John's Gospel, Jesus repeatedly uses "I am" statements, climaxing in the claim in John 8:58 that "before Abraham was, I am." There is no doubt that this intentionally echoes the similar "I am" statements of

Yahweh in the book of Isaiah.[6] The implication was not lost on Jesus' hearers—they set out to stone him for blasphemy.

Very soon after Jesus' death and resurrection, the early church was referring to him and addressing him in terms which had previously applied only to Yahweh. The early believers called him Lord, the Greek word *kyrios* being the one regularly used in the Greek version of the Old Testament for the divine name Yahweh.

The apostolic church "called on his name" in worship and prayer. That was a phrase used in the Old Testament for invoking the presence and power of God in worship (e.g., Ps. 116:12f., 17). Stephen at the point of death declared that he saw Jesus standing at the right hand of God sharing in his divine glory (Acts 7:55). Paul, in an act of instinctive evangelism, called on the Philippian jailer to "believe on the Lord Jesus" if he wanted to be saved (Acts 16:31).

Elsewhere Paul could theologically justify such confidence by quoting Joel 2:32: "Everyone who calls on the name of the Lord shall be saved." Joel was unquestionably referring to Yahweh. Paul, just as unquestionably, was referring to Jesus Christ as the agent of God's salvation for Jew and Gentile alike (Rom 10:13).

Possibly the most remarkable identification of Jesus with Yahweh comes in Philippians 2:5-11, the hymn of Christ's humility and exaltation. It is widely agreed that these verses were probably not originally composed by Paul but were part of a Christian hymn he incorporates here. They are thus early evidence of Christian convictions about Jesus.

The hymn finishes by saying that God has given to Jesus "the name that is above every name" (v. 9). In biblical terms, that could only mean the name that belonged to God—Yahweh himself, the name so often simply rendered "Lord" in the Old Testament. So the next verse probably means to combine that implied name with the name Jesus itself. At the name belonging to Jesus there will be universal acknowledgment of his lordship:

That at the name of Jesus every knee should bow,
in heaven and on earth and under the earth,
and every tongue confess that Jesus Christ is Lord
to the glory of God the Father. (Phil 2:10-11, NIV)

We are so familiar with this (from a well-known hymn!) that we perhaps are not aware that in fact this is a partial quotation of words that were originally spoken by Yahweh about himself, from Isaiah 45. And in that context, the point of the words was to underline Yahweh's uniqueness as God and his unique ability to save:

There is no God apart from me
a righteous God and a Savior;
there is none but me.
Turn to me and be saved, all you ends of the earth;
for I am God, and there is no other.
By myself I have sworn,
my mouth has uttered in all integrity
a word that will not be revoked:
Before me every knee will bow;
by me every tongue will swear.
They will say of me, "In the Lord alone are righteousness [salvation]
and strength." (Isa. 45:21b-24a, NIV)

This declaration by God comes in the most unambiguously monotheistic section of the whole Old Testament. The magnificent prophecies
of Isaiah 40–55 assert again and again that Yahweh is utterly unique as
the only living God in his sovereign power over all nations and all history, and in his ability to save. This early Christian hymn in Phil. 2,
therefore, by deliberately selecting a Scripture from such a context and
applying it to Jesus, is affirming that Jesus is as unique as Yahweh in
those same respects. This is clear from the way the "name" of Jesus is
inserted at the crucial point where Yahweh would otherwise have been
understood. Jesus *is* Lord and will ultimately be recognized and acknowledged as such by all.

Another interesting factor here is the surrounding religious contexts of both texts. In both cases, Isaiah 45 and Philippians 2, it is actually
religious plurality. In Philippians, the uniqueness of Jesus is asserted in
the midst of the religious plurality of the Greek and Roman world of the
first century C.E. But it uses the same language and terms as the uniqueness of Yahweh himself had been asserted in the midst of the pluralistic,
polytheistic environment of Babylon in the sixth century B.C.E.

I question, therefore, whether the rediscovered (but not new) religious plurality of the twentieth century C.E. gives us any adequate
reason for departing from affirmations made in both Testaments in
similar contexts. At least we should be aware that if we insist on relativ-
izing Jesus out of deference to surrounding religious plurality, we not
only take leave of the New Testament witness to him but also jettison the
Old Testament foundations on which that witness was built.

In assessing the impact of Jesus we can go back further than this
early Christian hymn in Philippians. Paul's first letter to the Thessalonians is regarded by many scholars as his earliest, and if so, it would be the
earliest of all the writings that eventually came to form the New Testa-

ment. It is dated variously between C.E. 41 and 51—that is, within ten or twenty years after the crucifixion.

In Thessalonians Paul talks about Jesus in remarkable ways, with the obvious assumption that the Christians in Thessalonica already accepted and agreed with what he says. That is, it was already part of the worship and teaching of the church. Paul speaks of "the Lord Jesus Christ" in the same breath as "God the Father" (1 Thess. 1:1, 3). He can even address prayer to both together (3:11-13). Jesus is "God's Son," who will come to bring in the final act of judgment and salvation (1:10).

In the Old Testament, that last great final day was described as "the Day of the Lord [Yahweh]" (e.g., Joel 1:15; 2:11, 28-32; 3:14). The expected coming of Jesus has transformed it into the Day of the Lord Jesus (1 Thess. 4:16–5:2). And Jesus is our salvation in that day because he both died and rose again (1:10, 4:14) to save us from that judgment (1:10, 6:9).

We can get just too familiar with this kind of language in the letters of Paul and other New Testament documents, with the result that we do not see how astounding it is. Such was the impact of Jesus, such was the power of the memory of his amazing life and words, such was the experienced reality of his risen presence and power, that almost immediately, as shown in Acts (which, though written later than 1 Thessalonians, describes the earliest followers of Christ in Jerusalem immediately after the resurrection), Jesus was being exalted, worshiped, prayed to, and talked about alongside the one true living God of the Jewish Scriptures. The infinite "difference" of Israel's God had been amazingly transferred to, or rather extended to, Jesus of Nazareth, their human contemporary.

I stress this because today there is still a widely held popular view that the New Testament itself makes no claims about the deity of Jesus. It was only centuries later that the church, under the influence of Greek philosophy, came to regard him as divine and formulated a Christology of incarnation. We are asked to imagine a simple, homely Jesus, somewhat embellished by Paul and only deified in the later legends of the church.

Unfortunately this caricature of historical reality (for that is what it is) receives some credibility from the work of certain schools of biblical scholarship and is regularly put forward by advocates of religious pluralism as the accepted view of serious biblical scholars. But there are masses of evidence to show this will not stand as a truthful account of the early years of the movement that emerged from those first witnesses to Jesus of Nazareth. Fortunately, there are many good books available to help us think more clearly and accurately on this matter.[7]

When we put together both of the above sections, then, what emerges is a fully biblical portrait of the difference that was prepared for Jesus in the Old Testament and the difference he made even to the heirs of that tradition in the New Testament. The impact of Jesus was such that those who encountered him came to realize not merely that the Messiah had indeed come but also that in Jesus of Nazareth they had encountered Yahweh, the God of Israel. So powerful was this realization that, incredibly for monotheistic Jews, they could take the step of applying to Jesus Scriptures that had referred to Yahweh.

In Jesus, then, the uniqueness of Israel and the uniqueness of Yahweh flow together, for he embodied the one and incarnated the other. So he shares the identity and fulfills the mission of both.

The Difference Jesus Should Make to Us Now

What is needed if we are to bear such confident witness to Jesus in our contemporary world? I would suggest that at least three things will need careful attention and that we need to look to Jesus for the power to energize and sustain us in them. I began by reminding us that Jesus claimed to be the truth. All our witness on his behalf is thus, at a great variety of levels, witness to the truth. We ought to make at least the following commitments in relation to our witness to the truth.

We Commit Ourselves to Clarify Our Thinking

We confess that there is a great deal of confusion in the minds of Christians regarding the subject matter of this symposium. Much of the confusion is caused by the cultural captivity of the church itself and our inability to think outside the imposed limits of what is plausible to the world in which we live.

In the face of such confusion we need to help our church regain its confidence by enabling believers to think clearly in the following areas.

We need to understand ideological pluralism's roots

We commend the writings of Lesslie Newbigin and others in enabling us to recognize the process by which, for three hundred years, Western culture has adopted a dichotomized worldview which inserts categorical cleavage between object and subject, facts and values, the empirical and the transcendent, knowledge and belief, public and private, secular and sacred. The result of the long Enlightenment project and its fruition in modernity has been to demand dogmatic certainty in the first realm of each polarity and equally dogmatic uncertainty in the second. As Wilbert Shenk puts it, God, religion, and morality founded on both, become marginalized to the periphery of culture from the central position they once occupied.[8] Denied objective reality, no truth claims can be advanced for certain in relation to them. Only relative beliefs can be entertained.

However, just as we have begun to address the smorgasbord culture and supermarket mentality regarding religion that modernity fosters, we now have to face the postmodern flight even from the claimed certainties of Enlightenment dualism. We confront the denial of *any* objectivity anywhere: "Truth (with a capital T) is dead." "There is no supreme meta-narrative." The world of cultures and religions—and science and secularism, is a carnival of fascinating floats passing by. Enjoy what you can but claim finality for none.

If we are to communicate Jesus into such a culture (or virtual anticulture), we need a thorough understanding of it, and so we commit ourselves to the hard work of deep reading, listening, and engagement. This has always been the missionary task, since Paul stood up in Athens, and it remains a major challenge for us. We must understand the questions, and the sources from which they even become questions, before assuming that we know the answers.

We need to think biblically about religions and salvation

Religions. We must avoid simplistic, blanket assumptions that flow from ignorance or prejudice—that all religions are much the same and basically good; or that all religions (except Christianity) are totally of the devil and are systems of unrelieved darkness. Neither extreme is biblical.

Actually, the Bible is not greatly concerned about religions as systems or structures. It is concerned with human beings before the living God. It affirms two basic truths about human persons, both of which are reflected in human religions: first, that all are created in the image of God, are conscious of God, are capable of responding to God, and in all kinds of ways reflect their Creator; and second, that all are sinful and in rebellion against God, seeking to hide from God and to pervert God's truth, preferring the influence, power, and lies of the evil one. Human religions, then, simultaneously manifest both aspects of human nature—that which is good, God-seeking, and God-reflecting, and that which is evil, demonic, destructive, and oppressive.

As human constructs, all religions—like all cultures—can be vehicles of both good and evil. In all religions humans seek their Creator and also hide from him. This seems to me to be just as true of the peculiarly Western cultural religions of Enlightenment modernity (which has produced many "goods" as well as their perversions) and pluralism (which can be either the positive framework of social tolerance that provides an opportunity for the Gospel or the oppressive coercion of political correctness).

Salvation. We need to do some more hard thinking about what it means, in the context of modern and postmodern culture, to call on people to be saved. In relation to the plurality of religions, however, one question in particular needs to be cleared up. We are often asked to give a yes or no answer to the question, "Is there salvation in other religions?" I now refuse to answer the question without challenging its basic assumption.

The question takes for granted that salvation is something you get through a religion. Thus, the point to argue over is which religions, or how many, actually get you salvation. But the Bible seems to come against such assumptions head on. There is salvation in *no* religion.

Religion does not save anybody—God does. And the Bible is the story of what God has done in human history to save his whole creation, including fallen humanity. The Gospel is good news, not a good *idea*. So if we still want to affirm in some sense that there is no salvation in "the other religions," we must do so *not* on the grounds that they are inferior as religions to our religion, so ours wins. Rather, they are not salvific because they do not tell the story of what God has done to save people. The uniqueness of the gospel is the affirmation of the events that it proclaims and the good news that in those events God was reconciling the world to himself so that forgiveness and life can be offered to the repentant believer.

We need to think about the relationship of gospel to culture and about mission's cultural goals

The most conspicuous area of controversy at the conference from which this book originated was generated by Linford Stutzman's vision of "cultural hegemony."[9] On one hand, Stutzman wants to say only that if Jesus is truly the supreme Lord, then persistent witness to that truth should have culture-transforming effects for good. On the other hand, Stutzman's phrase generates suspicion and discomfort among his fellow Anabaptists, who remember the persecution their forebears suffered in the name of the lordship of Christ, at the center of a massive cultural hegemony.

There is a paradox here, however. Surely it was at least in part the courageous missionary and martyr spirit of early Anabaptism that eventually moved Western culture toward a more tolerant expression of faith, from which many benefited—not least in the New World. Would I be wrong to suggest an irony if modern Anabaptists, the heirs of believers whose uncompromising commitment to the lordship of Christ achieved cultural transformation, if not hegemony, were to retreat from the current form of that struggle for fear of the stigma of triumphalism?

Perhaps Stutzman's call can be best appreciated by persons immersed in mission in cultures outside the West. The Gospel *has* transformed cultures in recent history and living memory. Perhaps the conversion of Europe from its pre-Christian paganism lies too far back for us to appreciate it as much as we should, or perhaps the history of Christendom has polluted the picture too much for us to appreciate the transformation at all.

Doubtless the issues I have listed are only a few of those that require clearer thinking. The first and greatest commandment is that we must "love the Lord our God with all our heart . . . ," which in Hebrew means the mind, intellect, and will, more than the emotions. If we will not think, we will shrink.

We Commit Ourselves to Contending for The Truth

Pacifism is central to Anabaptist identity and commitment. Yet this should not make us nervous of the very biblical language of struggle, warfare, conflict, and victory. Our weapons are not carnal, but we do have weapons and we are in a battle (2 Cor. 6:7, 10:4f.).

Confident witness in today's culture calls for Christians to be willing to contend for the truth of the Gospel. This will mean at least the following: that we recognize the conflict over truth as a dimension of spiritual warfare, that we are prepared to attack error as well as defend truth, and that we are prepared to suffer.

The spiritual battle that rages between truth and falsehood is as old as fallen humanity—it goes back to the garden of Eden. And Paul characterizes human life in general as tending to exchange "the truth about God for a lie" (Rom. 1:25). Human minds are darkened and perverse, and the marks of satanic deception are to be found in all religions, including many institutional and cultural manifestations of Christianity in history. To struggle for the truth, therefore, is to engage the spiritual forces that surround the one who is "a liar from the beginning."

Paul seems to have been particularly faced with this struggle in Ephesus, from which he wrote 2 Corinthians. He notes both the spiritual power that blinds people and the spiritual light that God shines through the Gospel but at the same time points to the human duty of "setting forth the truth plainly" (2 Cor. 4:2, NIV). Similarly, in 10:1-6, he speaks of demolishing arguments and, in the same breath, demolishing strongholds. Clearly Paul saw no dichotomy between intellectual arguing for the faith and an encounter with spiritual powers.

Would that we had the same healthy synthesis today! For the battle for truth is spiritual warfare, with ideologies and massive cultural assumptions and plausibility paradigms that capture people's minds and hearts. So our struggle must be spiritual and in prayer, as well as intellectual and in debate.

Furthermore, the language of warfare must never be perverted into carnal triumphalism. On the contrary we must repent of all forms of historical and contemporary coercion. Spiritual warfare has no place for arrogance, superiority, bitterness, or personal attack. Significantly, Paul's most rhetorical passages about his warfare for the truth are framed with poignant descriptions of his own weakness (4:7ff.), suffering and marginality (6:3-10), and the "meekness and gentleness of Christ" (10:1).

We must be bold to expose error and fallacy

It is my conviction that effective and humble Christian apologetics can take the offensive. Surely we have the example of the prophets, Jesus, and Paul in their exposure of lies, hypocrisy, and false arguments. We can tackle head on some of the weaknesses in the apparent plausibility of the regnant ideology of pluralism. Indeed, pluralism at its best encourages us to do so.

We can challenge pluralism's relativistic illogic[10] and its epistemological arrogance. Pluralists want to say that no religion perceives or contains the truth about reality as it truly is in itself. But how do they themselves know this? They claim to know a lot about what they say nobody can know and presume to arbitrate as to what all other religions may or may not have truthful knowledge about. But what epistemological privilege or vantage point gives the pluralist the right to deny access to ultimate truth to any position other than his or her own? There is a hidden arrogance behind the apparent humility of pluralism, which quickly manifests itself in dogmatic intolerance of those who disagree.

We can challenge pluralism's cultural myopia. Modern Western pluralism as an ideology is a product of a particular cultural development in modern post-Enlightenment Europe. Yet it claims to have the key to all human knowledge and religion. But by what right? Pluralism relativizes *all* religions (not just Christianity), in the name of a worldview and a particularly Western, reductionist view of truth and reality that is not shared by the vast majority of the human race. While pluralism claims anti-imperialistic respect for all other cultures and religions, it becomes yet another form of Western cultural and intellectual pride.

So we as Christians, along with those of other faith traditions, have every right to challenge pluralism at every level—roots and fruits.

We must be prepared to suffer

In spiritual warfare there is a cost. The conflict between God and truth on the one hand and the serpent and lies on the other has never been a polite discussion. It can be painful, violent, and costly. Throughout history, whether first-century Jerusalem or Rome, sixteenth-century Zurich, or twentieth-century eastern Europe, those who call Jesus Lord and refuse to compromise that lordship with other claims to authority have suffered for it.

It is another paradox that the very freedoms we enjoy in Western democracies are themselves the fruit of that odd mixture of Gospel truth and Enlightenment "liberations." Yet, with that typically human capacity for turning good into oppression, pluralism is becoming a dogma as intolerant and repressive as the bigotry it claims to oppose. I personally wonder how much longer Western religious freedoms will last.

In my own nation, Britain, I would not be surprised if evangelism among religious and ethnic minorities were to be declared unlawful, under the guise of racial harmony. Are we prepared for that? And are we prepared to be obedient to the great commission despite the legal consequences—like the first followers of Jesus?

I hope Christians in the Anabaptist tradition will provide resources out of their own experience to encourage and stiffen the resolve of other branches of the church. And I hope we in the West will at last be willing to listen in humility and learn from sisters and brothers in the majority world, where such suffering and dangers for the sake of Christ are an accepted part of daily reality.

We Commit Ourselves to Renewed Living of the Truth

A characteristically Mennonite note is the importance of living as well as speaking the truth. It has also been said, of course, that the converse is true: sometimes Mennonites don't preach what they practice. However, if we are to strive for confident witness in our pluralistic world, then we must renew our commitment to the life that authenticates the truth of what we proclaim. How is this to be done?

We must recapture the courage of previous generations

We can look to immense achievement of two particular generations of believers—the New Testament church and the first generation of Anabaptists. One faced the combined world of Jerusalem and Rome—hostile Judaism and imperial power—as well as the surging sea of first-century religious plurality. The other faced the combined world of Rome, Wittenberg, Geneva, and Zurich—the might of Christendom, reformed and unreformed. In both cases, their missionary courage from utter powerlessness "turned the world upside down."

We must regain confidence in the historical truth of the Gospel

Without confidence in the Gospel, we will never live the Gospel. Yet we have so often succumbed to the pressure to privatize it into a subjective solution to personal needs or problems. We sing the chorus with the line, "You ask me how I know he lives? He lives within my heart." Wonderfully true, but not at all the way the apostles answered the question. What we smilingly affirm as a personal experience of the heart, they proclaimed as a publicly witnessed event of contemporary history.

The gospel was facts, events, something that had happened and been witnessed and recorded. As noted above, the gospel is good news, not good ideas, or even ideals. We must recover confidence in that objective having-happenedness of the gospel story which is the *sine qua non* of all its spiritual meaning.

The good news is to say, "God so loved the world that he gave his only Son." It is to affirm, "God was in Christ reconciling the world to himself." It is to marvel that, "while we were yet sinners, Christ died for us." And it is likewise to be convinced that "if Christ be not raised, then our message is empty and your faith is empty." Such massive realities are what is at stake in our confidence in the gospel.

By affirming it in this straightforward way, also, we get away from the potential arrogance of treating the Gospel as something we possess or can take some credit for. Strictly speaking, we do not say "We have a gospel. . . ," as though it were something we invented or owned, but rather "There is a gospel." That gospel confronts all of us with the ultimate reality of the God who is the judge of all, the lover of all, and who died for all—and rose again! Let us renew our commitment to recovering the simple power of the gospel story and the church's confidence in its redemptive effectiveness over against all substitutes.

We must pray for the renewal of the church and our own lives

The church should be "the plausibility structure for the gospel." Lesslie Newbigin had insisted on this; in his prophetic challenge, this was one of his most significant points. That is, it is the community of life and practice that makes the gospel believable.

For many Western people, the gospel is not so much untrue as simply implausible. It makes no sense in the dominant paradigm of our cultural assumptions and lifestyle. And people can see no viable alternative to the dominant cultural norms—unless the church provides it. The life of the church should demonstrate that the gospel is not only true but that it actually works (which is a more pressing criterion in the modern world).

This takes us full circle back to the theme of witness. The church is called to witness to the difference that Jesus makes when Jesus is Lord, just as Israel was called to witness to the difference of Yahweh as God. Israel was to be a light to the nations. We are given the identity and task of being "the light of the world." The most powerful way to communicate Jesus is to live like him—a task and a privilege open to every Christian. Then the world can see the difference and make the choice—light or darkness—for which all are responsible before God.

Notes

1. The author originally prepared this chapter as a live response to the papers that were later revised to form this book. His assignment was to focus on the uniqueness of Jesus in scriptural terms and then to respond to the preceding papers with a statement of commitments that ought to emerge from the presentations. Some of the material included in this chapter is more fully developed in his books *Knowing Jesus through the Old Testament* (Downers Grove, Ill.: InterVarsity Press, 1993) and *Thinking Clearly about the Uniqueness of Jesus* (Crowborough, Monarch: 1997).

2. E.g., Amos 9:7; Deut. 2:20-23; Ex. 9:13-16; Isa. 10.5-19; Jer. 27:5-7; Isa. 44:28–45:13.

3. See Chapter 2 of this book, "God, Justice, and Religious Pluralism in the Old Testament."

4. The importance of the theological linkage between Israel and Jesus has been given its most thorough treatment in the prolific writings of N. T. Wright. See especially the first two volumes of his project on Jesus and Paul, *The New Testament and the People of God* (London: SPCK, 1992) and *Jesus and the Victory of God* (London: SPCK, 1996).

5. Again, the work of N. T. Wright is of immense help in enabling us to feel the depth of the Jewish worldview and the breadth of their expectations at the time of Jesus. See especially *The New Testament and the People of God*, Part III, 147-338.

6. This comparison has been thoroughly examined by David Ball, "The 'I am' Sayings of Jesus and Religious Pluralism," in *One God, One Lord: Christianity in a World of Religious Pluralism*, 2nd ed., ed. A. D. Clarke and B. W. Winter (Grand Rapids, Baker; Carlisle: Paternoster, 1992), 65-84.

7. See, for example, the following works of established and reputed scholars in the New Testament field: R. T. France, "The Worship of Jesus: a Neglected Factor in Christological Debate?" in *Christ the Lord: Studies in Christology presented to Donald Guthrie*, ed. H. H. Rowdon (Leicester: IVP, 1982), 17-36; idem, "Development in New Testament Christology," *Themelios* 18.1 (1992): 4-8; J. B. Green and M. Turner,

eds., *Jesus of Nazareth Lord and Christ: Essays on the Historical Jesus and New Testament Christology* (Grand Rapids: Eerdmans; Carlisle: Paternoster, 1994); M. Harris, *Jesus as God: The New Testament Use of "Theos" in Reference to Jesus* (Grand Rapids: Baker, 1992); L. Hurtado, *One God, One Lord: Early Christian Devotion and Ancient Jewish Monotheism* (London: SCM; Philadelphia: Fortress, 1988); idem, "The origins of the worship of Christ," *Themelios* 19.2 (1994): 4-8; I. H. Marshall, *I Believe in the Historical Jesus* (London etc: Hodder and Stoughton; Grand Rapids: Eerdmans, 1979); idem, *The Origins of New Testament Christology* (Leicester and Downers Grove: IVP, 1976, 1990); C. F. D. Moule, *The Origin of Christology* (Cambridge: CUP, 1977); B. Witherington III, *The Christology of Jesus* (Minneapolis: Fortress, 1990); N.T. Wright, *Who Was Jesus?* (London: SPCK, 1992).

8. See Chapter 9 of this book, "The Church in Pluralistic North America: De-centering Conviction."

9. See Chapter 11, "Confident Witness for Cultural Transformation."

10. See especially Chapters 1 and 12.

CHAPTER FIFTEEN

You Know
that We Love You:
Concluding Reflections

Don Jacobs

I have often meditated on the witness of the apostle John. The writings we have from him are reflections from one who spent a lifetime serving his Lord Jesus but was still trying to pull all of life's knowledge and experience into a cogent whole.

Like John I continue to work toward an understanding of the truth and grace that are in Christ Jesus. The Gospel John knew and proclaimed was being assailed in his day just as in ours. One can detect the struggle in which he was engaged as a witness to Christ. Many of his problems would have been over had he simply acknowledged that there is a pre-existing Logos, a moral force in the universe, which has many icons—Jesus being but one. That would have bound Jew and Gentile together. They all worship or acknowledge the Logos in some form or other.

However, John knew that the pre-existing Logos was a *person*, not a force or an idea. The Logos is Jesus Christ of Nazareth, born of a woman, the Messiah of God, crucified as a common criminal, buried, and raised from the dead. John parted company with all who would seek a proto-religion which undergirds all religion. For him it was a fruitless search because Jesus Christ has appeared. In almost breathtaking clarity and conviction he wrote, "The Word became flesh and made his dwelling among us. We have seen his glory, the glory of the One and Only, who came from the Father, full of Grace and Truth" (John 1:14).

It was costly for John to insist that Jesus Christ is the "One and Only." His religiously pluralistic neighbors might have expected a more tolerant and "enlightened" view from John, the noted mystic. John's argument is based on many pillars, the center of which is that the essential problem is alienation from God and from each other. Sin, both inherent and willful, causes this alienation. John insists that there is only one effective, eternal, all-gracious way for sin to be dealt with—through the Cross and Resurrection of Jesus Christ. That self-giving death on the Cross and the powerful demonstration of the assent of God in the Resurrection is unique, unrepeatable, and sufficient for all persons everywhere for all time.

John insisted that we must believe right. He kept pounding on that. Doctrine was important for John. He used the term fifty-four times in his Gospel alone. There is a telling scene there on the Gentile shore of the Lake of Galilee. The crowds who have been miraculously fed ask, "What must we do to do the works God requires?" Jesus answers, "The work of God is this: to believe in the one he has sent" (John 6:28-29).

Readers of this volume will be left with many thoughts to sort out. Some will be discarded. Others will be accepted wholeheartedly. Others will be modified to fit into the reader's scheme of things. Most importantly, a book such as this can help us focus on what we truly believe.

Of one thing I am convinced: it does matter what we believe. Two themes carry the weight of John's comparable convictions. He emphasizes them repeatedly: "Love one another" and "Believe." Too often we reinterpret "love" to mean that we believe nothing lest our beliefs create a barrier between us and the loved one. Or we easily swing the other direction, clinging to our particular idea of the truth even if it means hating others. John declared that Jesus is full of grace and truth. The Cross of Christ is the full expression of the unconquerable love of God and the eternal justice of God against sin. The Cross is where truth and grace met. Now Jesus is the Way, the Truth, and the Life.

We are always learners and will be until we go to glory. We do well to examine our beliefs. But there is more. Having said all he had about belief, John closed his Gospel with a scene we do well to ponder. It took place on the shore of that lake where Jesus tested his disciples' faith repeatedly. Could they trust Jesus? When the storms raged and they were fearful, he was quick to point out the purpose of it all—to build faith. "Oh, ye of little faith." The words ring in our ears even now. We too need faith. On that sea the disciples learned great lessons in faith, as do we who learn from watching them.

Returning to the lakeside, as the first rays of the morning sun began to clear the night fog from the surface of the water, Jesus gathered firewood and caught a few fish. He began to make breakfast for these disheartened disciples who had toiled all night but had caught no fish.

We have felt holy awe at the words spoken next by Jesus, resurrected Lord, Lamb of God; the words burn still in our hearts. Jesus didn't ask if Peter believed in him. That had taken place long before on that hilltop in the Gentile lands of Caesarea Philippi. There Peter had believed correctly. Now Jesus had a more searching question. "Do you love me?"

Peter felt the pain of that question pierce his heart. For that question called for a response that went beyond doctrinal belief. It went beyond an understanding of God's marvelous grace. Yet it included all of this. Listen again. "Do you love me?"

When we love someone, we do not dissect the person, rejecting this or that as we see fit. I love my wife—heart, soul, mind, body, and all that comes with her. Love encompasses the entire relationship.

Peter was changed forever when he said, "You know that I love you." And we are changed forever when we hear the Lord's most intimate question, "Do you love me?"

You can certainly remember such times in your own life. I well recall my first encounter with Jesus Christ. It was on the campus of Eastern Mennonite University between the Administration Building and the Chapel. That meeting changed my life. I believed. No doubt about that.

Nevertheless, many years later, on the shores of Lake Victoria in Tanzania, while a struggling missionary, that same Jesus visited me again with a question similar to Peter's. He did not ask, "Do you like your work? Are you getting on well with the language? Are you witnessing effectively in this culture? Do you have meaningful quiet times? Are you praying lots? Are you reading the right books? Do you feel comfortable with these people here?" No. Those were the questions that I was asking. Jesus cut through all that. "Don, the son of Paul and Trella Jacobs, do you love me? Do you love me? Do you love me more than these?" I was undone. However, in that "undone-ness" I was remade.

If I love Jesus, how can I fuss about his view of the universe? If I love Jesus, how can I dispute his view of me? If I love Jesus, how can I have a love which is greater? If I love Jesus, will I not reach out and gladly accept all his gifts? If I love Jesus, will I not want to guard my relationship with him so jealously that I will allow nothing to come between us? If I truly love Jesus, I will cling to the cross, experience the resurrection, and have a new song in my heart for him every morning and every night.

Listen to that loving, almost pleading voice. "It is good to examine your belief, but my heart yearns for your love. Do you love me? Do you truly love me?"

We respond with Peter, "You know that we love you." Jesus' heart is warmed.

Select Bibliography

NOTE: To make this select bibliography as useful as possible to students of the book's key issues, the goal has been to include the main sources used by chapter authors as well as significant additional sources referred to in the text or recommended for background reading. More specialized sources can be found in chapter notes.

Allen, Diogenes. "The End of the Modern World." Christian Scholar's Review 22, no. 4 (1993): 339-47.

Anderson, Gerald. "Theology of Religions and Missiology: A Time of Testing." In The Good News of the Kingdom: Mission Theology for the Third Millennium, edited by Charles van Engen, Dean S. Gilliland, and Paul Pierson. Maryknoll, N.Y.: Orbis Books, 1993.

———. "Theology of Religions: The Epitome of Mission Theology." In Mission in Bold Humility: David Bosch's Work Considered, edited by Willem Saayman and Klippies Kritzinger. Maryknoll, N.Y.: Orbis Books, 1996.

Anderson, Norman. Christianity and the World's Religions: The Challenge of Pluralism, Downer's Grove, Ill.: InterVarsity Press, 1984.

Bauman, Zygmunt. Postmodernity and Its Discontents. New York: New York University Press, 1997.

Bediako, Kwame. Christianity in Africa: The Renewal of a Non-Western Religion. Maryknoll, N.Y.: Orbis Books, 1995.

———. "The Unique Christ in the Plurality of Religions. In The Unique Christ in a Pluralistic World, edited by Bruce J. Nicholls. Grand Rapids, Mich.: Baker Book House.

Braaten, Carl E. No Other Gospel! Christianity Among the World's Religions. Minneapolis: Fortress Press, 1992.

Braswell, George W. Jr. Islam, Its Prophet, Peoples, Politics and Power. Nashville, Tenn.: Broadman and Holman Publishers, 1996.

Caputo, John D., ed. *Deconstruction in a Nutshell: A Conversation with Jacques Derrida.* New York: Fordham University Press, 1997.

Clarke, A. D., and B. W. Winter, eds. *One God, One Lord in a World of Religious Pluralism.* Cambridge, England: Tyndale House, 1991.

Clendenin, Daniel B. *Many Gods, Many Lords. Christianity Encounters World Religion.* Grand Rapids, Mich.: Baker, 1995.

Cragg, Kenneth. *The Call of the Minaret.* 2d. ed. Maryknoll: N.Y.: Orbis Books, 1985.

———. *Muhammad and the Christian.* Maryknoll, N.Y.: Orbis Books, 1984.

Crocket, William V., and James G. Sigountos, eds. *Through No Fault of Their Own?* Grand Rapids, Mich.: Baker, 1991.

Dasgupta, Surendranath. *A History of Indian Philosophy.* Vol. 1. London: Cambridge University Press, 1932.

Derrida, Jacques. *The Gift of Death.* Translated by David Wills. Chicago: University of Chicago Press, 1995.

Fry, C. George, James R. King, Eugene R. Swanger, and Herbert C. Wolf. *Great Asian Religions.* Grand Rapids, Mich.: Baker Book House, 1984.

Geertz, Clifford. *The Religion of Java.* Glencoe, Ill.: The Free Press, 1960.

Giddens, Anthony. *The Consequences of Modernity.* Stanford, Calif.: Stanford University Press, 1990.

Griffin, David Ray. "Introduction to SUNY Series in Constructive Postmodern Thought." In *Varieties of Postmodern Theology,* edited by David Ray Griffin, William A. Beardslee, and Joe Holland. SUNY Series in Constructive Postmodern Thought, New York: State University of New York Press, 1989.

Holland, Joe. "The Postmodern Paradigm and Contemporary Catholicism." In *Varieties of Postmodern Theology,* edited by David Ray Griffin, William A. Beardslee, and Joe Holland. SUNY Series in Constructive Postmodern Thought, New York: State University of New York Press, 1989.

Holland, Scott. "How Do Stories Save Us? Two Contemporary Theological Responses." *Conrad Grebel Review* 12, no. 2 (spring 1994): 131-53.

Hunter, James Davison. *American Evangelicalism: Conservative Religion and the Quandry of Modernity.* New Brunswick, N.J.: Rutgers University Press, 1983.

_____. *Evangelicalism: The Coming Generation*. Chicago: University of Chicago Press, 1987.

Kateregga, Badru D., and David W. Shenk. *A Muslim and a Christian in Dialogue*. Scottdale, Pa.: Herald Press, 1997.

Knight III, Henry H. *A Future for Truth, Evangelical Theology in a Postmodern World*. Nashville, Tenn.: Abingdon Press, 1997.

van Leur, J. C. *Indonesian Trade and Society*. Bandung, Indonesia: Sumur Bandung, 1960.

Lindbeck, George A. *The Nature of Doctrine: Religion and Theology in a Postliberal Age*. Philadelphia: Westminster Press, 1984.

Martinson, Paul Varo, ed. *Islam, An Introduction for Christians*. Translated by Stefanie Ormsby Cox. Minneapolis: Augsburg, 1990.

McClendon, James Wm. Jr., and James M. Smith. *Convictions: Defusing Religious Relativism*. Rev. ed. Valley Forge, Pa.: Trinity Press International, 1994.

Middleton, J. Richard, and Brian J. Walsh. *Truth is Stranger Than It Used To Be*. Downer's Grove, Ill.: InterVarsity Press, 1995.

Murphy, Nancey. *Beyond Liberalism and Fundamentalism: How Modern and Postmodern Philosophy Set the Philosophical Agenda*. Valley Forge, Pa.: Trinity Press International, 1996.

_____. "Philosophical Resources for Postmodern Evangelical Theology." *Christian Scholar's Review* 26, no. 2 (winter 1996): 184-205.

Newbigin, Lesslie. *Foolishness to the Greeks: The Gospel and Western Culture*. Grand Rapids, Mich.: Eerdmans, 1986.

_____. *The Gospel in a Pluralist Society*. Grand Rapids, Mich.: Eerdmans, 1989.

_____. *Truth to Tell: The Gospel as Public Truth*. Grand Rapids, Mich.: Eerdmans, 1991.

Noss, John B. *Man's Religions*. New York: Macmillan Publishing Company, 1980.

Orlinsky, Harry. "Nationalism–Universalism, and Internationalism in Ancient Israel." In *Translating and Understanding the Old Testament*, edited by Harry Frank and William Reed. Nashville, Tenn.: Abingdon, 1970.

Parrinder, Geoffrey, ed. *World Religions, From Ancient History to the Present*. New York: Facts on File Publications, 1971.

Phillips, Timothy R., and Dennis L. Okholm, eds. *Christian Apologetics in the Postmodern World*. Downer's Grove, Ill.: InterVarsity Press, 1995.

Pinnock, Clark H. *A Wideness in God's Mercy: The Finality of Jesus Christ in a World of Religions*. Grand Rapids, Mich.: Zondervan, 1992.

Placher, William. *Unapologetic Theology*. Louisville, Ky.: Westminster/Knox, 1989.

Prabhupada, A. C. Bhaktivedanta Swami. *Bhagavad-Gita As It Is*. Los Angeles: The Bhaktivedanta Book Trust, 1984.

Rommen, E., and H. Netland, eds. *Christianity and the Religions: A Biblical Theology of World Religions*. Evangelical Missiological Society Series #2. Pasadena: William Carey Library, 1995.

Sanneh, Lamin. *Piety and Power, Muslims and Christians in West Africa*. Maryknoll, N.Y.: Orbis Bools, 1996.

———. *Translating the Message, The Missionary Impact on Culture*. Maryknoll, N.Y.: Orbis Books, 1989.

Shenk, Calvin. *Who Do You Say That I Am?* Scottdale, Pa.: Herald Press, 1997.

Shenk, David W. *Global Gods, Exploring the Role of Religions in Modern Societies*. Scottdale, Pa.: Herald Press, 1996.

Spivak, Gayatri Chakravorty, and David Plotke. "A Dialogue on Democracy." In *Radical Democracy: Identity, Citizenship, and the State*, edited by David Trend. New York: Routledge, 1996.

Toulmin, Stephen. *Cosmopolis: The Hidden Agenda of Modernity*. New York: The Free Press, 1990.

Weaver, J. Denny. Review of *The Nature of Doctrine: Religion and Theology in a Postliberal Age*, by George A. Lindbeck. *Conrad Grebel Review* 3, no. 2 (spring 1985): 221-24.

Wright, Chris. *Thinking Clearly about the Uniqueness of Jesus*. Crowborough, England, 1997.

Yoder, Lawrence McCulloh. "The Introduction and Expression of Islam and Christianity in the Cultural Context of North Central Java." Ph.D. diss., Pasadena: Fuller Theological Seminary, 1987.

Yogananda, Paramahansa. *Autobiography of a Yogi*. Los Angeles: Self-Realization Fellowship, 1977.

The Contributors

Gerald H. Anderson, former Methodist missionary on the faculty of Union Theological Seminary near Manila, Philippines, is editor of the *International Bulletin of Missionary Research* and director of the Overseas Ministries Study Center, New Haven, Connecticut. Most recently he edited the *Biographical Dictionary of Christian Missions* (Macmillan Reference, 1998, and Eerdmans paperback edition, 1999).

Susan Biesecker-Mast is assistant professor of communication, Bluffton (Oh.) College. She has published in the fields of women's movement rhetoric and classical rhetoric.

Thomas Finger is professor of systematic and spiritual theology, Eastern Mennonite Seminary, Harrisonburg, Virginia. A participant on the Faith and Order Commission of the National Council of Churches since 1983, he has long been involved with the study of religious pluralism. He has authored several books, including his two-volume *Christian Theology: An Eschatological Approach* (Thomas Nelson, 1985-1989).

J. Nelson Kraybill is president, Associated Mennonite Biblical Seminary, Elkhart, Indiana. He has served as program director, London Mennonite Center in England, and is author of *Imperial Cult and Commerce in John's Apocalypse* (Scheffield Academic Press Ltd., 1996).

Elmer Martens has taught at Mennonite Brethren Biblical Seminary, Fresno, California, for twenty-five years. He has also taught short courses in over half a dozen overseas contexts. An Old Testament scholar, he has authored several books and served as one of six associate editors of the recently published five-volume *New International Dictionary of Old Testament Theology and Exegesis* (Zondervan, 1997).

John D. Roth is professor of history, Goshen (Ind.) College, director of Mennonite Historical Library at Goshen, and editor of *Mennonite Quarterly Review*.

Calvin E. Shenk, former missionary in Ethiopia, divides his time as professor of religion at Eastern Mennonite University, Harrisonburg, Virginia, and as Mennonite Church representative and scholar in Israel. His latest book is *Who Do You Say that I Am?* (Herald Press, 1997).

David W. Shenk is co-editor of *Practicing Truth*. He has served for nearly two decades as director of U.S. missions and then overseas ministries for Eastern Mennonite Missions, Salunga, Pennsylvania. He is now academic dean and professor of theology at Lithuania Christian College, Klaipeda, Lithuania. He is author of many articles and books on religion and mission, including the award-winning *Global Gods* (Herald Press, 1995) and *Christians and Muslims in Dialogue* (with Badru Katerrega, Herald Press, 1997).

Sara Wenger Shenk, former missionary in Yugoslavia, is assistant dean at Eastern Mennonite Seminary and a conference speaker. She is author of several books that address communicating faith across generations, including *And Then There Were Three* (Herald Press, 1985) and *Why Not Celebrate!* (Good Books, 1987).

Wilbert R. Shenk is a missiologist and professor of mission history and contemporary culture in the School of Missions, Fuller Theological Seminary, Pasadena, California. Shenk has served in mission administration and written or edited numerous books on missiology. From 1990-1993 he worked on The Gospel and Our Culture Project in Birmingham, England.

Linford Stutzman is co-editor of *Practicing Truth*. A former missionary in Germany and Australia, Stutzman is associate professor of mission and culture, Eastern Mennonite University. He also directs the John Coffman Center of Church Planting and Evangelism at Eastern Mennonite Seminary. He is author of *With Jesus in the World* (Herald Press, 1992).

Tite Tienou is professor of theology of mission in the School of World Mission, Trinity Evangelical Divinity School at Trinity International University, Deerfield, Illinois. For many years he has been president and dean of Faculte de Theologie Evangelique de L'Alliance Chretienne, Abidjan, Cote D'Ivorie. Tienou is a prolific writer, especially on the church in African context.

Chris Wright is an Old Testament scholar and principal of All Nations Christian College in Ware, England. He has authored several books on Christian faith, including *What's So Unique about Jesus?* (MARC, 1990) and *Thinking Clearly about the Uniqueness of Jesus* (Monarch, 1997).

Lawrence Yoder is professor of missiology, Eastern Mennonite Seminary. He has spent more than twelve years in Indonesia serving in mission and administration. He has written articles in both Indonesian and English languages on the history of the Mennonite Church in Indonesia.